Now retired, Robert Douglas worked a [illegible] as an electricity chargehand. Although he has lived in Northumberland for many years, he says you can take the boy out of Glasgow, but you'll never take Glasgow out of the boy. His first volume of autobiography, *Night Song of the Last Tram*, was a bestseller in hardback, and Robert has given many talks and readings from the book since its publication in 2005.

Praise for *Night Song of the Last Tram*:

'A terrific realisation of a wartime childhood . . . a fascinating piece of social history,'

George Hunter, retired history teacher, Glasgow

'Heart-rending, side-splitting, achingly nostalgic. In two days I'd read it all, scarcely able to put it down.'

Stuart J. Mitchell, Glasgow

'I laughed out loud at some parts, shed tears at others. I thoroughly enjoyed this book and recommended it to all my friends.'

Margaret T. Davis, Glasgow

'Beautifully written. I look forward to its sequel.'

Winifred Abrahams, Walton on Thames

'Brought back such a lot of happy memories . . . had me laughing aloud so much.'

Alice Hill, Paisley

'I both laughed and cried . . . the only disappointment came when I finished reading the last page.'

Alan Templeton, Ayrshire

'An evocative, atmospheric and moving work. I could not put the book down!' Revd F. R. Aitken, Ayr

'I felt I was transported back in time from the minute I opened it until I read the last page.' Elizabeth Hogg, West Lothian

'Beautiful, simple vignettes of daily tenement life made me feel, somehow, that era belonged to me.' Hamish McDonald

'I just couldn't put the book down until I reached the end. It was 1 a.m. and I was in danger of sleeping in for work next morning!' Agnes Larkin, Ayr

'I exclusively read autobiography – and it is one of the very best.' Susan James, Lewes

'How much I enjoyed reading *Night Song* . . . I laughed, cried, and lived every moment.' Rachel Booth, Glasgow

'*Night Song* is a wonderful story of childhood in Glasgow.' Jean Arrol Deegan, London

'It's a long time since I enjoyed a book so much. I will be recommending it to my friends.' Tracey Robson, Northumberland

'Made me laugh and cry in equal measure. So beautifully written.' Susan M. O'Farrell, East Lothian

'I thoroughly enjoyed the book. I laughed and cried throughout.' Linda Smith, Ayshire

Robert Douglas

Night Song of the Last Tram

A Glasgow Childhood

First published in Great Britain in 2005 by Hodder and Stoughton
A division of Hodder Headline

A Hodder paperback

13

A CIP catalogue record for this title is available from the British Library.

ISBN 978 0 340 83861 7

Typeset in Monotype Sabon by
Rowland Phototypesetting Ltd,
Bury St Edmunds, Suffolk

Printed and bound in the UK by
CPI Mackays, Chatham ME5 8TD

Hodder Headline's policy is to use papers that are natural,
renewable and recyclable products and made from wood
grown in sustainable forests. The logging and manufacturing
processes are expected to conform to the environmental
regulations of the country of origin.

Hodder & Stoughton Ltd
A division of Hodder Headline
338 Euston Road
London NW1 3BH

This book remembers my Ma,
Janet Douglas,
and
our tenement days.

Acknowledgements

With special thanks to Audrey Graham who first told me, 'You should write.'

And

The tutors and members of the W.E.A. Writers Group in Hexham, Northumberland, especially: Brendan Cleary 'tutor extraordinaire', Gellie Draper, Marjorie Graham, Margaret Hall, Pat Hirst, the late Philip Holden, Christine Lowes, Louie Marshall, Jadze Race, Chris Ractschus, Carol Richardson, David Wedderburn, Pat Hare and Kathleen Kenny.

Also

The late Ron Tierney for 'lending an ear' so often.

Extra special thanks to Philippa Collingwood for her indispensable input over the years.

Particular thanks to those of my readers who have generously given permission for parts of their letters to be reproduced in the front matter of this edition.

Finally, and most important of all, thank you to my wife Patricia.

All illustrations from author's private collection.

Contents

Hail the Conquering Hero

If my father, Robert John Douglas, had been killed in North Africa or Italy during the Second World War, I know that for the rest of my life I would have looked at the few photographs of him and mourned our lost relationship.

Unfortunately, he survived and came home.

I watched as Ma used the edge of her finger to open the newly delivered telegram. She looked at me and smiled.

'Your daddy's coming hame fae the army the day. He's due in at the Central Station this afternoon aboot four o'clock.'

'Is he hame for good?'

'Aye, that's him demobbed.'

This was exciting news, I was going to have my daddy in the house. No more having to look at the photos of him in the right-hand drawer of our Utility sideboard to remind myself what he looked like. It was September 1945. I was six years old and barely remembered him.

'Ah'm gonny wait ootside until he comes,' I announced.

'You've plenty of time,' said Ma; 'it's only eleven o'clock. Ah'll tell ye when it's gettin' near.'

She busied herself cleaning and polishing our tenement single-end. The linoleum was scrubbed then polished; the carpet taken out to the back court, hung over the railings and seven bells knocked out of it with the beater; all the brasses polished; the range black-leaded and its 'steels' emery-papered. We maybe only had one room, but it would be like a wee palace by the time he came home. Hopefully his return

My first photograph, taken around the end of 1939, before the Germans tried to bomb me!

would be less memorable than his departure some three years earlier.

When he was called up into the Royal Engineers in mid-1941, my father's embarkation for overseas in May '42 was not particularly auspicious. He had suggested to Ma that, 'It might be best if ye didnae come doon tae the station tae see me off, hen. Ah think it'll be too upsetting for ye.'

Ma pretended to go along with this kind thought, surmising that what he really wanted was his 'fancy woman' to see him off. Since early in their marriage – they'd wed in March 1938 – he had been seeing other women, and one in particular: Nell. Somehow Ma, Janet Douglas, had not only got to know her name, but also the fact that she was hefty-built and taller than my father. As he was just five feet two and three quarters – he always insisted on his 'three quarters' – Ma never referred to her as anything other than 'Big Nell'.

As they said their tender goodbyes, Ma was already working

out how much of a head start to give him. There was little thought given as to what she would do if she did find this woman deputising for her. She'd think of something.

Asking her friend and neighbour from the next close, Esther Sinclair, to look after me, Ma made her way by tram down to the Central Station, determined to see he got the send-off he deserved. She weaved her way through the hundreds of wives and sweethearts saying goodbye to their menfolk, until she eventually spotted my father locked in a farewell embrace with his paramour.

Ma, surprise on her side, immediately confronted them and proceeded to give the two of them a good old-fashioned Glasgow sherrackin in front of the crowd, loudly lambasting them and informing her shocked, but attentive, audience that, 'I'm his wife and the mother of his three-year-old son. This is his hoor, his fancy wumman. He'd rather huv her seeing him off than his wife and wean!'

Just as, in the movies, when the crowd draws back to form a circle so as Fred and Ginger can perform one of their exquisite routines, so the Central Station cast of extras drew back to leave Ma and the two red-faced lovers in the middle.

Attracted by the commotion, an inspector soon appeared. While Ma was distracted, Big Nell seized her chance, made a bolt for the exit and wasn't heard of again until 1946. Later, with the soldier at last off to the wars, and Big Nell missing in action, Ma returned home to Doncaster Street and, over a cup of tea, told Esther of her adventures.

'Och well,' said Esther, 'God's good. Wi' a bit of luck he'll no come back!'

That had all been more than three years ago. In the ensuing period his unit, 911 Docks Operating Company, Royal Engineers, had taken him through North Africa, Sicily and Italy. They had written to each other, made up, and were resolved to make a new start when he was demobbed. The big day had now arrived.

It was a sunny, late September afternoon. Since Ma had announced he would be home, time had almost stood still. I was in and out the house at fifteen-minute intervals and continually asking, 'Whit time is it noo, Ma?'

She looked at me. 'Mind, once your daddy's hame you'll huv tae start sleeping in your bed-chair. Daddy'll be in the big bed wi' me!'

This was a blow. I hadn't thought of that. For the last three years I'd slept every night in the recess bed with Ma, cuddling in on cold winter nights, pestering her to tell me stories, or just lying safe and warm in the dark until, as she'd forecast, 'The Sandman comes and sprinkles stardust in your eyes and sends you tae sleep.'

He always did. All that would be gone now. I was six and a half and couldn't remember *not* sleeping in the big bed with my mammy. I began to think it a pity the Germans hadn't hung on for another year or two.

The long afternoon trickled by with still no sign of my daddy. I sat at the edge of the pavement, lethargic in the warm, autumn sun. I tried, once again, to picture him, to get the feel of him, from the two brief memories I had – his hands around my waist as he'd lifted me into the dimly lit cockpit of a Spitfire on display in George Square during a 'Wings for Victory' week and sitting on his uniformed knee to have our photo taken in Jerome's Studio, before he went abroad. I still remembered how jaggy his army greatcoat was on the backs of my short-trousered legs.

Every now and again someone would turn the corner and my heart would give a little jump, but it was never him. I was determined to see him the instant he entered the street. It was now after four o'clock. I wouldn't go into the house or play with my pals in case I missed him. I thought about all the exciting things that had happened in our street that year: the big bonfire right in the middle of the road and everybody dancing and singing round it on VE Day. That had been great! Then the same again a wee while later for VJ Day. I'd liked VE Day best. Now my daddy was coming home. That would be the best thing of all. I wished he would hurry up.

There was the noise of a window being opened in the tenement opposite. I watched as Mrs Mulholland, who lived on the ground floor, placed a cushion on the window sill, rested her folded arms on it and leaned out to take the air. She looked up and down the quiet street. I ran over and sat on the sill of her adjoining window. For the umpteenth time I repeated my litany, 'Ma daddy's coming hame fae the Army the day.'

'Is he, Robert? That's grand. Will ye know him when ye see him?'

'Aye.' I extracted a small snapshot from my shirt pocket. 'See, he sent that fae Italy.'

She looked at the garish, hand-coloured photo of him with his neatly trimmed Ronald Colman moustache, and wearing his glengarry.

'Dae ye know ma daddy?'

'Oh aye, Ah know yer daddy awright, son.' She said it sort of funny. We blethered for another couple of minutes then, 'Look!' she said.

A small figure had just come round the corner by Lizzie's shop, glengarry on the back of his head, greatcoat open, kitbag slung over his shoulder and, I would find out years later, tablets in his pocket for the last few days treatment of the VD he'd recently contracted in the brothels of Bari.

'Daddy!' I ran, full pelt, toward him. He put down the kitbag, held out his arms and I leapt up into them. As I did so the inside of my short-trousered left leg caught badly on one of his greatcoat buttons. It was very painful. He kissed me on the lips; his clipped moustache was jaggy, it felt strange. I was only used to being kissed by women.

May 1942. Taken before my father goes abroad. I still remember how 'jaggy' his greatcoat was.

My tender inside leg was really smarting and I wanted to cry, but I didn't want my daddy to think I was a cry-baby. I bit my lip and fought back the tears – he'd think I was just happy to see him.

He carried me, and dragged his kitbag, through the close and into our house. Inside, he put us both down and I watched in delight as he and Ma kissed and hugged. I sneaked a look at my leg, the skin was broken and it still stung like hell.

I was too young to know what an omen was.

That night I lay in my bed-chair and listened to Ma and Da whispering and giggling in the dark. This was the first time I'd been in the bed-chair for years. The three thin, brown corduroy cushions offered little protection from the wooden slats; the buttons on the cushions dug into me. I turned on my side and tried to find a less lumpy bit. I wasn't half missing the big bed. To take my mind off my discomfort I thought back to the afternoon. As I'd waited for my father to appear I'd tried to recall the few memories I had of him. As I did so, other early events had popped into my mind. I now began to think about them again, and tried to put them in order.

I finally decided what was the earliest thing I could remember.

Earliest Memories

The melancholy wail of the air-raid sirens reverberate through the rapidly clearing streets and back courts. It's early 1941 and the raids are an almost nightly ritual the length and breadth of the country. The sirens are still sounding and Ma has barely finished pulling the blackout curtains when there is the expected knock on the door.

'That'll be Mrs McDonald.' I hear Ma open the door.

'Hello, Mrs Douglas.'

'Aye, in ye come, Mrs McDonald.'

The familiar figure enters. 'Hello, son, how are you the night?'

As I'm only two and a half she doesn't expect an answer. She gives me a wee smile, and I watch as she kneels down then crawls on all fours under our table. Once there, she makes herself comfortable on a cushion she's brought for that purpose. Mrs McDonald lives 'one-up' – on the floor above us. She has read in a magazine that under a table in a ground-floor room is a safe place to be during an air raid. Ma continues to sit by the range, sewing or embroidering, whilst I play on the floor. Now and again the two of them will have a little conversation. When I hear Mrs McDonald's disembodied voice coming from under our table it reminds me she is there, so I go over and lift the edge of the tablecloth. There she sits, cross-legged, in her wraparound peenie and a turban on her head with the knot at the front. When I lift the tablecloth she always gives me a wee smile and says, 'Keek-a-boo!'

*

At last the 'all-clear' sounds. Mrs McDonald emerges, stiffly, from her emergency shelter.

'Ah'll get away upstairs noo, Mrs Douglas. Thanks very much.'

'Not such a lang one the night,' says Ma as she sees her out.

'Naw, but the buggers might be back.'

'Well, if they dae, just come doon and give me another knock.'

'Are ye sure, Mrs Douglas? It might be late.'

'Och, it's nae bother, Mrs McDonald. Ah'll be wakened anywye if the sirens go off. We'll just huv a wee cup of tea and a blether; the wean'll be sleeping.'

'Oh, that's awfy good of ye. Ah might see ye later.'

Ma closes our door and we listen to the receding footsteps, then the bang of her door upstairs as she rejoins her husband and son, both called Archie.

Throughout this period of shared danger, the genteel proprieties – with Mrs McDonald and our other neighbours in the close – are consistently observed. It is always Mrs McDonald, Mrs Kinsella or Mrs Lawrie.

Because Ma has an infant child to look after, she is exempted from being 'directed into war service'. Although she hasn't a job, we manage all right. My father has given her an extra seven shillings and sixpence a week on top of the marriage allowance she gets from the Army. As our single-end is cheap to rent, she manages fine.

When the bombing gets heavier, Ma and me are evacuated to a farm near Dundee. The woman makes lovely yellow, iced biscuits using condensed milk. As I wander round the yard eating them I'm accompanied by some hens. At frequent intervals the cock bird startles me with his loud, piercing crows. We don't stay very long as the farm folk make it obvious they aren't too happy at having 'toonies' foisted on them. Increasingly there are raised-voice conversations.

'Would you mind asking if you want tae use the stove, or bile water!'

'Ah've got a bairn; ah'm trying tae wash his nappies as soon as ah can so as they'll not smell, otherwise that'll be another fault.'

Sniff! 'It's nice tae be asked.'

'There was naebody in the wash hoose; Ah thought it would be okay.'

Sniff!

It takes less than ten days for Ma to decide she is not staying where we are obviously not wanted. She'd rather be back in her 'ain house' and take our chances with the Luftwaffe. So we return to the city. Mrs McDonald is pleased to see us back. Losing the regular supply of iced biscuits is a blow.

We haven't long returned when Ma's mother dies.

For three days Granny McIntosh lies in her coffin, on trestles, in our single-end as people call in to pay their respects. Ma's three brothers, James, Bill and George, are all in the forces, so we have to take her. Her death, like the frequent air raids, doesn't make much impression on me. However, I do enjoy playing under the coffin, using the broad cross-struts of the heavy trestles as bridges to run my toy car along, making engine noises as I do. The voices of the mourners drift down to me.

'She'll be a sore miss, mind.'

'Ah've known her since we were lassies.'

'She looks that peaceful.'

As the mourners stand at the coffin, from my den underneath I assume that, as I cannot see their faces, they cannot see me. My invisibility enables me to inspect their footwear as they shuffle past. Dusty boots with brass eyelets are the norm for the menfolk; there's also the occasional broken lace tied in a big knot. I find those more interesting than clean, highly polished shoes. I recognise Granny Douglas right away as her long-since dulled and cracked patent-leather shoes put in an appearance; the small cuts on the sides of the toes – done to accommodate her bunions – announce who it is.

Eventually it dawns on me that everybody is getting to look in the big box, except me.

'Ah want tae see in the big boax.'

'Sshhh, ye cannae.'

'Ah want tae.'

'It's no nice for wee boys.'

'Ah want tae!' I start howling. That usually works. It does this time too.

'See, it's just yer granny. She's sleeping.'

I look down at the long, thin face, at her hair parted in the middle. I wonder why she lies there all day and never speaks to anybody.

'Will she be gettin' up?'

'No.'

'How no?'

' 'Cause she'll no.'

'Whit fur no?'

'She's no weel.'

I take a good look at her. 'Mibbe she's deid!'

The few mourners present try, unsuccessfully, not to laugh. Ma puts me down. I don't bother asking for another look. At night the lid is put on the coffin and the screws turned a few threads, then Ma and I go to sleep a few feet away in the recess bed. Three days later it's all gone. I don't half miss the trestles.

During this period Mrs McDonald, out of respect, has taken her chances with the Luftwaffe. Immediately after the funeral she resumes her communion with our table.

The Germans' main attacks are centred around the docks and industrial area. Only twice do they come anywhere near us;

they make an attempt to hit the BBC building in Queen Margaret Drive, just over a mile away, but only succeed in destroying some fine Victorian town houses opposite. Further up Maryhill, perhaps a mile, Kilmun Street is badly hit one night and there are heavy casualties.

Our table is never put to the test. As the war goes on the raids on Glasgow lessen until, by 1944, only the occasional single raider will make a desultory appearance on moonless nights, more nuisance value than threat. Mrs McDonald doesn't even get out of her bed.

The Night of the Unbroken *Windows*

During these early years of the war there were other things happening in our part of Maryhill. Unaware of them at the time, as I grew up I would often hear them being told. And retold.

Cocozza's Blythswood Cafe stood on the corner of Maryhill Road and Trossachs Street. It was very much part of 'oor bit'. Part of our lives. The Cocozzas were always referred to as 'The Tallies'. There was nothing derogatory or racist about it. It was a typical example of Glasgow's 'economy of speech'. The Blythswood Cinema was the Blythsie. The Unemployment Bureau was always the Buroo. Italians were Tallies. Ma would say to me, 'Away roon tae the Tallies and get me ten Capstan,' or, 'When we come oot the Blythsie we'll go ower tae the Tallies for a single nugget.'

Then came the June evening that showed the Cocozzas weren't just The Tallies. They were oor Tallies!

It had just turned dark when the mob, around twenty strong and mostly young men, came strutting the length of the Maryhill Road, smashing the windows of any shop or business with an Italian name above the door. The previous day, 10 June, Mussolini had invaded south-east France and brought Italy into the war alongside Hitler's Germany. A wave of anti-Italian feeling swept the country. Old Peter (Pietro) Cocozza, Italian-born, had been taken away that afternoon to be interned for 'the duration'. His two sons, Bertie and Rennie, born in Glasgow, were not subject to internment.

Cocozza's in 1967.

The mob stopped outside the cafe. As usual, a few local boys were standing blethering under the streetlight on the corner. At first they just watched developments.

'Hey, Eyeties! We're here tae put yer windaes in. You're no' gonny get stabbed in the back like Mussolini would dae it. We're gonny fuckin' dae it right in front of ye!'

There was a chorus of shouts, threats and other oaths from the rest of the vigilantes. Inside the shop, Rennie, the youngest, looked out at the gang from behind the counter. The family had feared this might happen after the previous day's treacherous act by Mussolini. Rennie ran out into the street to confront them.

'Look, ye have nae cause tae put oor windaes in. My brother, Bertie, wiz called up a month ago intae the RAF. Ah've already registered for the call-up. Ah'll be away maself as soon as ah turn eighteen. Ah'm daeing fire-watching at nights until they send for me.'

'You're fuckin' Eyeties jist like the rest o' them. Anywye, they've locked up yer auld man, huvn't they?'

'He's only locked up 'cause he wiz born in Italy. My father disnae support Mussolini; he's got nae time for him. Honest.'

'Aye, so ye say. C'mon, lads, let's put the bastard's windaes in!'

The mob was about to surge forward when Rennie, in a futile attempt to stop them, spread out his arms.

'My brother's already daein' his bit in the forces and ah'll soon be away. It's bad enough havin' my father locked up for nothing. It's jist no' fair tae smash oor windaes.'

So frustrated had Rennie become while trying to reason with his tormentors, he burst into tears. The gang of youths halted. There were murmurs of dissent from some of them: 'Och, mibbe we shouldnae dae their windaes.' 'It's a bit much tae dae their shoap when the *two* boys will soon be in the forces.'

The ringleader was still for it. 'The auld man's been put in the jail, huzn't he? They widnae lock him up for nuthin'. Ah'm for putting their windaes in!'

Rennie's tears had made the majority feel uncomfortable. The fate of Cocozza's windows hung in the balance.

As the confrontation unfolded, the four or five local lads continued to watch from under the streetlight. One of them, big Mick Hoban, now decided it was time to try and tip the scales. He strode over and stood beside Rennie.

'Look, ah've grown up wi' these two boys. We went tae school the gither, played roon the streets the gither. Them, and their faither, huve nae mair interest in that bastard Mussolini than ah huv.' As he spoke, the rest of the small group he had been standing with ambled over and lined up either side of him and Rennie. Mick continued, 'So, if ye want tae put their windaes in, lads – your gonny huv tae get by us.' He looked at the leader. 'These are *oor* Tallies!'

There now came further murmurs of dissent from, quite clearly, a majority of the would-be window smashers. Their spokesman realised he was beginning to lose his authority – and much of his aggression. Big Mick's nickname was well earned; he was built like a 'brick lavvy'.

The head vigilante looked up at Mick. He cleared his throat.

'Aye, well, if you boys can vouch for them, ah suppose that's good enough for us. We'll, eh, let them aff then.'

Behind him, quite a few members of his group had already peeled off and slipped away into the night.

'Right ye are, boys, we'll head off further doon . . .' He turned round as he spoke, to find his support had seriously declined. There was a further bout of throat-clearing, then, 'Well, anywye, it's getting a bit late, lads. Dae ye think we should mibbe call it a night?'

The motion was carried unanimously.

I was around twelve years of age when I first heard of the events of the 11 June 1940. By then it was already part of local folklore.

Cocozza's windows survived the war intact. As did the two sons. Old Peter was released late in 1943 when, after Mussolini was deposed, the new Italian government not only stopped fighting, but did a quick volte-face and came in on the side of the Allies! They were now, once more, *all* 'oor Tallies'.

Primary Colours

'Get up, son. You're starting school the day.'

'Ah'm no wanting tae.'

'Ye have tae. Everybody has tae go tae the school.'

'Ah'm no.'

It was a cold January morning in 1944. I wasn't going to be five until the next month, but Ma had arranged for them to take me early, otherwise it would be Easter before the next intake. Having lost the early-morning debate as to whether I'd be starting school or not, I was dragged out of bed and, greetin' and girnin' continuously, I was washed, force-fed and frogmarched the one hundred and fifty yards up our street and through the infants' gate of Springbank Junior School. I had known, of course, there was a school at the top of our street. Now and again I had even peered through the railings and watched the kids playing – but I didn't think it had anything to do with me. I thought Ma liked having me around the house. This was a serious turn of events: Ma was wanting rid of me!

Amid curious stares from most of the kids in the playground, Ma led me firmly by the hand up the stairs and into the dark, central corridor of the large building. Instantly there were new smells in the air: carbolic soap, lino wax and disinfectant. The smells of Glasgow's schools. We stopped at the first door on the left and Ma knocked.

'Come in!' We did. 'Ah, this must be little Robert.'

How did this auld wumman know my name? I'd never seen her before in my life. I looked at Ma; if the word 'chicanery' had been in my vocabulary, it would have sprung to mind. There had obviously been moves going on behind my back, and this early-morning delivery into the hands of strangers was the result.

The auld biddy sat down opposite me. 'So you have come to join us, Robert, have you?'

I didn't answer. Instead, I just looked at her. Elderly, thin, her hair drawn back into a tight bun, she immediately reminded me of Granny McIntosh in her coffin. But not as lively.

'I'm Miss Smith and you will be in my class, Primary One.'

As if on cue, all the kids began to file into the room and take their places. I decided not to make a fuss and allowed myself to be seated at a desk for now. Ma made her excuses and left and I managed not to shed a tear. Miss Smith turned her back and began chalking on the blackboard. As she did, the more experienced inmates began to whisper and some pulled and pushed one another and giggled.

Without turning round, Miss Smith said, in a loud voice, 'Some of you are forgetting I have eyes on the back of my head!'

The class quietened. Jesusjonny! I felt my scalp tingle. If my mammy had known this surely she wouldn't have left me here. I peered at the back of her head to see if I could spot the eyes glinting through her hair. This was the first time I'd ever heard of people with eyes on the back of their head. Maybe it was just teachers? I decided that the first chance I got I was off. But I would wait for the right moment. Ma was always taking me to the pictures with her, I knew that Bogey and Cagney never rushed things when they were planning a break from 'the pen'. My opportunity came sooner than expected.

A loud bell began to ring. Miss Smith looked up. 'Right, children. Playtime.'

We all filed out into the playground. I watched as my fellow inmates began running around and making lots of noise, especially the girls, who seemed to be doing screaming exercises. Two teachers hung about near the main door. I made a beeline for the gates – and got clean away. A couple of minutes later I opened our door and stepped in to give Ma a nice surprise. She was sitting reading a paper and drinking a cup of tea. She looked at me, then at the clock.

'Whit are you daeing here?'

It hadn't entered my head I wouldn't be welcome. That had just been the longest spell Ma and I had been apart since the doctor cut the umbilical! She didn't look pleased. I had to think fast.

'That auld wumman huz got eyes oan the back of her heid!'

'She needs them with you around.' She grabbed me by the wrist. 'C'mon, back tae school wi' you.' Wearing just her wrap-around peenie, and not stopping to put on a coat, she dragged me, howling all the way, back up Doncaster Street and into the playground. The kids were still out, so any who'd missed me arriving that morning got an action replay. She pulled me into the empty classroom. Miss Smith looked up from her desk.

'This yin has run back tae our dwelling!' Ma always tried to talk 'pan-loaf' when addressing doctors, teachers or debt collectors. Miss Smith opened her desk and brought out the tawse.

'Well, I'm afraid he will have to find out that he can't do things like that without being punished!'

She leaned over and whispered in Ma's ear. Ma nodded. I began to feel uneasy.

'Hold out your hand,' said Miss Smith.

I confidently looked up at Ma. This was when she would come to my rescue. Ma took hold of my arm, held it out and with her other hand began to open out my fingers so as my hand was palm-up, facing Miss Smith. 'Treachery' was another word I wished I knew. I watched as Miss Smith unrolled this thick, leather belt, black on one side, brown on the other. She held it vertically, and menacingly, over my hand.

'Now, you must learn, Robert, you don't run away from school.' She let the tawse fall gently onto my palm.

'*WWWHHHAAAaaaaa!*' There was no pain. There didn't have to be, the whole ceremony had been punishment enough. I looked at Ma through eyes brimming with tears. Surely now she would come to her senses. I was horrified to see she was trying, and failing, to suppress a laugh. What was the matter with her? In one short morning she had handed me over to this branch of Barlinnie Prison, now she was presiding over the Warden giving me a hiding. What had I done to deserve this?

Next morning I went, meekly, to school. There was nothing to be done. However, all was not lost. At the morning playtime on that second day I was swinging on one of the big, heavy gates. One of the kids swung the other gate shut, trapping my finger in between the two and turning a large flap of skin back, deep into the red flesh. It was very painful, bled like billy-oh, and Ma was called up to the school while I was treated for my war wound. (Well! There was a war on at the time.) It was almost worth all the pain for the loving tender care I got from Ma over the next week or so, though I never missed a day at school. At least it proved, after the trauma of that first day, that my ma still loved me and wasn't trying to get rid of me. As for Springbank School, it was a most wonderful part of my childhood. From the age of five until I turned eleven, the teachers there would instil in me an interest in learning and, most especially, reading. It was with great reluctance that I had to leave to go to the 'big school'. As for Miss Smith, she was in reality a kind and gentle soul, much loved by her pupils. I never did get to see beyond the hairnet and bun to confirm there were eyes on the back of her head. I didn't have to. I *knew* they were there!

Tell it to the Marines

'C'mon, gie me a wee dance, son.'

The Andrews Sisters are belting out 'Don't Sit Under the Apple Tree' from our big, wooden-cased radio with its mysterious station names like Droitwich and Hilversum. Ma takes both my hands in hers and tries to quickstep me round the limited space of our one room. She then picks me up and, holding me in one arm, the other outstretched holding mine, dances us around the table. At just twenty-five, she loves to dance. But it is 1944 and my father is in Italy. Even if he was here, she wouldn't get a dance. He doesn't like dancing.

Ma is always sure of a partner when my Uncle George is on leave. She has three younger brothers, James, Bill and George. James is a regular soldier, having joined the Highland Light Infantry in the late 1930s; he has already been wounded at the battle of 'Knightsbridge' in North Africa. After the death of their mother, Granny McIntosh, in 1941 when George was sixteen, he and Bill shared digs until 1943 when both joined up; Bill in the King's Own Scottish Borderers, George in the Royal Marines. George spends all his leaves at his 'big sister's', sleeping in my bed-chair. I adore him, resplendent in his Marine's uniform. Our room is always full of fun when he's on leave. I cannot believe how lucky I am that this handsome marine is *my* uncle. I follow him around like a puppy. He always makes time for me. When he talks to me, I glow. When his leaves are up, I shed tears. When Ma tells me he will be arriving again in a few days, I think of nothing else until he appears in our single-end – and turns it into a Hollywood film set . . .

Standing in his shirttails, Uncle George is, yet again, pressing his uniform trousers. We hear the click of high heels enter the close, and stop outside the door. Then the knock. He looks at Ma.

'If that's Ruby Robertson, tell her ah'm no in.' There is an even louder knock. 'Och Netty, go on. Ah'd dae it for you.'

Ma sighs as she heads for the door. We listen as she opens it.

'Oh, hello, Ruby.'

'Sorry tae bother ye, Netty. George wiz supposed tae meet me ootside Cocozza's at seven-thirty. It's efter eight, noo.'

'Well, he went oot sometime efter seven, Ruby. Mibbe he's away for a pint and got intae company. Ye know whit he's like.'

Uncle George peers at me through the steam and begins to make low, snorting noises, pretending to choke back a laugh and covering his mouth with a hand. I go into kinks of laughter and have to put both hands over my mouth as he shooshes me.

'Ah don't know why ye bother with him, Ruby,' says Ma in a louder voice, 'he's no reliable, hen.'

George puts on a shocked look as he points to himself. 'Me!' he mimes. I bury my face in a cushion to try and keep my laugh in.

'Well, ah'll gie him another ten minutes,' says the departing Ruby.

'Ah widnae even give him that,' says Ma.

George does a silent minuet, holding his shirt hem up with one hand whilst blowing kisses and waving 'bye-bye' with the other to the unseen Ruby. I writhe on the chair as I choke with laughter *and* take a stitch at the same time. As Ma shuts the outer door and begins to open the inner, George leaps back to the table and begins, nonchalantly, to iron and innocently whistle.

'Ooooohhhhh!' I am now in real pain as I try to get my laugh out, fighting for breath, tears streaming down my face.

Ma enters. 'Whit's the matter wi' him?'

George looks at me, as though for the first time. 'Poor wee soul, ah think he's having a fit. Should we send for the doacter?'

'Urghgurgle' is all I can say. Ma tries to keep a straight face.

'It's the polis we should be sendin' for, for you. The way you treat them poor lassies.'

George begins to put on his trousers. 'Och well, ah suppose ah'll have tae go. Duty calls.' He begins to button his high-neck tunic. I watch his every move, lost in admiration. Doing an impression of Charles Boyer, he speaks to his reflection in the mirror, 'Come with me to the Casbah, Dahling. You bring the cash – and I'll wait at the bar!'

Ma tuts as I, once more, begin to laugh helplessly, even though I don't understand the joke. I stop laughing and we both give him our undivided attention as he executes his final task. He takes hold of the small, navy-blue forage cap, with its red piping and Royal Marines badge. Opening it, he places it at a gravity-defying angle on the right side of his head, giving it a few settling-down wiggles. Ma and I hold our breath as he takes his hands away – and it stays put, clinging precariously to his blond, wavy hair.

He turns round. 'Well, whit dae ye's think, zat all right?'

Ma smiles. 'Aye, you'll pass in a crowd,' she says, a catch in her voice.

The uniform of the Royal Marines could have been designed for George.

'Right, ah'm away,' he says, 'ah'd better cut through the back courts and up Maltbarn Street in case Ruby is hangin' aboot, eh?'

Minutes later I watch from the window as my handsome uncle momentarily brightens up the grey, Glasgow landscape of wash houses and middens as he heads for another night out, Master Of All He Surveys. King of the World. He is eighteen.

Uncle George, Ma's youngest brother and my idol, taken in 1943. He is 18. The forage cap is, as usual, defying gravity.

It is not a good time to be eighteen. It is not a good time to be learning how to drive a landing craft on and off beaches. It is March 1944.

The evening passes so slowly.

'They'll no be long now, Ma, will they?'

'He'll be here when he's here.'

'Dae ye think he'll bring his pals again the night?'

'He might.'

'Ah think he will.' I am struggling to keep my eyes open. It is almost ten p.m. and it seems ages since I'd watched him go through the back courts to avoid the amorous Ruby. The soporific heat from the range begins to get to me . . .

I awake with a start. The room is full of people; instantly I'm wide awake. I feel a tingle of excitement in my stomach – it is going to be like last night, like every night when Uncle George is on leave.

They are all talking at the same time. I can smell the beer on the men's breath. The green screwtop bottles of McEwan's India Pale Ale clink cheerily together as they are brought out of the brown paper carrier bags and placed on the table. The 'carry-oot'.

'Where are the glasses, Netty?'

'Ah jist want a shandy.'

'Who's got a fag?'

'Gie the bairn a drink of ginger.'

'Lift they bottles till ah put a blanket oan the table, ready for the cards.'

'Is there anything tae eat, Netty? Ah'm starvin'.'

In a minute our little house is transformed. It isn't a tenement single-end anymore, it's one of the sound stages at MGM – 'Lights, camera, ACTION!'

'Make sure they blackoots are pulled proper.'

'Ah'll get them.' I watch as one of the girls stretches up to tug at the curtains, revealing shapely thighs as far as where the seams hit the tops of her stockings. The four girls all look like film stars to me: bright, print frocks; rich red lipstick; permanent waves and rouged cheeks. The heady smell of Evening in Paris mingles with California Poppy and displaces the air in the room. Two of the guys wear double-breasted suits, just like George Raft. The other is in army uniform and then, of course, Uncle George.

'Right! Let's get the game started.'

'Wait the noo, ah'll have tae go a place first. Where's the lavvy key?'

I try to recall a scene in *Down Argentine Way* where Betty Grable or Carmen Miranda asked Don Ameche for a loan of the lavvy key.

'Ah'll go with ye,' says another of the girls.

'So will ah,' says the third.

'They cannae go the length of themselves withoot huvin' tae go for a piss,' says one of the boys, shaking his head.

'Shhh, mind the wean,' says a girl.

'Is there a light?'

'Naw, you'll have tae take a candle,' says Ma.

She opens a sideboard drawer and produces a candle and box of matches. The three girls are barely gone ten seconds when there are screams and laughter from the close and all three come running back amidst a skitter of high heels.

'The candle's blew oot!'

'Here, take the matches with ye.'

At last, everybody settles round the table and the game begins. This is what I like best. I always get to sit next to Uncle George.

'Now, don't you bother your Uncle George,' says Ma.

'Ah'll no.' I'm hurt at even the very suggestion.

George puts his arm round me and squeezes me close, the entire company watch and smile. 'This is my Number One Pal.'

Is it possible to die from pleasure? This is pure happiness, sitting close to *my* Uncle George and watching him at work. He undoes the fastening on the high neck of his tunic. The forage cap is taken off. One blond lock obligingly falls onto his forehead. The cap is folded flat and placed under his left epaulette. Already the girls can't take their eyes off him.

The game is, nominally, Pontoon. In reality it is 'Can You Hang On To Your Girl?' George's companion of the evening sits very close to him on the other side. She already realises that, for her, the game is 'Can You Hang On To George?'

I bask in reflected glory as, once more, he effortlessly becomes the centre of attraction. He can turn the mere selecting of a card into a fine art.

Cigarette dangling from his lips, one eye half shut against the spiralling blue smoke, he takes a card from the deck, makes as if to discard it, stops, takes another look at it and mutters, 'Mmmmm?' Then, after a pause, he places the bottom corner of the *almost* discarded card just into the top of the cards he holds in his hand. Using the tip of his elbow he gently slides the card down amongst the others – whilst making a different sounding 'Mmmmmm!' The girls giggle while the boys try to think up ways to compete. As the evening wears on the atmosphere becomes electric. The aroma of female perspiration mingles with the scent of cheap perfume.

Eventually, sometime around midnight, I cannot keep my eyes open any longer. Ma puts me into my pyjamas, making sure none of the girls can see me undressed, and I'm bundled, unwashed, into the big bed. Lying on my side, still trying to see what's going on, the murmur of voices and soft laughter from young people trying to have some fun becomes the sweetest of lullabies.

Next to Ma I love my Uncle George *best in the world*. I wish he could be on leave for ever.

Flickering Memories

With my father in Italy, and Uncle George only appearing now and again to brighten up our lives, by mid-1944 Ma's main source of entertainment and relief from war, rationing and the blackout is – the cinema. Especially our local hall, the Blythswood. At least twice a week, from infancy, Ma takes me to the pictures with her. It soon becomes as much a part of my life as it is hers.

'Here!' Ma stuffs another piece of 'nugget' into my mouth as the drama on the screen nears its climax. I don't like nougat, but sweeties are rationed so it's better than nothing. Almost. Ma, her pal Annie Dunn, and the rest of the audience in the Blythsie are totally absorbed as Bogart tells Claude Raines, for the umpteenth time, that he hasnae got a clue where these 'Letters of Transit' are. Meanwhile, I've managed to prise my teeth apart.

'Ah'm needing the lavvy.'

'Ssshhhh.'

'Ah'm burstin'.'

'In a minute,' she hisses.

'Ah'm needing tae go!'

There are some tuts from surrounding patrons as I continue to drag Ma, and them, reluctantly away from Rick's Bar in Casablanca. Then Ma's regular saviour appears, in the tall, lanky form of Nicky, the *male* usherette. As he strides up the centre aisle Ma hails him, 'Nicky! Gonny take the wean tae the lavvy, he's burstin' for a wee wee.'

Nicky sighs. 'Aye, awright.'

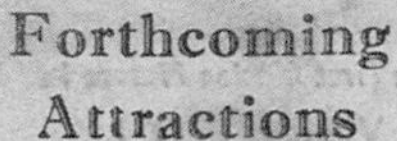
Forthcoming
Attractions

★

PUSHOVER
Black Horse Canyon
NAKED ALIBI
OVERLAND PACIFIC
PASSION
VALLEY OF THE KINGS
Return to Treasure Island
BETRAYED
DAWN AT SOCORRO

A programme for my beloved 'Blythsie', Ma's escape from the reality of wartime Glasgow.

To a ripple of sighs and mutterings, I make my way along the row then follow my leader. As we pass along the front of the screen I crane my neck to look up at the giant images. Claude is still havin' nae luck getting yon letters of transit off Bogie.

Nicky holds the side exit door open and we step, blinking, into the brightly lit, narrow corridor. A few more paces and we turn left into the small toilet. I breathe in the expected smell of strong disinfectant; at five years old I have already decided I really like it. I pull one leg of my short trousers up and to the side and start peeing, at an angle, into the stand-up urinal. I attempt to hit a Heinkel – really a fly – with the stream, but it continues to circle, unscathed. Nicky leans against the wall. He lives at the top end of Trossachs Street in one of the new type of tenement blocks, built just before the war.

'Will you be going away tae be a sodjer, Nicky?'

'Naw, ma eyes are too bad, they'll no take me.'

I look at him. He is probably only nineteen or so, but seems like a grown-up to me. Tall and very thin, he wears thick-lensed spectacles reminiscent of the bottoms of lemonade bottles.

'Are ye finished?'

'Aye.' I give my willie a good shake. Ma keeps telling me not to let any peeings drip onto my exposed inner thighs, especially in the winter. The cold wind soon makes them all 'scodded'.

'C'mon then.'

I follow him back into the hall. Claude's in the middle of telling Bogie what a scunner he is for no letting him huv them letters.

As well as the Blythsie, there are quite a few other cinemas within striking distance. A couple of hundred yards down the Maryhill Road stands the Seamore. I always find it a large and rather impersonal hall. Within a short tram ride are the Star, Roxy, Rio and the Grand. But, the Blythswood is by far our favourite. A small, comfortable hall without a balcony, it always seems snug and welcoming. The rear third of the cinema is raised three steps higher than the rest of the hall; these are the 'dear seats'. The Gibson family, who live on the Maryhill Road, practically run the place; Ma Gibson in the ticket kiosk, Pa Gibson keeping an eye on the queue and daughter, Betty, working as usherette and ice cream girl. For a large part of my childhood I assume that they own it. Only when I start at Springbank School and have James Gibson in my class do I find out that they just work there. Still, having James as a pal means a free entry now and again.

*

The wartime cinema is especially memorable, not least the community singing. A short, cartoon-like film is shown with the music of three or four of the latest hit songs playing in the background. The lyrics appear along the bottom of the screen and, as a little white ball bounces from word to word, the audience sing along with great gusto. For some reason, there are two which stick in my memory, both by the Andrews Sisters – 'One Meatball' and 'Ac-cent-u-ate the Positive'.

Sometimes during a show, a member of the audience would have to be contacted urgently. A message would be scratched onto a dark, blank piece of film: 'Mrs Fraser, 215 Maryhill Road, please report to the Manager's office.' And this would be inserted into the gate of the projector and appear superimposed on top of the movie being shown. If someone rose and made their way along a row, there would often be asides such as: 'Ah hope it's no bad news that soul's gonny be getting' or 'Oh, it's awright, she's been expecting her laddie hame oan a forty-eight-hour pass, that'll be him.'

There is, of course, a strong sense of patriotism during the war years. When the National Anthem is played at the end of the show, heaven help anyone who doesn't stand until the last note fades. If spotted trying to slip out they will be subjected to quite caustic remarks. As the end credits roll on the last film it is all right to make a beeline for the exit, but once the anthem strikes up you are expected to stand still. Then comes the stampede for the doors.

When Ma and me come out the Blythsie, if Ma has enough money we will head across the street into Cocozza's Cafe. There, hopefully, we will find a seat in one of the booths with their etched-glass partitions and marble-topped tables. Almost invariably we'll find ourselves sharing with neighbours.

'Huv ye jist come oot the Blythsie?'

'Aye, it was rerr the night, wizn't it.'

'Oh aye, ah never miss wan of Bogie's pictures.'

Maria Cocozza appears.

'A macallum (two scoops of ice cream with a dash of raspberry essence) for the wean, Maria, and a plate of hot peas for me.'

Peas are unrationed, so if someone is feeling peckish it is a regular thing to indulge in a plate of hot peas – with plenty of salt, pepper and vinegar. With their propensity for giving the diner wind, not for nothing have they earned the nickname 'musical fruit'!

'C'mon,' says Ma. 'It's nearly eleven, time we were in oor beds.'

We say our goodnights and walk the couple of hundred yards along Trossachs Street and left up Doncaster Street to Number 14.

'Will we huv a wee cup of tea and a slice of toast before we go tae bed, Ma?'

Ma sighs. 'See you, ah cannae get ye up in the morning, and ah cannae get ye tae go tae yer bed at night.' She reaches for the poker and stirs the fire back to life. Minutes later we are eating thick slices of toasted 'plain' bread spread with butter and apple jelly, washed down with mugs of hot, sweet tea.

'Get yer teeth cleaned before ye go tae bed.'

I open the round, pink tin of Gibbs dentifrice, wet my small toothbrush under the cold tap and, with a circular motion, rub the bristles on the hard block of toothpaste until it begins to foam.

'Give your face and neck a wash, tae.'

'Ah'm only going tae bed, Ma.'

'Get it done.'

I strip to the waist and, after a fashion, wash the designated areas. Soon, pyjama-clad and carrying the current week's *Beano*, I climb over Ma and get into the back of the recess bed. Somewhere in the middle of page two, 'Lord Snooty and His Pals', the Sandman gets me while I'm not looking. I vaguely remember Ma gently lifting the comic off my face.

A night at the Blythsie, a booth in Cocozza's, then fall asleep cuddled into Ma in the back of the big bed. Ah widnae call the King my uncle!

Transports of Delight

I only ever had one bad experience on a tram.

Ma and me were sitting just inside the lower saloon, on the three-seater bench seat. Opposite, on the two-seater, were two elderly ladies. I was three years old. The tram had stopped at the lights on the busy junction of St George's Cross.

'Ma, what's that?'

Ma casually glanced at the line of vehicles behind us, trailing back up the Maryhill Road.

'That's a motor car.'

The two ladies watched in interest.

'Nooo, not that. That!' I pointed.

The Glasgow dowagers smiled benignly as they listened to this attractive little boy in the blue beret and dark, belted mac. I noticed their interest and knew I was the centre of attraction. I gave an exaggerated sigh.

'Oh, you mean the lorry,' said Ma, also responding to the women's interest by beginning to talk pan-loaf again.

I shook my head vigorously. 'Nawww, the fuckin' van!'

One of the matriarchs emitted an audible 'Ohh!' The smiles froze on their faces. Ma turned a deep red, to the roots of her hair. By good luck for her – bad for me – the tram was still held by the lights. I instantly felt the mood had changed but couldn't figure why. I'd only used one of the new words I'd recently picked up from my pals, now that I was allowed to play out in the street. In one swift unbroken movement Ma grabbed me by the arm and, my toes only occasionally touching terra firma, whisked me straight off the tram and into the nearest close where she gave me the proverbial 'good hiding'. I had just discovered there was such a thing as Bad Words.

From as early as I can remember I loved 'going for a hurl on the tram'. Glasgow Corporation bus services ran up and down the Maryhill Road. Alexander's buses, with their painted bluebird on the side, were a regular fixture on the run from Dumbarton to the city. Yet, I don't ever remember pestering Ma to take me on a bus. In 1949 the trams were discontinued on Garscube Road and replaced by trolleybuses. The cobbled setts were covered in smooth tarmac and the trolleybuses were silent and well sprung and glided away as though on castors. They did nothing for me. I don't think I took more than half a dozen trips on them, just for the novelty, before I was back round the Maryhill Road waiting for a tram.

All during my early childhood Ma just had to say, 'Dae ye fancy a wee run on the tram?', and my pals would be abandoned, games left unfinished, comics folded to be read later. What was their magic?

We had been visiting Rosie McGuire, an old school pal of Ma's, who lived on the south side of the city. Around ten p.m. we left her warm house and stepped out into a cold, damp winter's night. Leaning into the wind, we made for the tram stop. The road was almost deserted of both traffic and people. The wet tramlines shone like silver ribbons. As though it had been waiting for us, sleet began to swirl down. I watched it curl past the streetlights and wished I was home and getting ready for bed. Like all five-year-olds I was wearing short trousers. I pulled up my navy-blue woollen socks, with the two white bands at the top, as high as they'd go. But there was still a gap and my knees were getting wet.

'Aw, Ma, ah hope there's a tram soon.'

'Aye, me tae, pal.' She stood me behind her, stretched her

arms back and pulled me in close. The blustery wind still tried to find me.

'Ah hope it's a new caur, Ma, they're alwiz nice and warm.'

'The 'new' Coronation-type trams were streamlined and had automatic doors which opened and closed to allow passengers on and off. The 'auld' trams had open platforms and their heaters never seemed to be very efficient.

I occasionally looked out from behind Ma and peered into the murk, longing for that first sight of a tram. Even an auld caur would be welcome. Ma flicked the gathering sleet off the top of my head before it melted. At last I was rewarded.

'Here's a caur coming, Ma!'

'Are ye sure?' She paused. 'Aye, so it is, son.'

It slowly came nearer.

'It's a new wan, Ma. Great!'

The tram stopped, the doors swished open and we clambered onto the platform. The sleet tried to swirl in behind us but the door rattled shut and cut it off. Already I felt warmer.

'Shake your coat to get most of it off.'

We stood on the platform for a moment stamping and brushing off the remnants of a winter's night. The conductor retreated a step or two into the saloon to escape the small blizzard. We soon followed him and took a double seat. Ma put her arm round my shoulders and pulled me in close; I gave an involuntary shiver as I began to defrost.

'Mmm, we'll soon be nice and warm, son.'

'Aye.'

The journey would be around forty minutes. As with every tram I rode my eyes began to wander around the saloon, taking in the art-deco light fittings, the jagged pattern on the cut-moquette upholstery, the leather straps with ivory-coloured, plastic hand grips for standing passengers to hang on to. I never failed to read all the notices with their dire warnings of twenty-shilling fines for spitting; reminders not to alight until the tram is stationary; and numbers showing how many standing and sitting passengers were allowed.

It wasn't long until the steamy warmth, creaking woodwork and gentle swaying, allied to Ma's arm round me, all conspired to send me to sleep. But seconds later I was shaken to a heavy-eyed wakefulness.

'C'mon, son, it's oor stop next!' During those few seconds the tram had travelled halfway across the city! How did they do that?

The Gentle Art of Queuing

Our door was knocked and opened at the same time.

'Netty, are ye in?' Esther Sinclair, Ma's pal from Number 4, popped her head round the room door. 'Ah'm no stopping, it's jist tae let ye know Guthrie's the butcher has got his quota in. He's got some sausages and liver tae. Ah know you're registered wi' Guthrie's, so ye'd better get roond there pronto.' Esther liked cowboy pictures.

'Thanks, Esther, ah'll go straight roond. C'mon, son.'

Ma took our ration books from the sideboard drawer and placed them in her well-worn, red Rexine shopping bag. Minutes later we were dodging trams as we crossed a busy Maryhill Road. Already a queue had formed outside George Guthrie's.

During the war, and for some time after, there were two aspects of life in which there always seemed to be queues. In front of cinemas when word got out that, 'There's a rerr picture oan at the Blythswood/Seamore/Roxy this week; don't miss it.' And outside food shops when it was known they'd just had a delivery.

With all meat, sausage, eggs, sugar and other commodities strictly rationed, it was essential for housewives to make sure they got their weekly allowance – if it was available. As refrigerators were something only glimpsed in American movies, foodstuffs and milk quickly went off if kept. Ma and all other wives had to shop on a daily basis for their requirements. Customers had to register with a butcher and grocer and could only shop with them.

*

Ma and I tagged on to the end of the line at the butcher's. It ran along the counter, then the length of the far wall and finally stretched back to the door. Next but one in front was Annie Dunn, further along stood Lena Robertson deep in conversation with Mary Nelson. Within minutes Irene Barrie joined behind us.

Since rationing had been imposed, queuing had become a part of shopping. As you waited your turn the time had to be passed. What better way to pass it than having a good blether? It didn't matter whether you knew your fellow 'queuees' or not.

Lena leaned out from the line; she was about five in front of us. 'Wiz aw that noise comin' from your close oan Setterday night, Netty?'

'Naw, next yin up. Top flat.' Ma looked knowingly at Lena.

'Big Ella, ah suppose?' Lena seemed to vibrate as though her engine was running. Another witness for the prosecution came forward.

'Who else?' Meg drew herself up to her full five feet as she spoke. Meg lived up the same close as the accused. She looked around, as if to make sure she wasn't going to be overheard. I wondered if she hadn't noticed the shop was full. As Meg, confidentially, leaned inward, so did the entire queue, including folk who'd never even met the subject of the character assassination. George Guthrie placed his arms on top of the counter so as not to miss anything.

'Hoose wiz full of Yanks!' *Sniff!*

Meg regained the vertical, the queue followed as one. Lena adjusted her ample bosom with the backs of her forearms.

'S'not the first time, mind. Gettin' tae be like the forty-ninth state up therr nooadays.' She engaged in some more righteous bosom adjusting, then she leaned forward, the assembled company following suit. 'Ah'll tell ye's whit else ah've heard.' She paused for dramatic effect. Ma pulled me in close, put one hand over my ear and pressed my head, and other ear, against her coat. Whatever was about to be divulged was obviously 'not for my ears'. Lena took a final, imperious look around. She had them; you could have heard a sausage drop. 'Ah huv it oan good authority that Big Ella is . . .' she lowered her voice and soundlessly mimed, 'three months gone!' There was a chorus of 'Whit?' from one or two who'd never been on a lip-reading course. Lena held up three fingers and spoke a bit louder, 'Three months,' then mouthed the word 'gone', and to make sure there was no mistake, moved her hand in a curving motion in front of her stomach. 'Ah wid imagine it'll be called Tex!'

As the laughter died down Ma let go of my head. I tugged her sleeve.

'Ma, Big Ella's no been gone three months, ah saw her in the street yesterday.' I was extremely gratified as the queue went into fits of laughter, though Ma wouldn't tell me why.

There was a good war film on at the Blythsie and queues at both the 'dear end' and the 'cheap end'. The dear-end one was smaller, so we joined it. It was a blustery night with an occasional spit of rain. It was only when you were near the front of the queue that you got shelter under the short canopy above the cinema entrance. Ma and I were so far back from the brightly lit canopy we were in the dark.

A voice came out of the shadows: 'Put the wean in the middle, oot of the cauld.'

There was a shuffling and a tunnel appeared. I was shunted into it, an unknown hand shoved a sweetie into my mouth, and the adults closed in around me – like a baby penguin in an Antarctic night. Now, only the odd wee breeze managed to reach my short-trousered legs.

Movement by the queue was intermittent. Folk went in and out of the cinema at odd times. They would quite happily go in in the middle of the main feature, watch it to the end, therefore finding out 'whodunit', sit through the rest of the show – newsreel, cartoon, second feature, 'coming attractions' – then watch the start of the main film until it came to the bit they'd already seen – 'C'mon, this is where we came in' – then make their exit. This meant folk were constantly leaving the cinema in twos and threes all evening and the assistant manager regularly appeared to call, 'A single and a double.' 'Two singles.'

As we slowly moved forward, with it being Glasgow, there were soon multi-faceted conversations going on between folk who'd never met before in their lives. One man mentioned he wanted to see the film – it was about the war in North Africa – because he'd served there with the Desert Rats. Another man came into the conversation because he'd served there with the Long Range Desert Group. As the queue trickled forward these two kept us all enthralled with tales of raids behind enemy lines and anecdotes of officers and men they'd known in common. With my vivid imagination, they put pictures in my head which the film would find hard to match.

As we neared the head of the line we were entertained for a few minutes by a couple of down-and-out buskers. As was the case with back-court singers and newspaper sellers, I found I could not understand a word the busker sang. His mate managed to tap-dance without moving. Then, of course, after their 'turns' they came along the line with an empty bunnet held out and a monotone, 'Thankyooverymush ladiesangennlemen' and picking up a few coppers here and there, including one from Ma.

At last we got in, just in time for the main feature, *Five Graves to Cairo* starring Franchot Tone. Then, all too soon it seemed, the picture finished, the Blythswood emptied and we were strolling home. Ma didn't have enough money for a visit to Cocozza's.

'Ma, ye know what?'

'No, what?'

'Ah think listening tae yon two men in the queue wiz even better than the picture.'

She smiled. 'Dae *you* know what?'

'No, what?'

'Ah think listening tae yon two buskers – wiz better than the picture!' But long before she finished the sentence the two of us were in stitches.

Uncle George: D-Day + 42

I was wakened by voices. Still tired, I managed to open my eyes. I'd have a look to see who our early-morning visitor was then drift back off to sleep. Ma was cooking at the range and talking to them. I lazily turned round in the big bed and, with my last reserves of energy, craned my neck to have a look.

'Uncle George!'

Stripped to the waist, braces hanging down, he was in the middle of a wash and shave at the sink. He turned.

'Hiyah, pal!'

Instantly wide awake, I dived out of bed, ran over and sat up on the lid of the coal bunker, next to the sink.

'Ah never heard ye come in. Was ah sleeping?'

'Ye were as sound as a wee top.'

I looked at him. It was just wonderful to see him, I was fizzing with excitement. He turned to Ma.

'Gonny gie me a cup of hot water oot the kettle, Netty?'

I watched as he put a pinch of salt in it, stirred it, then took a tentative sip.

'Whit dae ye dae that for, Uncle George?'

''Cause it's good for ye. Flushes yer system oot. But ye have tae drink it first thing in the morning, before ye have yer breakfast.'

I resolved to start doing that, too. Anything my Uncle George did must be good. I watched as he drew the safety razor, in short strokes, over his jaw. I could hear the blade scraping against the tough bristles. I wished I was old enough to shave. He rinsed the razor in the soapy water filling the blue-rimmed, enamel basin. He then began to wash, lathering his face and neck vigorously, rinsing it off, then rubbing his wet hands under his oxters. I tried to memorise every move. That's how I'd wash in future. Turning on the single, brass tap he cupped his hands under the stream of cold water and splashed his face, making blowing noises as he did. I didn't fancy that so much, but, if Uncle George did it I'd have to do it too.

Finished, he flicked his hands at me, sprinkling me with beads of cold water. Laughing, I jumped off the bunker and ran out of reach. It was great. My Uncle George was back.

Ma laughed too. 'Aye, he's feart of watter, that yin.' I could tell she was happy. She had her baby brother back.

I continued to watch his every move as he finished what he called his 'morning ablutions'. I noted the hair under his arms and on his chest; I hoped I'd be hairy when I grew up.

'Ah've got something for you!'

'Have ye, Uncle George. Whit is it?'

He went over to his kitbag, rummaged in it, then handed me a large, square object wrapped in silver paper. I pulled open the foil at one end and revealed an enormous block of chocolate.

'Oh Ma, look!'

Sweets were stringently rationed. I wondered how I could show this windfall off to my pals – without giving them any.

'That's Navy chocolate. That's what we use for making oor cocoa.'

'What do you say?' Ma reminded me.

'Aw, thanks a lot, Uncle George.'

'Ah've got something else for ye, a wee war souvenir.' His tunic was hanging on the back of a chair. He reached into one of its pockets, then placed a small, light object in my palm. 'Do ye know what that is?'

I looked closely at it. Triangular-shaped, about the size of a half-crown, it looked like glass but was too light and its edges were rounded. It had a brownish tinge and, inside, there were little brown bubbles which meant you could hardly see through it.

'Is it melted glass?'

'Nearly right,' said George. 'It's a piece of Perspex from the canopy of a German fighter that crashed on the beach in Normandy.'

'Wow! Did the plane go on fire?'

'Aye, that's why it's aw melted.'

I rubbed my thumb along the smooth edges and looked even closer at the brown bubbles trapped inside.

'Gee! Wait till ma pals see this.' At five, I didn't make the connection that a young German pilot was probably burning at the same time. 'Thanks a lot, Uncle George.'

It was September 1944, George's first leave since Normandy.

It would be years later, from talking to his brothers James and Bill, that I would find out about George's experiences on D-Day.

On 6 June, having turned nineteen less than a fortnight previously, Marine PO/X 113748 McIntosh. G. (Combined Ops), has the task of driving an LCI (landing craft infantry) on and off Juno beach with one load of troops after another. Once the large troopship has been emptied he, his crew and landing craft will return to England aboard her.

No amount of training has prepared them for the maelstrom of 6 June. Battleships and cruisers lie offshore sending salvo after salvo over their heads as they flit back and forth in their tiny craft. Destroyers and corvettes race up and down even nearer shore, the crack of their 4·5s almost as loud as the frightening sound of the large capital ships loosing off eight-gun broadsides from their eighteen-, sixteen- and fourteen-inch main armaments. Bombers fly low overhead to drop their bombs just inland from the beach; fighters fly even lower as they zoom in to strafe individual targets. German fire from gun emplacements and dug-in field guns regularly straddle the landing craft as they head for shore. Nearer the beach, machine-gun and rifle fire from German troops rattles off the side of their fragile LCI.

Increasingly they pass half-sunk tanks and landing craft, some on fire. Bodies of dead and wounded soldiers float on the water and litter the beach. Noise, death and mayhem surround them as they make trip after trip. There is only one thought on their minds – will we be next?

At some time during the day their craft is hit and disabled and they have to scramble ashore. They will spend the next *six weeks* stranded on this Normandy beach, under long-range German shellfire night and day and regularly strafed by Luftwaffe fighters on tip-and-run raids before they eventually get back to the UK. They are commandeered by the Beach-master – the officer responsible for all movement on and off the beach – and used as runners and general dogsbodies.

George will later tell his brothers that, though this was bad enough, worst for him was being ordered to clear the dead off the beach. What had once been young men like himself now lay like so much butcher-meat: parts of bodies, entrails, limbs, brains. He could not bring himself to touch them. Not sober.

He and his mates take to pillaging the abandoned houses along the beach. As this is France, there are copious amounts of wine and cognac to be had. In his own words, 'We stayed drunk the whole six weeks.' It is the only way he can handle the sights and sounds of this extended nightmare. It is also the start of a lifelong drink problem.

'Ma, whit's the matter wi' Uncle George, he disnae play wi' me as much as he used tae?'

'Och, he's maybe got a lot on his mind. Don't you pester him.'

'But even when he brings his pals back wi' him, he disnae have a good laugh like he used tae.'

'Now, jist you listen tae me. There's a lot of things happened to yer Uncle George since he was last hame. He just needs peace and he'll soon be back tae his auld self; don't you keep bothering him.'

Soon Uncle George's leave was almost over. It was still great to have him in the house, but, it had been a big disappointment to me. He just wasn't full of fun anymore. He'd sit with a newspaper in his lap, not reading it, just staring into space. On previous leaves he waited till the evening before he went out for a drink. Now he went out at lunchtime, came back and slept it off, then went out again in the evening. He seemed restless when in the house during the day. No longer did his uniform get its daily press.

Still, this was Saturday. Ma had said he could bring his pals back to the house tonight for a farewell do. Surely it'd be good tonight.

The four 'movie stars' from his last leave reappeared, plus a new one – complete with Veronica Lake hairdo. Two of the four original blokes were back, and three new ones. All tried to liven the party up. To no avail.

'C'mon, George, gie us a wee smile.'

'Ah know, we'll let him win a couple of hands, that'll dae the trick.' It didn't.

George tried to smile, but as the evening wore on, the more he drank the more morose he became. As usual, I sat beside my hero. I wished and willed him to somehow get back to being what he had always been – the centre of attraction, with the girls hanging on his every word. I was at a loss to know what had happened to my glorious uncle.

It was late in the evening. I was beginning to get sleepy, but still hoped for a minor miracle. Any second now he would spring to life; maybe the next mouthful of beer would do it. The rest of the party were trying to enjoy themselves in spite of George, but his presence was a damper. He'd left the card game earlier saying, 'Och, ah'm fed up playing cards,' and now sat on a fireside chair. I sat on the other side of the range, opposite him.

Suddenly, 'Ah'll show ye's ah'm no frightened of anything!'

The conversation at the table died. All heads turned to watch as he moved his chair so that he sat four-square in front of the fireplace.

'What are ye on aboot, George?'

'Ah'll show ye's all, ah'm no fuckin' scared of anything.' This was said in slow, measured tones. As he spoke he was searching through his tunic's breast pockets.

'George, naebody has said a word about ye; we've all just been trying tae have a wee game of cards and a bit laugh. C'mon back tae the table and have a wee gemme. C'mon.'

'Ahaa!' In triumph George brought his hand out of his pocket and held it up in the air. Between two fingers he held a small bullet. 'Just watch this.' He reached out and dropped the bullet into the centre of the hot coals. There was a moment's silence.

'Fuck me!'

There was the sound of chairs, in unison, scraping backwards from the table; one fell over. Most of the girls let out little screams, a couple of guys laughed. They all made for the door. George moved his chair even nearer to the fire. As usual I had been watching my hero's every move. Now things were livening up; this was better.

'C'mere, you!' Ma grabbed me by the wrist and yanked me off the chair, saying to George, in passing, 'See you, ya silly bugger!'

There was a log jam at the door as all our guests tried to get through it and into the small lobby, then open the outside door to the close – and safety.

A male voice said, 'Ah cannae get the outside door opened, there's too many in the lobby. Back up intae the room.'

'Yur joking, in't ye?' said another male voice.

'Ye should be lettin' aw us lassies oot first, ya bastards!' suggested a female.

'Fuck off!' said a gent.

Ma made a beeline for the recess bed. She lifted the valance and we crawled under. A second later the valance lifted again and we were joined by 'Veronica Lake', she blew her cheeks out. 'Talk aboot wimmen and children first; did ye see them?'

By now we could hear the excited chatter from the rest of the company; they had made it out to the close. Billy shouted from the lobby, 'George, come oot here; that's bound tae go off any second.' Ma added her voice to the pleas: 'George, will you stop being so bloody—' There was a terrific BANG! Most of the girls screamed, including Ma. We heard footsteps coming back into the room.

'Is he awright?' shouted Ma.

'Aye, but there's bloody cinders everywhere.'

The room quickly filled up and everyone dashed around trying to locate, and return, most of the fire to the fireplace. Uncle George brushed the ash from his uniform and hair. He appeared to have cheered up considerably.

'See, "The Man They Couldnae Kill", that's me. Ah wiz stuck oan the beach in Normandy for six weeks, so another wee bullet disnae make any difference. Ye jist saw for yerselves, no frightened of anything.'

'Naebody said ye were, yah eejit,' said Ma.

'Ah well, jist in case anybody did,' muttered George.

'Where did the bullet finish up?' enquired one of the girls. A search was instituted and it was found, deeply embedded, high up in the frieze near the gas meter. It was left undisturbed.

Next morning, somewhat subdued, Uncle George headed down to the Central Station to catch his train back to Chatham. Before departing he borrowed a pound from Ma for a drink en route. As ever, I sadly watched him go. His leave had been a terrible disappointment to me. I fervently hoped that next time I saw him he would, once more, be my old Uncle George – King of the World, Master of All He Surveyed.

Victory in Europe Day

'It's VE Day the morra; there's gonny be a party in the street.' Ma sat at the table shelling peas into a bowl. 'Open wide!' She shoved a pea into my mouth.

'Whit's a VE Day?'

'The Germans have surrendered. Mr Churchill says the morra's tae be called VE Day. "V" stands for Victory and "E" stands for Europe so, it's Victory in Europe Day. It's gonny be a holiday all ower the country wi' folk havin' parties and celebrating.'

'Even doon in England?'

'Aye, doon in England tae.'

I pondered on all this information. 'Are we no fighting the Germans anymair?'

'Naw, they've gave in, and they'll have tae dae what they're telt in future and start behaving thurselves. A bit like yerself,' she added. As I opened my mouth to reply to this slur she force-fed me another pea.

'So, when we go tae the pictures, will there be nae mair fighting on the newsreels?'

'Well, there'll be some, 'cause we're still fighting the Japs. But you'll no see any mair fae Germany. That's aw finished noo.'

This was a disappointment. At the age of six, I'd never known the weekly newsreels without their war reports, usually illustrated with exciting footage of German trains, planes and ships being bombed and strafed as we put them on the retreat. Jeez, I really liked it. It was gonny be pretty dull now. Avoiding another pea, I made for the door.

'Ah'm away tae see if ah can find oot whit's gonny be happening.'

I emerged from the shade of our close into a bright, warm street. Jim McDonald, Tommy Dunn and Tommy Finegan were already out, busy making enquiries. There was a definite feeling of 'something going on'.

'Did ye's hear aboot us beating the Germans and this VE Day thing they're gonny have in the street the morra?'

'Aye, it sounds like a rerr terr, eh?'

'Dae ye know whit ah've heard?' Tommy Dunn looked at the three of us. 'Noo that the war's finished, the Corporation are gonny get rid of the baffle walls.'

'Whit for?'

Tommy shook his head, disappointed by my ignorance.

' 'Cause there'll be nae mair bombs, will thurr? So they're no needed.'

I looked up the street. Four feet away from each close mouth, parallel with the edge of the pavement, stood a solid brick wall, six feet tall, six feet wide and two feet thick. If a bomb landed in the street they were supposed to deflect the blast away from the close in case any folk were sheltering there. For some reason, the baffle walls on the other side of our street weren't brick-built. They were constructed of corrugated iron sheets held together by a frame and filled with sand.

'They should just leave them,' said Jim; 'they're smashing for hiding behind when we're playing sodjers!'

As we spoke we suddenly heard wee Mrs Docherty's window going up. She lived one-up across the street. We wondered what we'd done – usually her window going up meant she was about to get on to us. Her son, John, came out of the close; we got ready to run. Maybe we'd done something yesterday and we'd forgotten about it? We looked at one another. John turned his back to us and looked up at his mother.

'Right Ma.'

She threw down one end of a long string with small red, white and blue pennants on it. He walked straight across the street and, attaching the string to a nail on top of a clothes prop, held it up to Granny Smeaton who was waiting at her window. She tied the string to a newly hammered-in nail on her sill.

A couple of hours later the street was festooned with bunting which had last seen the light of day at the 1937 Coronation. Union Jacks and blue and white Scottish Saltires waved from a dozen or more windows. Old men and young boys, us included, went foraging round shops, factories and middens for fuel until, by evening, a bonfire at least fifteen feet high had grown in the middle of our street. As the day wore on the atmosphere became electric until, by mid-evening, there were spontaneous parties going on in quite a few houses. As bedtime loomed my pals and I were still out in the street, hoping our mammies would forget the time and let us enjoy all the activity as music, singing and laughter drifted down to us from the many windows. The darker it got, the brighter the street became. Then I realised why – nobody was bothering to pull their blackout curtains. There was no need to; there would be no sneak German raider over tonight.

In the morning, as usual, I reluctantly emerged from sleep. Ma was already up. I lay half dozing until, from somewhere, the memory of all the fun and excitement of yesterday popped into my head.

'Aw Ma, it's that VE thing the day, in't it?'

She laughed. 'Ah was wondering when it would dawn on ye. Feart in case you miss anything, are ye? Don't worry, all the fun disnae start till the efternoon.'

'Whit fun will there be?'

'Jist you wait and see. There's gonny be a party in the street later on.'

'Will they be lighting the bonfire?'

'Naw, that'll no be lit till it gets dark. Nae use lighting a bonfire during the day, it's best at night.'

'Can ah stay up late tae see it?'

'Oh aye, you'll be staying up late the night. This is a special day, pal. You don't get many days like this.'

After a bolted breakfast, and giving my face a 'cat's lick' at the sink, I was soon running out into the street. I sat on the steps at our close mouth while I took it all in. It was wonderful. My street was full of colour, it had been transformed. Even more flags and bunting had appeared. Everything was in Technicolor. And the bonfire was bigger than ever.

I decided to stay sitting at the close mouth to watch all the comings and goings. The close, or entry, ran from the street through the width of the building to the back court. Halfway along its length the stairs led off up to the three upper landings. Three families lived on each of the landings plus three inside the close. Twelve families in all. We all gave our address as 14 Doncaster Street. Our single-end was in the close. The windows faced into the back court, with a view of wash houses and middens and the back of the Maltbarn Street tenements. I sometimes wished we looked out into the street. It would have been more interesting.

The wind was in the right direction that day and was being funnelled through the close, giving a pleasant breeze as I sat and watched all the preparations.

As it neared midday, Annie Dunn came out and began marshalling her troops. The men were sent up to St Cuthbert's Church to borrow the long, folding tables and chairs and benches from the hall. These were set up in the street. Right in the middle of the street! Surely if the polis came they'd say, 'Ye cannae dae that!' They did – but they didn't. They just smiled, had a blether with Annie for five minutes, then went on their way. It seemed you could do anything you liked on a VE Day.

By one o'clock, sandwiches, cakes and jellies had been produced along with all the plates and cutlery needed. By two o'clock, all us kids were sitting at the tables getting tucked in – just like Lord Snooty and His Pals in the *Beano*. Our mammies were in close attendance, occasionally reaching over us for their share. In jig-time the foodstuffs, washed down by cups and mugs of ginger, vanished from the scene. The next couple of hours were taken up by games and community singing until, around four-thirty, the borrowed tables and chairs were returned to a relieved caretaker, who'd had visions of some of them finishing up on the bonfire.

Things quietened down after the party. The men who'd built the bonfire were adamant it wouldn't be lit until dark, sometime around nine p.m. To make sure none of the older boys were tempted to light it earlier, a watch was kept on it for the rest of the afternoon and early evening.

I spent the hours until the bonfire would be lit on tenterhooks, continually in and out the house in case I missed anything.

'You're like a hen on a hot girdle,' said Ma.

I'd listen to the radio for a while, or read. Every half hour or so I'd run out to the close mouth in case things were livening up. At last, shortly before nine, for the umpteenth time I ran back into the house.

'Ma! Ma! Lots of folk are beginning tae gather roon the bonfire, they must be gonny light it soon.' I was jumping up and down.

'Are ye sure?'

'Aye, honest. Since ah was last oot there's lots of people have come oot their hooses and other wans have come intae the street from other streets. Hurry up, Ma, we'll miss it.'

She rose, put on her coat, paused, then took it off again.

'Ma, whit are ye daein'? We'll miss the bonfire.' I was practically running on the spot at the door.

'Ah shouldnae need ma coat once the bonfire gets going. C'mon then.'

We came out of our close and stood on the pavement.

'See! Didn't ah tell ye, Ma.'

A large crowd surrounded the unlit mountain of wood, old furniture, fruit boxes, cardboard and paper. Everybody in our street was out, including some well wrapped-up invalids who hadn't been over the door for years. There were many I recognised from neighbouring streets which weren't having a bonfire. I felt somehow proud that Doncaster Street had made the effort. Most of the men, some in uniform, had drifted back from the pub with, of course, the mandatory carry-oot – McEwan's Pale Ale – and bottles of lemonade to make shandies for the womenfolk. The scene was set.

Dusk at last began to change into night. There were occasional outbursts of 'Why Are We Waiting?' In the middle of one chorus there was movement as a section of the crowd began to part, then came a shout.

'*This* is why ye's are waiting!'

A few men came through the newly cleared gap carrying someone over their heads.

'Ye's cannae light the fire until we've got Adolf up where he belongs.'

I took a closer look at the 'man' they were toting. He was dressed in what looked like an old Glasgow Corporation Tramways uniform, his face a painted mask with the unmistakable toothbrush moustache and hair combed over the forehead.

'Let's get Adolf up therr on top so as we can make it hot for the bugger!'

The crowd cheered in agreement, then cheered even louder as

one of the younger men clambered up the unstable pile and deposited the Führer on the pinnacle.

Then it was time. The moment I'd been waiting for since the previous day. Four or five men thrust lit papers into the bonfire's base. Loud 'hurrahs' echoed off the tenements and baffle walls. Slowly at first, then spreading faster and faster up the mountain, the flames took hold. Soon the crowd began to draw back as the heat increased.

'Look, Mammy! The flames are gettin' tae Hitler.'

I watched in delight as the dummy was first obscured by smoke and then, as the flames climbed higher the smoke cleared and I could see him again.

'Look, Ma, he's went up!'

With a gentle *whoosh* the Ubermeister of all German Tram Conductors self-ignited. He seemed to defy his fate for a moment until, with a lurch and a flurry of sparks, he fell to the side.

There was a great roar from the crowd and a uniformed soldier near me said, 'Burn, ya bastard!' His wife, or girlfriend shushed him. 'Wellll,' said the soldier, and they both laughed.

People began to join hands and dance round the fire, first one way then the other. As they skipped, sometimes almost running, they sang the usual party songs – 'Bee Baw Babbity', 'She'll Be Coming Round the Mountain'. Other groups, who couldn't get near the fire, formed their own circles and did the hokey-cokey. As the evening wore on folk who were known to have a good voice were cajoled into doing a turn for the assembled company. Later still, a wind-up gramophone was produced and an impromptu dance began. Now and again someone would ask Ma to dance. She didn't need to be asked twice; it had been a long time since she'd had a 'proper' dance.

After a couple of hours some of the older folk returned to their houses but continued to watch the celebrations in comfort – leaning out of their windows, their folded arms resting on a cushion on the sill. By midnight the fire had shrunk considerably. In a fit of bravado some of the young men, egged on by the girls, began to take a run at the fire and leap through the still considerable flames. All went well until John Dinning from one side, and Alec McFarlane from the other, not being able to see one another through the flames, jumped at the same time and met head-on in the middle! To cries of horror from the spectators they plunged down and vanished into the heart of the flames. A split-second later the cries turned to shrieks of laughter as the two of them exited like V-1s, trailing showers of sparks behind them, then danced in a frenzied jitterbug, waving their arms as they brushed dozens of embers from their clothes and shoes. Except for singed eyebrows and hair they were none the worse for the experience.

It was almost one a.m. when Ma persuaded me into going to bed. I just didn't want it to end. As she led me by the hand towards our close I kept looking back, intent on drinking in every last image of this wonderful happening in our street. The bonfire had long since collapsed from its great height but still continued to burn brightly. After all the years of not knowing anything other than the blackout I'd never seen our street lit up at night. I still wasn't used to the streetlights being on and people not bothered about pulling their curtains so that the lights from their windows spilled out onto the road. It was strange to be in a street that wasn't blacked out anymore. Some folk still danced, but now slowly, holding each other close, the girls resting their heads on their man's shoulders. Most people just stood around in groups, talking softly, all gazing into the embers as though looking for something, or deep in thought. I wondered why. Suddenly I remembered something.

'Mrs Paton didnae come, Ma.'

'Naw, it would be too sad for the poor soul. What has she got tae celebrate?'

Mrs Paton lived round the corner in Hinshaw Street and she and Ma were quite pally. Her daughter, Georgina, was in my class at Springbank. Just over a week ago her husband, advancing deep into Germany with his unit, had been killed in action. I thought some more about it.

'That's a shame, Ma, in't it. If the war had just finished aboot ten days ago, Mr Paton would still be alive and Mrs Paton would've been at the bonfire the night.'

Ma put me, unwashed, into my pyjamas and straight to bed. Minutes later she climbed in beside me and I cooried into her.

'It's been smashin' in the street the day, Ma, huzn't it?'

'Aye, it's been great.' She reached up and turned the light off. 'C'mon, it's late, cuddle in and get tae sleep.'

I lay in the dark and listened. The sounds of music, laughter and singing drifted in through the close. I could see it in my mind's eye. I knew this had been a special day. A *very* special day. My daddy, far away in a country called Italy, should be able to come home soon. That'll be really great.

Striking the First Blow

'Why does ma daddy no play games wi me or tell me stories like ma pal's daddies do?'

Ma thought for a moment. 'Some daddies aren't so fond of doing things like that, son. They sort of, ahhh, haven't got the time.'

I would also like to have asked why I'd been wakened up two or three times, late at night, by them shouting and bawling at one another. Somehow I felt I shouldn't.

My father had been demobbed for over two months now. He'd returned to his job as a goods porter for the LMS at College Goods Station. He had been working there when he was called up, and they'd had to give him his job back when he was demobbed. He'd also, from what I'd picked up during their arguments, resumed seeing Big Nell – last seen absconding from the Central Station three years previously. But the main disappointment for me was the fact that he appeared to have no interest in me whatsoever. At the cinema, in books, and at neighbours' houses, daddies played with their weans. Mine didn't.

I wasn't the only one who seemed to be 'in his road'. There was his mother. Quite a few of my pals had their granny living with them as part of the family. My granny didn't even have a house of her own; she lived in a home. Granny Douglas was the only grandparent I knew, the others all having died within a short space of time early in the war. I'd just managed to glimpse Granny McIntosh in her coffin. That was the only memory I had of her. Her husband, my grandfather James McIntosh, a

Ma and me.

journeyman brass finisher, had also died early in the war. I had no memory of him at all.

Granny Douglas had been born Jean McCrindle, in Girvan, the daughter of fisherfolk. When my grandfather, Robert John Douglas, had died in 1941 she'd taken to the drink. The following year she'd been evicted from their house, in nearby Northpark Street, for rent arrears. She'd had no option but to move into the almost Dickensian Salvation Army Shelter for Women, in Clyde Street by the Broomielaw.

At the time of her eviction in 1942, her four sons, Tommy, Bill, Jack and Robert John (my father), were all in the armed forces. Her only daughter, Jean, had married around 1937 and promptly moved away, never to be heard from again. Her four sons all returned safely from the war – with the exception of Jack, who had lost an eye in North Africa. Their mother remained in the home. She would stay there for the rest of her long life.

*

All during the war, and after, she would call at least once a week at our house. She would always sit on the first chair you saw as you entered the room, just three feet or so from the door, next to the sideboard. No matter how cold the day, or even if she'd been caught in the rain, she never sat any nearer to the fireplace. This was as a courtesy to Ma. It was known that the women's shelter was – as my father always put it – lousy! She also, for the rest of her life, never wore anything other than the mourning clothes which had been bought back in 1941 when Granda Douglas had died. As the years wore on, so did her clothes – including the fox fur she always had round her neck. As I grew up I watched them become shiny and threadbare. She had a permanent musty smell around her, which she tried to mask, unsuccessfully, with cheap perfume.

By the time she'd paid for her accommodation at the home, to ensure her bed, the rest of her meagre pension was split between food and her favourite tipple, the cheap wine known as Red Biddy. When her money ran out toward the end of the week she'd come up to our house as she knew that Ma, in spite of rationing, would always give her something to eat, even if only bread and jam and a cup of tea.

She would eat anything at all. In summer, as we had no fridge, milk would turn sour in a couple of days or less. If she saw Ma about to throw a half-pint of sour milk down the sink she'd say, in her strong Ayrshire accent, 'Dinnae dae that, gimme it here.' Ma would hand her the bottle of yellow, curd-like milk. With our faces screwed up, we'd watch her drink it in two or three gulps, put the bottle down and wipe her lips with the back of her hand. 'Lovely! Dinnae forget, jist keep any sour milk for me. It's a shame tae waste it.'

Mostly she'd come in the afternoon when my father was at work. I'd come in from school to see this plump little figure, all in black, cloche hat, fox fur and rosy red cheeks, sitting just inside the door. Except for a rolled-up gamp, it was 'Grandma Giles' come to life. Now and again my father would come home early.

The three of us heard his footsteps in the close, then the key turning in the lock. Granny stuffed the last piece of sandwich into her mouth. I watched her tense as the inner door opened. She was the first one he saw.

'Oh, it's you, is it?'

'Aye, hello, son.' She didn't have any teeth so she was still trying to finish the sandwich.

'On the bloody mooch again, ah see!'

'It was just that last slice of corned beef,' said Ma. 'It would have been off by tomorrow.'

'Ah've told ye before, if ye keep feeding her she'll jist drink the money she's saved.'

As he spoke, his mother was drinking her hot tea as fast as she could. My father turned to her.

'C'mon, it's time ye were away. Ah want tae get washed and huv ma dinner in peace.'

Granny put the cup, still with some tea in it, back in the saucer. She rose, stiffly, to her feet.

'Thanks a lot, Netty. Ah enjoyed that wee bite.' She opened the room door. 'Cheerio then.'

'Aye cheerio,' said my father. 'Shut the door behind ye.' She had hardly closed the outer door when he turned to Ma. 'Whit huv ah told ye aboot feedin' her?'

'It was less than a full slice of corned beef; it was just aboot on the turn. It would have been thrown oot. Ye surely don't grudge yer mother a wee sandwich?'

'Never mind whit ah grudge, jist listen tae whit ah'm fuckin' telling ye. We've got enough tae dae looking efter oorselves withoot feedin' her. The more ye feed her the more she huz for drink.' He took the full kettle from the hob over to the sink and

1938. Ma and Da: Janet McIntosh and Bobby Douglas, in their courting days.

began washing himself. Ma set the table and began cooking the dinner. He'd been home from the army less than three months, already I knew he'd be in a mood the rest of the evening. For a few weeks now I'd sometimes been wakened up at night by him and Ma arguing. I'd be scared, so I'd lie with my eyes tight shut, willing them to stop. Sometimes I'd hear a slap – and Ma would start crying. I didn't look. I didn't want to see him hitting my mammy. He'd started to shout at me a lot when he came from work if I got in his way, or did something wrong. He frightened me. I wished he was still in the Army.

We sat down for our dinner; one of Ma's specialities – mince and doughballs.

'Were ye busy doon the station, the day?'

'We're alwiz busy.'

'The wireless is good the night. *Happidrome* at eight and *ITMA* at nine.'

'Mmm.'

'Can ah have another spoonfy of mince, Ma?' She reached for the spoon.

'Let him serve himself. He's six; time he wiz daein' things for himself.' Ma withdrew her hand.

'Take some yourself,' she said.

I reached over, took a spoonful of mince and brought it toward my plate – leaving a trail of gravy and mince on the tablecloth.

'Look at the useless cunt!' My father shook his head. I felt myself go red; there was real venom in his voice. As I returned the spoon it slipped out of my fingers and clattered noisily into the dish. More mince splashed onto the cloth.

'*Whamm!* I hadn't expected it and didn't see it coming. He'd quickly reached over the table and belted me on the side of the head. This was the first time he'd hit me. It was so sudden. I swayed on my chair and almost fell off. I caught my breath, and at first didn't cry. For a second I wasn't quite sure what had happened.

'Don't hit him like that,' said Ma.

'Ah'll fuckin' hit 'im anywye ah want.' The shock had worn off now and I began to cry.

'There's nae need tae hit him as hard as that.'

'Ah'm his father and if ah want tae hit 'im ah'll hit 'im.' He looked at me. 'Shut the fuck up, you.'

I continued to cry. He stood up, reached over and grabbed me by the back of my shirt collar.

'Get yourself undressed and intae that bed-chair.' He dragged me off my seat, banging my knee painfully against the table leg. Nothing like this had happened before. I was badly frightened and began to shake.

'Nothin' but a fuckin' mammy's boy; time he had a bit of discipline.'

'For Christ's sake! All he did was spill some mince ontae the tablecloth. He's no used tae serving himself.'

'Aye, because you fuckin' mollycoddle 'im. That's why he's never bothered aboot me since ah came hame; you've turned 'im intae a mammy's boy.'

'You never make any effort tae be pals wi' him. He'd love it if you'd play games wi' him. He's said to me umpteen times, "Why does ma daddy no play games wi' me?"'

'Aye, well he'll huv a wait. Ah'm no wasting ma time wi' a mammy's boy.'

'Naw, if ye spent half the time on him that ye spend on yer hoor, Big Nell, ye'd get on better . . .'

The argument escalated as I hurriedly put on my pyjamas, unfolded my bed-chair and got into it in case he decided to hit me again.

Ma was getting the better of him verbally so, to get away from her unanswerable charges, within half an hour he put his jacket on and headed for the pub. Later that night I would be wakened up as, bolstered by the drink, he restarted the argument to try and get the better of it. Eventually Ma would let him have the last word so as we could all get peace and quiet to go to sleep.

Doctors and Dentists Are Bad For You

'*Oooyahooyah* OOYAH!'

'Ah've hardly touched ye,' said Ma.

'Ye have.'

Ma shook her head. 'God only knows, ah hate it when ah have tae stick an Elastoplast on you – ah know that two or three days later ah'm gonny have tae go through this pantomime tae get it off.'

I sat with my foot in a basin of warm water while Ma gently 'plooted' the almost detached plaster. We had now entered the second day of trying to get it off. Ma finished another two minutes' plooting with the water then, pulling gingerly at the edge, gained an almost immeasurable fraction of an inch. I accompanied her with a non-stop chorus of '*Oooyahs*', but half of it still clung, malevolently, to my shin.

'Aw, that'll dae the noo, Ma. Ah'll jist pull ma sock up over it and go oot and play wi' ma pals for a while.'

'That's whit you think. You're staying here till it's aff.'

'But this is the worst bit, Ma; it'll take ages.'

'It'll just have tae.'

I looked down in great apprehension. We were now at the piece of gauze in the centre. The dried blood had welded it to the scab.

'It'll need plenty of plootin', Ma. If ye pull it too soon it'll take the scab off.'

About an hour later the plaster reluctantly gave up its hold. Ma looked at my tear-stained face.

'Ah've never seen anybody like ye in ma life, talk aboot

"cowardy, cowardy custard". The next time ah've got tae take a plaster off you, ah'm gonny invite all yer pals in tae watch the carry-on of ye, and see whit ah've got tae put up with.'

I looked at her. 'Ye widnae.'

'Ah would. In fact, ah'm gonny!'

It was bad enough when some ailment was treated at home. But I lived in constant fear of developing something which meant a visit to the doctor or dentist.

'We're going doon tae the Dental Hospital this afternoon.' Ma smiled benignly. 'Dae ye remember when the dentist came tae the school and had a wee look at your teeth?'

'Aye.'

'Well, they want a wee look at them doon at the Dental Hospital. It'll mean a nice wee hurl on the tram.' That was the clincher.

'Oh, awright then.'

'Yer daddy's coming tae.'

I never read anything into the fact he was coming. It was late 1945 so I wasn't that used to having him around. I never smelled the rat. Unknown to me, Ma had received a letter saying I needed to have five baby teeth extracted: top row, front. Knowing my tendency toward outright terror where medical procedures were concerned, they'd decided that lying – right up until the last minute – was the best method to get me down there.

We sit on a wooden bench in a rather austere corridor. It is all wood panelling, majolica tiles and art-nouveau door plates and handles. To save electricity there are no lights on. The long corridor is dull and gloomy, a minimum of daylight filtering in from windows at either end. Overall is the smell of disinfectant and . . . what? Noises from distant rooms and feet walking along other, probably similar, corridors can just be heard. I get the feeling there are lots of other people in the building. Ma and Da seem to talk low, and clear their throats a lot. Probably didn't like talking in this big, echoing place.

There are two other children, a boy and girl, waiting with their parents. The adults try to make conversation, but it keeps petering out. The two kids are probably around six, too. We soon start talking and showing each other the comics we've brought. The corridor doesn't bother us; now and again the adults have to shoosh us.

A nearby door suddenly swooshes open and a heavily starched nurse in a red-striped uniform leans out and calls a name. The little girl is taken to the door by her mother. Only the child is wanted.

'I'll see you in a few minutes, darling.'

The girl looks a little bewildered as the nurse puts a firm-but-gentle hand behind her. The big door swooshes shut. That unidentified smell is stronger after the door had been opened. The wee boy and I look at one another, then continue our conversation. We are just beginning to enjoy ourselves when – *swoosh*. The face of the starched nurse appears, with a false smile.

'She's ready now.'

The wee lassie's parents rise quickly and go to the door; there is some movement behind it. The wee boy and I suspend negotiations so as to watch.

'Thank you very much.'

'She'll be fine, a little bit groggy for a while.'

I wonder what 'groggy' means. The door closes and the parents turn. The daddy is carrying the girl! We've just been playing with her; now she's lying motionless in her father's arms. I wonder why he said 'Thank you very much' to somebody who's just handed him back his daughter on the brink of death. There is something wrapped round her mouth. That strange smell hits me again. I don't like it. The wee lavvy in the Blythsie smells better than that. My new pal and me look at each other. Our eyes carry two messages – There's something no very good going on in there, and I hope you're before me!

The parents with the wee lassie who is dying slowly walk along the corridor, talking softly to her. Nae good talkin' tae her, mister, I thought, she cannae hear ye. Anyway, I'm just here to be looked at. Comforted, I start talking to my new pal again and we are soon absorbed. *Swoosh!* That door again, and the nurse's head. We stop talking. She calls a name. Great! It's not mine. The wee boy looks at me. Our friendship is obviously finished. He vanishes through that door. The smell is definitely coming from there. Seconds after my ex-pal passes through, there are muffled sounds like there is a bit of a rammy going on. It doesn't last long; soon all is silent. I'm left with just adults. I pretend to look at my comic. I begin to get very bad feelings as to why I'm there. I feel trapped, as I know I can't start causing any bother. My father is with us, he'll just hit me.

Less than five minutes later there is another *swoosh*. I hate that sound.

'He's ready.' I watch in abject fear as his parents collect his body. I look up the other end of the corridor, hoping other families have come in while I wasn't looking – and they're all before me. No. We're the only ones left. I wish I was somewhere else.

'Ma?'

'What, son?'

'Ah'm just here tae be looked at, in't ah?'

'Yes, they just want to have a look at your teeth.' Even though there's nobody about ma has automatically gone into pan-loaf. It's the grand building that's doing it.

Swoosh!

'Robert Douglas.'

There's a stab of fear in my stomach. I use up my last chance: I lean forward and look at my father. Maybe it's him; he's Robert Douglas, too. Ma gives me a gentle push.

'Come on, it's you.'

I find myself walking toward the door on somebody else's legs, Ma behind me. The Starched One takes over.

'Come along, Robert.'

She's doing that firm-hand-on-the-back thing. The door swooshes shut *behind* me. We are in a wee lobby, facing another door. No wonder we could hardly hear a sound. The inside door has a sign on it. I try to pronounce it to myself: *theeter*. No. Maybe *thee-at-er*. I give up. Starchy gives me a stepmother's smile. We go through the inner door into a big room. I wonder if I should try and run for it. The room is almost bare. There's a funny, padded bench contraption with lots of stainless-steel legs and struts. A man with a white coat on stands beside it.

'Hello, Robert. Would you like to come and lie on here for me so that I can have a little look at your teeth?'

Would I fuck, I think to myself. Ah want ma mammy and ah want tae go home. I say nothing. The dentist and his starched assistant lift me up onto the bench, where I lie stiff as a board and increasingly terrified. He has something in his hand. It looks like a brown rubber ring with a red rubber pipe coming out the back of it. The pipe goes all the way up to a connection in the ceiling; halfway up its length it runs through a bit that looks like a rugby ball.

'I'm going to put this on your mouth, Robert, and I want you to take big deep breaths for me and see if you can blow up that balloon.'

He points to the rugby ball. The Smell is really strong now. It must be coming from that thing in his hand. He moves toward me with it. I turn my head away, I don't want that on my face. The dentist puts one hand, fingers open, on top of my head. I feel his fingers pressing on my skull and sliding on my hair as he tries to turn my face round. How could my ma send me in here? I vow never to forgive her. If I get out alive.

'Ah'm no wantin' that on ma face; stoap it, ya fuckin' bastard! Ah want ma mammy.'

Starchy Red Stripe tuts. 'Really! These children.'

'You can fuck off tae!'

She gives a mega-tut. He gets the mask over my mouth; The Smell is everywhere. It does come from this rubber thing. I begin to feel sick.

'Take big deep breaths, Robert. It will soon be over if you do.'

'Let go, yah big bastard, fuck off!'

Because I'm swearing I have to take breaths – the only thing to breathe is The Smell. Suddenly, from a distance I can hear a strange sound – *zwingzwingzwingzwing*. It's coming nearer. Inside my head there is a pounding. I begin to feel dizzy, the *zwingzwings* get louder and they're joined by bells, big, deep, sonorous bells, like in the film *The Hunchback of Notre Dame*.

'That's a good boy, Robert, big deep breathssssss . . .'

'Letglo yahfrookinbigblastward . . .'

I awake feeling sick, then become aware I'm not in my bed. I try to clear my head. I don't know where I am. I can feel cold air on my face and knees. The fresh air begins to clear my head a little. I'm on my father's back! He's giving me a 'coal-carry'. Ma has her hand on me in case I topple backwards. As my senses clear further I begin to feel pain in my gums. I remember where I've just been. A towel is wrapped loosely round my mouth. I move my head back and the towel stays lying along my father's shoulders – there's a big, red circle of blood on it, just like a Japanese flag.

'Oh! He's beginning to come round.'

I recognise Ma's voice. At the same time I realise what they've just let strangers do to me.

'Yah rotten blastwards!'

My father laughs, Ma tuts – just like Starched Nurse. I don't care.

'Ah've never been so black-affronted in ma life,' says Ma.

'Rotten big blastards, ye said they were jist gonny look at me.'

'Ah could hardly keep fae laughing,' says my father, 'specially when the dentist said, "He has a rather colourful vocabulary for six."'

'Ah did not know where tae put maself,' says Ma.

'Well,' says my father, 'it's the anaesthetic. Some people who've never swore in their lives eff and blind like troopers under it.'

I look around to see where we are. Up ahead I recognise St George's Cross. It'll be half an hour before we're home. I just want my bed.

'Why are we no on the tram? Ye said we wid be going on the tram.'

''Cause the dentist said the fresh air wid dae ye good,' says my father. He paused. 'Mibbe stop ye fae sweering.' He laughs out loud. Even though I feel dreadful, I get a little surge of pleasure. I've made my father laugh for the first time.

Ma rubs my back. 'Och, ye were ma brave wee sodjer, wizn't ye, son?'

'Ah wiznae a brave wee shodler, ah wiz scared.' I lay my head down on my father's shoulders and bury my aching mouth in the towel. The blood has gone cold. 'Ah'm no talkin' tae youse. Ah'm never gonny talk tae youse again.' My gums are starting to throb, but I manage to doze off.

At long last we get to the house and, tired and traumatised, I'm put to bed. I'm left with a sore mouth – and a lifelong fear of the dentist.

*

Me aged 6. Not long after the nightmare visit to the dentist. I'm reluctant to smile and show the gap.

My sixth year was proving to be a memorable one. Mostly for bad reasons.

'Ma, gonny look at ma leg, it's got a wee sore bit on it?'

'Mmmm, it's mibbe a wee bite. Ah hope it's no the start of a boil.'

I felt a pang of fear. I'd heard about boils. Now and again one of my pals would get one. My Uncle Jack had had one on the back of his neck about a year ago. It had given him some gyp until they'd cut it. The words 'boil' and 'lanced' went together. Every time I heard the word 'lance' it put bad pictures in my mind. That night, when I went to bed I prayed very hard it wouldn't be a boil. It was.

'Ah'd better take ye up tae see Dr McNicol. It takes the doctor tae treat a boil.'

'Ah'm no wantin' tae see him, ah don't like him!'

'Oh, don't talk nonsense, Dr McNicol is a smashing wee

doctor. You should think yourself lucky you're oan his panel. Lots of folk want tae be, but he's full up.'

'They can huv ma place.'

Ma fixed me with a stern look. 'Yer gaun!'

We sat in the small waiting room with its mis-matched chairs and the smell of antiseptic. Or was it disinfectant? I looked around at the collected coughs and wheezes. Now and again I glanced down at my painful leg and my feeling of dread increased. Ah bet he wants tae lance it. Dr McNicol hadn't long been in practice at this little surgery on Maryhill Road, but already he'd made his mark as an efficient GP who had no time for malingerers, or the workshy. Within a few months of his arrival most of the long-term sick were either back at work, or had changed their doctor. This was 1945, before the National Health Service.

'Just go in, Mrs Douglas.' Ma propelled me along in front of her.

'Hello, what's the problem?' We hadn't even sat down yet.

'I'd like you to take a look at his leg, Doctor.' Ma was straight into pan-loaf.

While he examined my shin, I inspected him. He was a small man, aged around thirty, with wavy hair and a three-piece suit. Ma thought he was great and was especially taken by his quick little smile. 'He just turns it oan an' off like a light switch.'

'Yes, it's a boil!'

A great stab of fear went deep into my stomach. I felt myself go weak. Everything was now out of my control. I was in the hands of doctors and mammies. Dr McNicol sat back in his chair.

'I'll give you a note to take to Mr Angus, the chemist. He'll give you kaolin to make a poultice. Bring him back in two days' time – it should be ready for lancing.'

I almost passed out when I heard the word I'd been dreading.

I knew that in two days' time I'd probably die of fright right in front of him as soon as he came near it with anything sharp. It would serve the two of them right.

'We'll soon get this cleared up for you,' said the doctor. The wee smile flashed on and off. Well, at least Ma would go away happy.

'Thank you very much, Doctor.' Ma handed over the half-crown consultation fee.

'Have you used kaolin before?'

'No, Doctor.'

'The hotter the poultice, the better it will work and draw everything to a head.' He looked at me. 'Do you know where kaolin comes from?'

'The Gestapo!' I wanted to say. 'The chemist's?' I said.

The wee smile lingered longer than usual; Ma was certainly getting her half-crown's worth.

'No, the main basis is mud from the River Nile. Do you know where the River Nile is?'

I thought quickly. 'Doon the Toon, near West Nile Street?'

He nearly laughed. Ma will probably force another two-and-six on him if this keeps up.

'No, the Nile is in Egypt.'

We received the normal smile as we got up to leave. A few minutes later we were out on the Maryhill Road heading for the chemist's. My thoughts were all of fear.

'Ma, ah'm no wantin' tae huv hot poletisses. And ah'm no gonny get it lanced!'

'You'll have tae.'

'Ah'm no gonny.'

'Dae ye want tae lose your leg?'

'Ah'm no bothered.'

'Don't talk bloody nonsense.'

'It's ma leg. Ah don't huv tae huv it done if ah don't want tae.'

Ma stopped dead in the street. 'Listen, you've got a boil and you're gonny have it treated. We'll be back tae see Dr McNicol on Thursday – and that's final!'

'Mmmmmmmm!' I gret and girned all the way down the Maryhill Road, in and out the chemist's, along Hinshaw Street and down Doncaster Street until, just before we got to our close, Ma gave me a clout which shut me up – for a while.

The next two days were dominated by Ma heating the kaolin up in a pan, spreading it on a piece of lint, covering it with gauze, and trying to get me to sit still long enough to get it on the boil while some heat remained.

'*Oooyahooyahooyah!* It's too hoat.'

Ma withdrew the poultice, which had only been in the vicinity of my shin, and tested it with the back of her hand.

'Too hot? If it gets any caulder it'll huv bloody icicles hangin' from it.'

'It's burning!'

'It's no burning. Look!' She held it against her cheek.

Reluctantly I allowed her to place it on the boil and secure it with a bandage. Long before morning it would be down round my ankle. As the days passed I watched in horror as the boil got redder and redder, then began to develop a yellow head. At all times it was painful and throbbed, especially during the night. Then Thursday arrived.

In a state of abject terror I found myself entering Dr McNicol's surgery. Ma quickly took the dressing off. The doctor reached down, lifted my leg up and rested my foot on the edge of his chair, between his legs. A bad move. I checked that he didn't have any weapons in his hands.

'Yesss, that's quite ready. That'll clean out no bother at all.'

He firmly held my leg with one hand. I felt trapped. He reached over with his free hand to open the lid covering a small, stainless-steel container. I watched as he lifted out a slender, shiny knife-like instrument which had been lying in some red liquid. A terrible fear, solid inside my stomach, began to take me over. I watched as he shook excess liquid off the instrument back into the tray. As he turned toward me light glinted on the scalpel. I'd seen enough.

'*Waaagh!*' I was up and off the chair in a flash and got myself behind a solid table at the far end of the room. As I'd kicked off from the starting blocks I'd pushed hard on the foot between the good doctor's legs. He'd given an '*Ooof!*' and now looked a bit red in the face. Ma and he still sat in the same positions, looking at one another. There was a moment's silence.

'Come back here immediately!' said Dr McNicol – in a voice slightly higher than when we'd come in.

'Ah'm no.'

'I promise you won't feel it; it will be very quick.'

'Don't care, ah'm no lettin' ye dae it.' I looked at Ma.

Her face was scarlet; she spoke. 'Oh Doacter, ah'm awfy sorry. Ah alwiz huv the awfyist job wi' him when he's no well.' In the midst of all the drama Ma blew her cover by forgetting to speak pan-loaf.

Dr McNicol put Excalibur back in its container. 'Well, I'm sorry, but I've no intention of chasing him round the surgery with a scalpel in my hand.' This was music to my ears. 'You're not very brave, are you?' he said.

'Ah don't want tae be.'

He shook his head. I thought I detected the glimmer of a smile, his balls must be getting better. He looked at Ma.

'Just keep poulticing it. Eventually it will be ready for cleaning out. It's essential you get it all out. You *must* get the root. If you don't, it will almost certainly recur. Use plenty of antiseptic with everything you do.'

As we left the surgery, with me on guard in case it was a ploy to catch hold of me, I caught a glimpse of the doctor heading for the sink. I thought I detected a slight limp. I didn't care. I'd escaped from under the knife.

Ma and I headed for the chemist's again. I felt a great weight had been lifted from me.

'Ah've never had such a showing up in ma life, ah'll never be able tae look that man in the face again.'

I tried to look contrite. I couldn't.

Next morning when I awoke, the boil didn't seem so sore. I reached down. My leg was wet. I pushed back the covers.

'Ma, ma boil's burst!'

She came over and inspected it. 'Right, we're gonny get it cleaned oot while the going's good.' She looked me in the eye. 'Now, listen tae whit ah've got tae say. Ye didn't want it lanced – ye didn't get it lanced. Is that right?'

'Aye.' I knew what was coming.

'So, ah'm gonny have tae clean it oot for ye. Ah'll be as gentle as ah can *but*, ye heard whit the doctor said, we have tae get the root *out*. Don't start any of yer baby stuff, just grit yer teeth.'

I watched as she fetched some warm water, antiseptic and gauze pads. I shut my eyes, gripped the arms of the chair. And gritted my teeth.

'Right! Ah've got it, ah've got the root.'

'Ahhh.' I let out a breath I didn't know I'd been holding. 'Gie's a look.' I wanted to see this bad little get that had caused me so much trouble. She held the pad up. 'Ooooh! In't it horrible?' I looked at my leg. The boil was still red and raised round its edges, but the centre had collapsed into a hole. It looked like a small, spent volcano.

'See, now that wisnae too bad,' said Ma; 'you were good there. Why can't ye always be brave like that?'

'Don't know.' I shrugged my shoulders. But I was pleased with the praise.

Ma threw the pad with the root in it onto the fire. I watched as the flames enveloped it. I hoped that, somehow, it could feel it.

*

Later that day we heard my father's key in the lock. I'd been anticipating him coming home from work, though he was already fed up with his job at the station and was always complaining. As soon as he opened the inner door and came into the room I was ready.

'Daddy, we got ma boil burst and cleaned oot – and ah didnae cry!'

He didn't look at me. He looked at Ma, a sour smile on his face. 'What's he wantin', a fuckin' medal?'

Ma didn't reply. I looked from one to the other. I could feel tears coming into my eyes. I blinked them back.

Drew

It was the early summer of 1946 when Drew and his parents moved into Doncaster Street. We didn't know his name then. Whenever we saw him, with his mother, somebody would say, 'There's that wee new boy again.' Then the long summer holidays started and, as ever, we would be out playing in the streets and back courts from morn to night until, usually between nine and ten p.m., as dusk was falling, you'd hear 'the cry of the Mammies'. Windows would go up, figures in wraparound peenies and turbans would appear at close mouths to shout names.

'Jim! Billy! Come on, time ye were in.'

'Aw Ma, jist another ten minutes.'

'Never mind another ten minutes. *Now!*'

Slowly, greetin' and girnin' all the way, we'd reluctantly abandon the street and head for our close. Days were never long enough.

As we ran about the street that summer we'd often catch a glimpse of the new boy coming back and forth, always with his mother. Like me, he was an only child. As they passed by he'd look longingly at us as we played rounders, kick-the-can, or cowboys and indians. When they entered their close he would actually lean back so as to catch the last possible glimpse of us, his mammy holding him firmly by the hand.

Maybe she just had a feeling.

It was a Saturday morning, not too long after the long holidays had ended and school restarted. A few of us were out in the street. The wee new boy was standing at his close watching us. Alone.

'Hey, therr's that wee boy. He's no with his mammy.'

'Will we ask him if he wants tae play?'

'Aye, go on.'

'Dae you want tae play wi' us?'

'Aye.' He walked over, shyly.

'Whit's yer name?'

'Drew.'

'Whit age ur ye?'

'Five.'

'Are ye at the school?'

'Aye, ah've just started, so ma mammy and daddy say ah can come oot tae play now.'

He was a small five, lots of freckles on his face and with a really short short-back-and-sides for the summer – like most of us. The hair on top, which had been spared, was a mass of tight curls. Up until now there had been only two younger than me in our gang. I was seven. Now there was Drew.

For the next few weeks he was always out playing with us after school and at weekends. He was a quiet wee boy, quite happy to tag along but determined to keep up with us when it came to games, or running, or climbing.

It was a Saturday. I came out of the children's matinee at the Seamore and walked up the Maryhill Road and back to Doncaster Street. It was around four o'clock and still light. As I turned into our street, John, one of the Sinclair twins, came running over.

'Huv you just came oot the pictures?'

'Aye, it wiz great, Hopalong Cassi . . .'

'Did ye hear aboot wee Drew?'

'Naw, whit aboot 'im?'

'He's been drooned in the Kelvin!'

'Jeez! How did it happen?'

John told me the story. Tommy Dunn and three or four others had decided to go to Kelvingrove Park, one of several green areas within easy reach of our bit of Maryhill, which is in the north-west of the city, sandwiched between the Forth and Clyde Canal and Ruchill Park to the north, and the River Kelvin and Kelvingrove Park to the west. Drew, however, had been forbidden to leave the street.

'Can ye no ask yer mammy?'

'She'll no let me go. She says ah'm too wee tae go far away.'

'Well, don't ask her. We'll jist be away an hour, she'll no miss ye.'

'Well, if it's jist an hour, 'cause if she finds oot ah've been away I'll no get oot tae play again.'

En route to the park plans had changed. It had been decided to let Drew see one of our favourite places for playing. They'd climbed over the wall into a secluded, heavily wooded piece of ground near to an abandoned flint mill. We went there regularly and it was always known as 'ower the wa'' (over the wall), because you had to climb a fairly high stone wall to get access. The River Kelvin ran through it. That day the Kelvin, normally placid, was in spate after a few days of heavy rain. During a game of soldiers Drew had hidden behind bushes at the river's edge and, somehow, fallen in. His friends watched in horror as the tumbling, swift-flowing water quickly carried him away under the Belmont Bridge and out of sight.

The following day, those of us who hadn't been there went down to the scene with those who had. With the morbid curiosity of children, we got them to point out where Drew had fallen in. In my vivid imagination I could almost see him slowly turning just under the water, his patterned Fair Isle pullover and curly topknot occasionally breaking the surface as he was carried away.

The bridge over the Kelvin, not far from the place where Drew was playing on that fateful day.

For years to come, every time we played 'ower the wa'' I would look at that spot and think – *that's where wee Drew fell in.*

Within weeks his broken-hearted parents, now childless, moved out of the street. It was shortly after that when I realised none of us knew his surname. During that couple of months when he'd played with us, he had just been Drew. Had 'Drew' been short for Andrew?

It's now over half a century since that tragedy. Those of us who remember him, those of us who survive, are now in our sixties. He's still that little boy in short trousers, woollen socks fallen down to the top of his boots. Fair Isle pullover, summer haircut, and a freckly, bonny wee face. And he's still Drew.

Davie, Big Dan and Three Cross Doubles

'Who's that man, Ma? He's always in the Mulhollands' close.'

'That's Davie the Bookie,' said Ma.

'Whit's a "bookie"?'

She sighed. 'Ah thought ye might ask that.'

For the next five minutes she patiently explained, in great detail, the job description of a street bookie. I was just about to let it go when she made the mistake of giving him his full title: 'So ye see, that's whit a bookmaker does.'

'A book*maker*!' I looked up at her. 'Diz he make books as well as taking bets oan the hoarses?'

She looked heavenward. 'Jesussufferin'jonny! Dae you alwiz have tae know every fart's end!'

'Aye.'

Between Ma's explanation, asking my older pals and keeping Davie under surveillance, by the time I was seven I just about had it all worked out. I'd often amble through the close while Davie was taking a bet and talking to a customer. As I passed them I'd hear snatches of strange conversation – 'first four favourites across the card', 'a yankee' and, the one I liked best of all, 'three cross doubles'. I hadn't the least idea what they meant, but it all sounded very adult and mysterious. It seemed a rather interesting occupation, not to say exciting. The excitement coming whenever the polis decided Davie was due for one of his periodic 'liftings'.

Before the law changed around 1960, betting was only allowed at the racetrack. Lots of folk liked a bet, but couldn't afford the time or expense of travelling to the racecourse. Solution: illegal street bookmaking. Davie supplied a service. He carried out his public-spirited work in the Mulhollands' close, directly across the road from mine. Most of his working day was spent in the close itself, walking back and forth keeping an eye open for the polis whilst taking the occasional bet. At the bottom of the street his sole employee, auld Duncan, stood at Lizzie's corner keeping his eye on Doncaster Street and Trossachs Street. At the first sight of 'the Law' Duncan would either give Davie a hand signal or, if his boss was out of sight in the close, a piercing whistle, which Davie never failed to hear. When the warning came Davie would, as part of a long-standing arrangement with the Mulhollands, enter their house through the ever-open door, close it behind him and sit down as though visiting Mrs Mulholland. Auld Duncan, meanwhile, would saunter off in the opposite direction to the polis.

If it was an attempted raid and the police knocked on Mrs Mulholland's door, the betting slips would be thrown on the fire. Only when they were well ablaze would the door be opened and surprise feigned at this visit from the Maryhill Constabulary.

Sometimes the Law would try other tactics; coming in over the roofs of the wash houses from the Maryhill Road back courts. Other times two plain-clothes officers would come strolling down the street. As most Glasgow policemen were at least six feet tall at this time, they were easily spotted. Even weans sitting up in prams had been known to let the dummy fall out of their mouths as they exclaimed, 'Therr's the polis, Mammy!'

My pals and me always liked it when those two big betting days came around – the Grand National and the Derby. Davie was exceptionally busy as everybody, so it seemed, had a wee flutter. Including my ma and da.

My father sat at the table, the *Daily Record* opened wide in front of him. As he studied the runners and riders for the Grand National he sucked on the end of a stubby pencil.

'Right, ah'm gonny have sixpence to win oan Deference and thruppence each wye oan . . . Fortune Hunter. Whit aboot you?'

Ma came over and stood for half a minute looking at the runners, drying a cup with the tea towel at the same time. 'Put me sixpence on Sheila's Cottage.'

My father shook his head. 'That's got nae chance, it's aboot twenty tae one.'

'Ah don't care,' said Ma; 'it's a nice name. Sheila's Cottage'll dae me.'

My father sighed as he wrote it down on the roughly torn piece of brown envelope he was using as his 'line'. He finished by putting his nom de plume: 'Wee Sab'.

There were no betting slips with tear-off carbon copies at this time. Any old piece of paper was used to write out a bet. The important thing was to put your nom de plume on it so as the bet could be identified as yours. At the close of the day's racing Davie would separate all the winning lines from the losers. A list would be made of how much money each was due – alongside the sum of money would be written the punter's nom de plume. You had to quote it to get your winnings.

Later that day I would join the queue waiting to be paid out and ask, 'What's to come for Wee Sab?'

Sheila's Cottage had romped in!

Whenever the favourite won the National or Derby, it always made it more exciting for us kids. As it meant Davie had a lot of winning punters to pay out, he would use a different method to speed things up. He would sit at Mrs Mulholland's kitchen window, facing into the back court, and there would be a queue, of cinema proportions, snaking away from the window. My pals and me would sit on the wash-house roof to watch all the comings and goings as each punter would approach the window, whisper their nom de plume – you didn't want anybody to know it – and Davie would tick his list then pay them out.

It was a few years later, around 1950, when Davie would break his leg 'in the line of duty'! It had been a normal day: Davie pacing to and fro in the close, taking the occasional bet, and auld Duncan at his post outside Lizzie's shop. A saloon car turned in to the top of Doncaster Street, the end furthest from auld Duncan, and came cruising down the street. As it approached the Mulhollands' close the driver hit the brakes. Before it had stopped, two young, uniformed constables leapt from it and made a dash for the close. Davie hadn't time to enter the Mulhollands'. With a cry of 'It's no ma turn, ya bastards!' he raced into the back court and attempted to get away over the wash houses and into Maryhill Road. As he was in his early fifties, and handicapped by the weight of coin in the pockets of his old gabardine mac, Davie was certainly not favourite to win the 'Glasgow Polis Steeplechase'. As he was just about to clamber over one of the high walls separating two back courts a young PC grabbed hold of his ankle. Davie wrenched it free and his momentum carried him over the wall and he crashed onto the tarmac surface on the other side, breaking a leg.

Next morning, after a slight delay while he appeared at the city magistrates' and was fined, Davie, in plaster and on crutches, was back in the close and open for business.

Further up Doncaster Street, John McDonald had recently acquired a car. More accurately, had recently acquired a mechanical disaster. John's pride and joy was a 1930 'baby' Austin. To the rest of the street it was known as 'the biscuit tin on wheels'. It seemed to spend most of the time at the pavement, with its bonnet up, and John tinkering with the engine. On the infrequent occasions when John took it for a run it would sometimes make it to the end of the street. Other times it would be gone for an hour or so, but would return being towed by another vehicle.

It was around five p.m. on a Saturday. Davie, still on crutches, was painstakingly making his way down the street. John McDonald had just managed to get the 'biscuit tin' going. Spotting Davie, John obligingly pulled over, opened the door – the window was stuck – and asked, 'Can ah gie ye a lift, Davie? Ah'm just aboot tae go for a wee run.'

Davie stopped, leaned on his crutches, and slowly looked over this early example of the car maker's art. The Austin stood, vibrating heavily, great clouds of blue smoke issuing from its exhaust, the occasional backfire disturbing the peace. Straight-faced, Davie shook his head, 'Naw, it's awright, John –' he paused – 'Ah'm in a hurry,' and resumed hirpling down the street on his crutches.

The Mulhollands were a good-living, Catholic family and regular worshippers at the large chapel on Hopehill Road. They seemed to have no ethical problems over the arrangements with Davie the Bookie. And why should they?

The only problem Mrs Mulholland ever had was Big Dan, her Irish husband – and that was only on a Friday night. Dan was a hard worker, devoted husband and doting father to his two daughters, Rose and Margaret. But, when he finished work on a Friday and was heading home with a full pay-poke in his inside pocket, he usually couldn't resist nipping in to Ye Olde Tramcar Vaults on the corner of Hopehill Road for a couple of pints – just to lay the dust and clear the throat, you understand. Trouble was, after a week's hard graft those pints slipped down without touching the sides, and wasn't the craic powerful good on a Friday, too?

Next time Dan looked at his watch it was seven o'clock and he'd better be gettin' home or the dinner would be on the back of the fire, and herself standing there, waiting, with her engine running. So, after taking fond farewells of his companions of the last hour or so, Dan would head for home – with just a quick stop at Cocozza's to buy some sweeties for the girls – and a box of Milk Tray for management.

It was around ten past seven on one typical Friday when Dan negotiated the last turn and started up Doncaster Street. Mrs Mulholland was already on sentry duty, leaning out of her downstairs room window. As soon as the errant Dan hove into view she turned her head and called back into the house, 'Rose! Margaret! That's your father finally appeared. Away and get him in as fast as ye can afore he black-affronts us.' She lifted the cushion she had been leaning on during her vigil and closed the window.

My pals and me had spotted Big Dan as soon as he turned the corner. The three of us made a beeline for him. We loved talking to him on a Friday night; he was always full of fun and was like a mixture of Victor McLaglen and Barry Fitzgerald with a few pints in him.

'Hiyah, Dan' we chorused.

He stopped, but continued to sway gently. As usual his bunnet was on the back of his head, his jacket open. He was a plasterer or painter and always wore white bib-overalls. He regarded us with a whimsical eye.

'Hello there, bhoys, aren't ye's the fine fellows so ye's are.' He looked at each of us in turn; he'd known us all since we were born. 'And are ye's good lads to yer mothers?'

'Aye Dan, we always are.'

His eyes moistened, he reached in his pocket, brought out a handful of change and after a painstaking sort, gave us all a threepenny bit each. 'Ah, now that's good, that's good.' He pointed a finger at us. 'Ye should always be good to yer mothers.' He looked up. 'Oh Jayz!' He had spotted Rose and Margaret bearing down on him. He held a finger to his lips. 'Shhh. Oh bhoys, I'm in trouble now, here's the childer coming, they'll be escorting me into the presence of herself. I'm about to fall into the hands of the womenfolk, God help me.' He shook his head. 'She'll be waiting there with a face like fizz.'

Rose and Margaret took up post on either side of him and gently linked their arms through his. 'C'mon, Daddy, come in and get your dinner, you're late.'

Dan pretended he hadn't seen them coming. 'Ah! It's the childer.' He looked at us. 'This is me gurls.'

'Aye, we know, Dan.'

He leaned to the left and right and tried to kiss them, but they drew back, not wanting to be kissed in front of us and in the street. Dan turned to us, mock sorrow on his face.

'Did ye's see that, bhoys? Me own darlin' gurls and not wantin' to give their daddy a kiss.'

'We'll give you a kiss in the house, Daddy,' said Margaret, the youngest.

'Now isn't that worth going home for, lads?' asked Dan.

Slowly, but surely, the girls pushed, pulled and persuaded Dan in the general direction of their close. Now and again a neighbour came into the street and passed the trio. Dan would have to exchange a few pleasantries and enquire if the neighbour, who had known them since infancy, had met his dowters.

We watched in amusement and laughed at his good-natured Irish craic until, at last, the girls got him to the close and then into the house.

With Dan gone the street seemed a duller place. Then the thought hit me – why couldn't I have had a father who was like that when he'd had a drink?

From Far Samarkand

'Hey!' said John Purden. 'Ah nearly forgot tae tell ye's, the roadmenders are coming intae the street the morra. They'll be here for a few days tae put a new surface doon.'

'Great!' Our spirits rose. Now this was something to look forward to.

Every few years, like an Arab caravan, the Corporation Roads Department would trundle into the street and set up camp. 'Greetings! we have come to give you a lovely new road.' For the next few days the place would be in a glorious state of uproar as they spread their trappings all over. The tar boiler, a trailer full of blocks of tar, or was it treacle toffee? Two small mountains, one sand, one chippings. Then there was the 'Morgan the Mighty' of machines – the steamroller. Just sitting there on the back of the low-loader, it exuded power. Fired up, steam issuing from every orifice, I expected it to start pawing the ground before flattening everything in sight. Yet, in spite of all its attributes, the steamroller wasn't my favourite of all the exotica on show; no, my affections were reserved for the Nightwatchman's Bothy. With such a name you'd expect a hut. It wasn't, it seemed to be just part of a hut – had someone stolen the rest of it? This piece of Corporation wonderment was a wooden wall, ten feet tall and fifteen feet wide, with short sides at either end. A bench seat ran its entire length and, on top, a canopy jutted out a yard or so to give shelter to those seated below from all but driving rain. Under the cover of this overhang, on various nails and hooks, hung assorted bunnets, jackets and overalls. Beneath the long bench seat, which was attached to the wall, sheltered a jumble of tackety boots and wellies. The whole shebang looked like a hut – with three quarters missing!

The auld 'watchie' would take over early evening, as the dayshift ended and quiet descended on the street. If the rain or wind were blowing in the wrong direction – into the open shelter – he would get some of the day men to manhandle it round to a better position before they went off. He'd then set about the first task of his long shift: lighting the brazier.

For his first few hours he would not be alone. Within twenty minutes of him taking over there would be four or five of us ensconced either side of him on the long bench.

'If ye want anybody tae go a message for ye, mister, wan of us will go.'

At last, night would begin to fall. We didn't feel as if we were 'assistant watchies' until it got dark.

'Can we light the candles in the lamps for ye? We've done it before, mister.'

As dusk melded into night we'd sit, faces lit and warmed by the glow of the burning coke, talking softly so as not to spoil the mood and get chased away by the man. The pulsing fire would continually draw our eyes and spark our imaginations with half-glimpsed pictures. Then it would be time to observe one of the traditional ceremonies of the working man. Brewing-up. The watchie would fill his tinny from a can of water one of us had fetched from our house. Placing it on top of the brazier, he'd bed it into the glowing coke. In no time at all it would boil. He'd open one end of his oval, brass tea-and-sugar tin and spoon a couple of measures of dry tea onto the bubbling water. Hooking a stick through its curved metal handle, he'd lift the tinny off. The brew would be stirred, sugar added – from the compartment at the other end of the tea-and-sugar tin – and milk poured in from an old medicine bottle. A bit of rag would be wrapped round the tinny to protect his fingers as he ate his piece and washed it down with hot, sweet tea.

If it was a cold night we'd lean back and snuggle into the dusty jackets and overalls left by the dayshift men, and watch the scurrying breeze occasionally turn the coke white hot. Now and again the unseen fumes would catch our throats and make us cough.

'Them fumes can kill ye, in't that right, mister?'

The old man would nod in agreement. We'd all contemplate the fire for another wee while.

'Ah widnae mind being a watchie when ah leave the school, wid you?'

'Me neither, it's a smashin' job. When ye finish in the morning you've got the rest of the day tae yerself.'

The old man laughed and almost spilled his tea.

Eventually, one by one we would be called in until, around ten o'clock, the watchie would be left to doze the long, draughty night away.

A Tenement Christmas

I was seven and still believed in Santa. Now and again some of the older kids would say, 'Santa Claus isnae real, it's your mammy and daddy that buy the presents!' I always refused point-blank to believe it. If they persisted I used to run off and not listen to any more of this heresy. I loved everything to do with Santa and Christmas, especially the last couple of weeks before the big event. Regularly there would be yet another reminder and I'd think to myself, Christmas will soon be here, and get another lovely tingle of anticipation.

Although I loved Christmas and went to Sunday School at St Cuthbert's Church in our street – when Ma could get me out of bed – we certainly weren't a religious family. My parents believed in God, but didn't like to bother *him*. Ostensibly we were Protestants, though we never went to church. Not even for Christmas services. Nor did we have any interest in that other Glasgow religious movement, football. It was played on a regular basis in the street, but rarely by me. I always found our street games too rough. When I had the ball, without fail someone would soon have it off me. If teams were being picked I'd be the last to be chosen.

Occasionally I'd go with some of my pals up to Firhill Park to see Partick Thistle – 'The Jags' – play. Within twenty minutes I'd be bored and would spend the rest of the first half collecting empty beer bottles lying on the terraces. At half-time I'd make my excuses and leave, take the empties to the nearest pub and hopefully raise enough money for the pictures.

Whether at school or playing round the street, I cannot recall any fights or arguments amongst my pals over Rangers v Celtic. To me there were always more important things than football. Sorry, Mr Shankly!

Ma and me were sitting in the Blythsie. As usual, in between the double feature there were the newsreel, cartoon and 'coming attractions' – it was funny how next week's film always promised to be better than this week's – and, as it was December, they always showed this festive 'short'. The same one every year, with the same message:

The Management and Staff of this Theatre wish all our patrons A Merry Christmas and a Happy New Year.

And I used to think, that's awfy nice of them. What I liked best about this festive short was the black and white montage that was going on *behind* the Manager's good wishes. The screen, divided into four quarters, showed four little films at the same time of what was, obviously, a very English, middle-class Christmas somewhere in the Home Counties. I would sit there totally absorbed, wishing I was there. Wherever it was, rationing didn't seem to exist. For the audience in the Blythsie in 1946, however, coal and most foodstuffs were still severely rationed. But while my little short was on I would have a warm glow as, lulled by the soundtrack of carols, I'd drink in the little vignettes up on the screen: Top Left: A family of children and adults are in their living room dressing the tree. As they hang baubles on its branches they are just about being melted by this roaring fire in the grate. Top Right: Family groups, all warmly clad, file up a snowy path to church. Bottom Left: A dozen or so kids sledge and throw snowballs at one another. A cheery snowman looks on. Bottom Right: A front door opens to reveal children standing on the path singing carols amidst gently falling snow. Apple-cheeked, they wear thick woollen coats and an assortment of scarves, 'pixie hoods' and knitted caps all with festive motifs in their patterns. Santa must have brought them a stash of clothing coupons amongst their prezzies.

Caught up in all this, I was dragged back from the Home Counties when a Glasgow voice two rows away said, sotto voce, 'They've probably aw got a sprig o' holly sticking oot their arses!'

Later, as Ma and I exit into a wet, windy Maryhill Road I carry the afterglow from those idyllic Christmas scenes back home with me.

'Aw, Ma, in't it nice of the Manager tae take the trouble tae show yon wee picture tae wish us a Merry Christmas every year?'

'Aye, it's awfy good of him.'

'Widn't it be great tae have a Christmas like yon folk in the film, eh?'

'Aye, it would. But they're aw well-aff people, yon.'

'Did ye see aw the stuff they had for eating on the table?'

'Aye, ah seen it.'

We come into the house. It is cold, the fire has burned right down and is nearly ready to go out. Ma lights a couple of gas rings to heat the room up, then begins raking the bottom of the bunker to try and scrape up enough dross and wee bits of coal to get the fire going again.

'Ah hope Christy Bain the coalman is round the morra. We didnae get any last week, so ah might be able tae sweet-talk him intae letting us huv two bags.'

As Ma talks about the coalman she reminds me of something I've been wondering about. Why is coal still rationed now that the war is finished? It's the same with sweeties and food and loads of things. Ma says she needs a new coat – but she hasn't got enough clothing coupons. You'd think they wouldn't need to ration things now. It's a year and a half since the war ended.

Anyway, there are much more important things to ask Ma about.

'Did ye see the amount of presents that were under yon tree? There was a big heap. They must aw get aboot eight presents each, yon weans.'

'Christ! Are you still on aboot that wee fillum?'

'Aye. Ma, how come Santa gies some weans mair presents than others?'

'Ah don't know. Mibbe they're well-behaved weans.'

The fire is burning up a bit, now. The gas rings are still giving out their steamy warmth. I take my coat off.

'But ah'm quite well behaved, Ma, in't ah?'

'Here.' She hands me a fork which has a slice of plain bread impaled on it. 'Toast that for yerself while ah brew the tea.'

'*Ah* think ah have been quite well behav—'

'Are you gonny shut up aboot weans and presents! Ye just have tae take whit Santa brings ye. If ah hear another word aboot presents ah'm gonny put another letter up the chimney and tell him no tae come here this year. Somebody else can get your presents.'

'Okay, Ma.' Jeez, ah'd better no say any mair. Imagine gettin' up and findin' Santa's no been.

Next morning, before school, I go round to the paper shop for my *Beano*. I feel a little frisson of anticipation as I'm handed it: the title 'The Beano' is covered in a coating of snow which runs down the sides of the letters. The snow is lovely and rounded and looks like big, plumped-up bolsters. As I slowly walk back home I take a glance inside. The title 'Lord Snooty and His Pals' is dripping with snow, too. I go straight down to the bottom of the page to have a look at the very last caption. As expected, Lord Snooty and all his chums are wearing paper hats and sitting round a large table which is laden with turkey, plum pudding and mince pies. They have also kindly invited some friends over from the *Dandy*. Desperate Dan is one of them. His cow pie has a piece of holly stuck in it. Christmas is definitely coming.

At last, Christmas Eve. In the morning it snowed, and now, just coming up for nine in the evening, it is freezing hard. I kneel up on the coal bunker and look out into the sombre back court. Most of the lights are on in the tenement windows that I can see. I try to imagine all the activity going on behind the steamed-up glass. What little light spills down into the back courts illuminates the hard-packed snow. The wash houses and middens take kindly to this white mantle; their stark lines softened. At the opening of each midden the snow has been churned into a brown slush as folk empty their ashes during the day.

I bet it's a good job being a midden man. Once you've emptied your first midden, that's your training done. Every midden is the same, a wee brick-built lean-to attached to the wash house. They all have three or four square-sided galvanised bins inside teeming with rubbish. I wonder why they always empty the bins at night? You never see the bin men's faces 'cause they all wear miner's helmets and lamps. As they troop in and out of the closes, the bins on their backs, if you look at them the lights blind you. They all have their trouser legs tied below the knee – to stop the rats running up. Maybe it's not as good a job as I think.

Elsewhere in the back courts, in the gloom I can see the various trails of footprints, now frozen, of all the people who passed through the back during the day. If you pick out an individual set you can follow them. Some are just taking a shortcut; some head for a wash house then stop, because the person climbed over it and into the next street. It's easy to spot where kids played for a while, the snow all churned up, then the tracks of two or three of them as they head back out to the street again. So many tracks, criss-crossing and heading off in all directions. You can go into the back court tomorrow and see where you and your pals walked yesterday. Without knowing why, I feel sad. Come the thaw, it'll all be erased. I wonder if anyone else thinks like that. My thoughts begin to ease off. I become conscious of the radio playing behind me. I turn back to the warmth, away from the cold air which hangs round the window.

'You'll no see much oot there, son.'

'Mmmm. The snaw makes things aw nice and clean the first day, doesn't it, Ma?'

Ma gives a soft laugh. 'You're a funny wee boy at times, you.'

I look round our house. A big fire burns in the range, there's a variety programme on the radio, a multi-coloured paper chain which I made at school garlands the mantelpiece. A few streamers of 'tinsel' – in reality surplus ex-War Department 'window', dropped by the RAF to confuse German radar – hangs from the green plastic light shade in the middle of the ceiling. We never have a tree; they are too dear.

'You'd better get your stocking hung up; you'll be going to bed soon.'

'Aw, Ma!'

'Never mind "aw, Ma," you'll have tae be in bed and sleeping or Santa willnae come.'

'Ah'm gonny stay awake and see him this year.'

'Ye said that last year.'

'Aye, but ah'm bigger noo, ah'll be able tae stay awake this year.'

I go to the sideboard drawer and, after a search, pull out a long, grey woollen sock. With a couple of large safety pins, and some help from Ma, I hang it from the brass rail under the mantelpiece. 'Slide it along a wee bit; it's too near the fire.' I move it.

At last, Ma persuades me to go to bed. My father is away working on the hydroelectric scheme at Loch Sloy in the Highlands. Ma and him haven't been getting along this last few months. Not only more rows than usual, but he has taken to hitting her when he comes home drunk on a Saturday night. I tend to get hit during the week when he's sober. He isn't coming home for Christmas. Ma suspects he'll have got in tow with some fancy bit up there. His absence is as good as a Christmas present as far as I'm concerned and, as a bonus, it means I'm back in the big bed with Ma instead of my lumpy bed-chair. Heaven!

I lie, under cotton sheets and a pile of blankets, cuddled into Ma's back. The light is out but the red glow from the range illuminates our little kingdom. Ma has spent the day getting the house ready in case we have any visitors during the holiday. The brightly patterned linoleum has been scrubbed, then polished with Mansion. All the brasses gleam – courtesy of Brasso. The range has been black-leaded with Zebo and the steel hinges and fittings emery-papered until they shine, as my father would say, 'Like a shilling on a darkie's arse!'

I snuggle closer into Ma until our heads almost touch on the bolster we share. The springs and mattress sag, so we tend to roll together anyway. For some reason a picture of the frozen footprints in the icy back court comes into my mind. I hope they'll still be there in the morning.

'Tell me a story, Ma. Go on, tell me a story.'

'Och, you and your stories.'

'Just for Christmas, Ma.' She sighs and turns onto her back. I know she's going to tell me one.

'Make it a nice long wan, Ma.'

Ma's stories are basically all the same. Poor girl meets rich boy, they fall in love, but there is *always* someone or something comes between. This might be his parents, her parents, an accident, an illness, a separation or some misunderstanding. In the end, of course, it always works out all right and they marry and live happily ever after. I thought Ma was a great storyteller and had been known to brag to my pals about her abilities. A few years later I would discover that she was recycling stories she had just read in the weekly *Red Letter* – the adult female's equivalent of the *Beano*!

As she often does when she is tired, she tries to get to the end of her story quickly. But I do my best to drag proceedings out by continually asking questions. On hearing that the young couple had dinner in a restaurant, I enquire, 'Whit did they have tae eat?'

'Ah don't know.'

'Well, it's your story, so ye should know.'

'Aaaaah, they had some chips.'

'*Chips!* Ye'd think they'd have something better than chips in a big restaurant.'

'Okay. They had ham and eggs. Is that better?'

'Aye, that's fine.'

Later, after their meal the young couple take a tram.

'Whit number wiz it?'

'Jesusjonny! Whit difference diz the number make?'

'Ah jist wondered if it wiz a Maryhill tram.'

'It wiznae. They were going tae Partick, so it wiz aaaaah – Number 18.'

There was a pause.

'It widnae be an 18. The 18 disnae go tae Partick – it goes tae Springburn.'

'For jumpin', sufferin' never mind whit . . .' Then the two of us go into peals of laughter. Ma keeps trying to say, 'It's murder polis trying tae tell you a story,' but it takes her five minutes before she can get it out. By the time she does, our sides ache and our faces are wet with tears. Eventually, Ma's voice, the warmth and the flickering glow from the coals dancing on the ceiling begin to take me.

Ma stops talking. I am too sleepy to protest. There is a noise from the fireplace. *It's Santa!* Instantly I'm awake and lean up on my elbow. At last I'm going to see him . . . It was the noise of the burnt embers collapsing in the grate. For a second I am sure that I'll see Santa taking my presents out of his bag. I lie back down, now wide awake.

'Aw, Ma, ah thought ah wiz gonny see Santa there.'

'It'll be a while before he comes. It's always in the middle of the night.'

'Gonny tell me another story?'

'Ah'm bloody sure an' I'm not. Ah'm exhausted after the last wan.' She turns round with her back to me. 'Just cuddle in and get tae sleep. Night night, don't let the bugs bite. If they bite squeeze them tight, night night.'

'Night night.' I lie behind her and decide to practise peering out of half-closed eyes so that Santa will think I'm sleeping when he comes. I'm determined to see him this year.

'Santa's been!' Ma's up and dressed, the fire's lit. 'Awww, ah've missed him again.' I lie back, tired, disappointed. Wait a minute – *he's been!* I fly out of bed. There are two brown-paper parcels on the fireside rug. My stocking bulges. I sit on the multi-coloured rug that Ma made. I tear open the first of the parcels.

'Look, Ma!' I hold up a shiny, clockwork car.

'Look, Ma!' The second parcel reveals an *Oor Wullie* annual and a jigsaw of Buckingham Palace. Inside my stocking are an apple, an orange, some nuts and a Mars Bar. I lay my new riches in a semicircle on the rug. 'See aw the things Santa's brought, Ma.'

'By, you're lucky. You'd better shout thanks up the lum.'

'THANKS, SANTA!' There's a slight fall of soot. For a second I wonder if he's maybe stuck up there. I look again at my new things. After breakfast I'll go round to all my pals' houses and see what he's brought them. I gather all my presents up and hold them on my crossed legs.

'Christmas is great, Ma, in't it?'

In my selfish innocence, I haven't noticed that Santa hasn't left anything for Ma.

An Early Ticket for the Steamie

'Time ye were putting that comic doon and getting tae sleep, son. We're up early in the mornin', mind; we're away tae the Steamie first thing.'

'Ah'll be up, Mammy, honest.'

'Mmmph! We'll see.'

I turned round in my bed-chair, trying not to shift the corduroy cushions and finish up lying on the slats. Once again I immersed myself in the 'madcap mayhem' of Abbott and Costello in *Film Fun*. I loved my comics. Not just at Christmas but all year. There was nothing I liked better than, when it was getting near bedtime, to suddenly remember – *I've got a new comic to read tonight!* The trouble was trying to resist devouring it as soon as I got it. I didn't just read the text, I pored over the artwork, especially in American comics like *Superman* and *Batman*. Sometimes I'd sit at the table and try to copy some of the illustrations.

Minutes later, somewhere in the middle of the 'daffy doings' of George Formby, I began to drift off to sleep; last thing I remembered was Ma gently lifting the comic off my face.

'C'mon, ah'll no shout on you again. UP!'

'That'sthefirsttimeyou'veshoutedonme.' It came out all weak and mumbly, I was too tired to say it any louder.

'First time! It's the *third* time and there'd better no be a fourth – or you'll rue it, boy.' She switched the big light on.

'Aaargh!' I had been lying face-up. For a split second it felt like someone had just stuck two school pens into my eyeballs. Even with them screwed up tight, the light still penetrated.

'Didn't ah tell ye last night tae put the comic doon and get tae sleep?' She sneaked over quietly and suddenly whipped the covers off, letting them fall onto the floor at the foot of the bed.

'Mmmmm.' I curled up into a ball.

'If ye get up now, and I mean *now*, ye can get yerself a comic tae take tae the Steamie. Whit wan is it that's oot the day?'

I sat up in bed, eyes still half shut. '*Beano*. *Beano*'s oot the day.'

'NOW!' She shouted. I staggered out of bed. 'I've boiled a kettle for ye so that's hot water in the basin. Don't forget your neck.'

Ma had taken a little charring job over at some toff's house in Hillhead from nine-thirty till twelve every morning. My father was working away again, thank God, but he wasn't sending her much money. This meant he was either drinking too much or had hooked up with some fancy woman. Probably both. Ma liked the family she was working for. The woman was very nice and her husband was boss at a company called The New Apothecaries Ltd. Her wee wage just helped keep us from going without, but it meant that when she had washing to do, we had to be up early so as she could go to the Steamie, get me ready for school, then get herself away to work.

'Now we havnae time tae waste. Away up tae Mrs Symington's and get four rolls, two of them well done, and two slices of corned beef. Ask her tae put it on oor line.'

It was just after six fifteen in the morning as I took the short cut through the back courts. There weren't many lights on. I made my way up the steep hill that was Cameron Street. The lights of the small dairy shone out into the damp mist like a beacon. I pressed the brass catch, pushed the door and as the shop bell rang I stepped into the familiar smell of fresh baked rolls, sliced meats and cheeses. Mrs Symington was in position behind her counter, green overall tied tightly round her waist and, like Miss Colman at the baker's, her hat, held by a hatpin, firmly on her head.

'Ma Mammy says could we have four rolls, two well done, an' two slices of corned beef, and would ye mark it on oor line till Friday, please.' I prided myself on being good at 'going a message'. I also, at eight, felt no embarrassment at asking for 'tick'. Everybody got tick, and Ma was known as a good payer. As somebody once said, 'Aw the local shops run like clockwork. Plenty of tick!'

Just after six-thirty Ma and I sat down to a roll on corned beef, followed by one on raspberry jam, washed down, of course, by a mug of sweet tea. Nectar of the Gods.

'Right, here's tuppence, away roon tae Deakin's and get your *Beano*. Ah'll get the dirty washing intae the bath while you're away. Hurry, mind, run aw the way.'

I ran off to the newsagent's, and minutes later stood at the counter as Mr Deakin busied himself cutting the strings on bundles of the *Daily Record* and the *Bulletin*s. Like all shops, Deakin's had its own smell: still-damp newsprint mingled with the aroma of pipe tobacco, snuff and firelighters. Mr Deakin was a man in his sixties. He always dressed in a well-worn, blue pin-stripe suit, a waistcoat which sported a silver 'Albert' and a silver pocket watch. The ensemble was topped off by a dark trilby hat. He leaned over the counter.

'Whit dae ye want, son?'

I held up two pennies. 'Could ah have a *Beano*, please, Mr Deakin.'

He surveyed the unopened bundles. 'Ah don't usually have tae get the comics oot as early as this. Let me see.' He made a lunge at a bundle and cut the string with his sharp knife, then riffled through the contents. 'No, no.' He rubbed his chin then pounced on another pile. 'Aha!' In triumph he drew out a pristine copy of that day's *Beano*. He looked at me with a serious face. 'You're

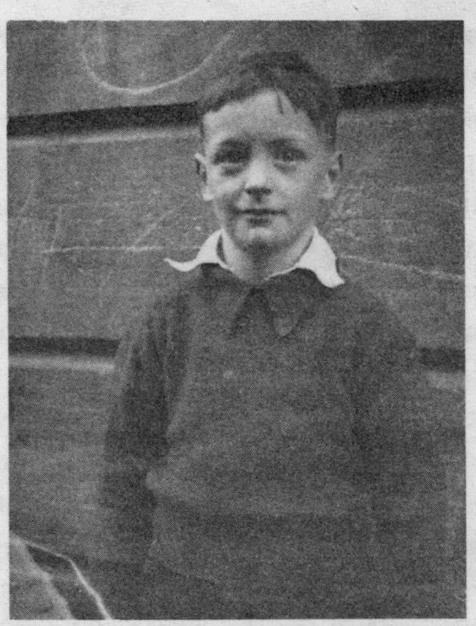

1946. Me aged seven years.

probably the first one in the city tae get a *Beano* this morning, dae ye realise that?'

'I felt my face go red at the thought of this honour. All those thousands of kids in Glasgow who would get this *Beano* today. But I was the first. 'Crikey jings!' was all I could say.

As I dashed into the house Ma was standing beside the galvanised bath, coat on, tapping her foot. I failed to read the signs.

'Ma, Mr Deakin says this is the first *Beano* tae be bought in Glasgow the day.'

'If you don't get a haud o' this bath and give me a hand, it'll be the first *Beano* tae hit the back o' the midden – unread.'

'Aye, right, Ma.' I tucked the comic inside my Fair Isle pullover and grabbed one handle of the bath. I knew she didn't mean it. But just in case.

With Ma, I retraced my steps up Cameron Street, past Symington's, and soon we were walking down the tunnel-like entrance to the Steamie. In the dimly lit entry, women passed one another in opposite directions, with outgoing clean and incoming dirty laundry. The methods of transport were various. Old prams were a popular choice; often with a tin bath perched on top. Some removed the body of the pram and sat the bath on the chassis, between the four wheels, then pulled the makeshift buggy with a piece of rope. One or two borrowed the wean's 'guidie' (home-made go-kart) and balanced the washing on the central wooden plank. A galvanised bath carried between two people, as with ma and me, was another favourite. Some folk struggled to carry the bath on their own, stopping every forty yards or so for a rest. Often as they neared the Steamie someone would lend a hand. Many, if they didn't have too much dirty washing, would bundle it into a sheet and carry it slung over a shoulder.

As we made our way down the dark entry, rickety prams rattling on the cobblestones mingled with greetings and brief conversations as friends and neighbours recognised each other in the half-light.

'By you're early the morning, Jessie. Zat you got yer washing done already?'

'Aye. Got visitors coming this efternin. His sister. If ah don't have the hoose like a new pin the crabbit-faced bitch will be sniffing aw ower the place.'

'Wiz that Mary Clarkson jist passed us, Jessie?'

'Aye, it wiz. Ah didnae think she knew where the Steamie wiz, that yin.'

'Aye, she's a stranger tae Oxydol, big Mary.'

As we entered the large washroom, we were enveloped in the warm, humid atmosphere of the tropics. All seemed very bright as the overhead lights bounced off the white, tiled walls. Spread along two sides and down the centre were the forty or so cubicles which the women hired. Each cubicle was divided from its neighbours by a six foot high, cast-iron partition. The top two feet of each partition was pierced, giving a lattice effect. This enabled the women to see those in the adjoining stalls as though in a confessional – or a prison. Each customer had the use of two china sinks with hot and cold taps, and draining boards either side. In a corner stood a metal sink with a steam pipe feeding into it, for boiling whites. Behind the rear wall of the cubicle was the dryer. A tall, narrow metal door was pulled out to reveal rails attached to it. Blankets were hung over them and the door slid back into the hot, dry cavity. Whilst the women got on with the rest of their wash, their blankets were drying.

Ma sat me up on one of the white-wood draining boards.

'Right, you get on wi' yer comic, pal.'

As she busied herself, I only half-read my *Beano*, spending most of my time watching what was going on around me and listening to the banter coming from the stalls.

'Dae ye think you'll get away for the Fair Fortnight, this summer?' Big Ella enquired of Lena.

'Naw, might manage a trip on the Govan Ferry – if the fare's still a penny.'

'Whit aboot you, Alma?'

'We're no going away, either. The money's gonny be spent on daein' the hoose up. Ah'm sick of the sight of it the wye it is.'

'Could be worse, mind.' Big Ella nodded in the direction of Lizzie McLeod: She dropped her voice. I lowered my *Beano*. 'Ye ever been in Lizzie's?'

There was a chorus of 'No!' Ella leaned forward.

'Never been in a hoose like it in ma life. You should see the state of it.' Ella shivered. 'Yer feet stick tae the carpet, there's not a cup in the hoose that's got a handle.' She paused. 'They had vandals break in last week while she wiz oot shopping – they left it tidier!' There was a roar of laughter.

'Aw c'mon,' said Lena, 'ah've told ye a thousand million times, Ella. Don't exaggerate!'

*

At one end of the large washroom stood three large, industrial spin-dryers. These were the sole responsibility of Wee Wullie – paramour to the downtrodden. Around thirty years of age, not much over five feet tall, and with a slightly lame left arm, Wee Wullie enjoyed being the sole male amongst so much perspiring womanhood. He was the only one allowed to load and operate the spinners. They had to be balanced in case the inner drum or casings were damaged. If too much weight was put on one side, when they reached high speed they went badly off balance and made the most frightening noise as the metal drum smashed and clanged against the outer casing. When this happened Wee Wullie had to make a dive and switch it off before something broke. Wullie liked to parade up and down in front of his charges, dark hair slicked back, clean white jacket on, as he awaited his next opportunity for . . . amour. The treatment each customer received was in direct proportion to how young and/or attractive she was. When Wee Wullie turned on the charm he was totally oblivious to the many pairs of eyes watching him through the latticework – or the running commentary on his performance.

'Look! Look! There's wee Margaret away ower tae the spinner. Will ye jist look at the state o' Wee Wullie trying tae lean ower the tap o' the dryer like it wiz a grand piano. Silly wee shite.' Those within earshot tried not to laugh too loudly in case they gave the show away. 'Oh, he's givin' her the big smile. Huv ye ever seen teeth like that? Like a set of burglar's tools. Is that no pitiful tae watch; he thinks he's George Sanders.'

For their visit to the Steamie the women wore a wide range of clothing. Wraparound peenies were much in evidence. Many favoured rubber aprons to try and keep their front dry as they leaned against the sink to use the washing board. Wellington boots were popular, and for the head, most had their hair tucked under a turban, the sweat trickling down their face and neck.

'Ye know whit, if sweating makes ye lose weight,' announced Big Ella, 'ah should be the size of yon Claudette Colbert by the time ah'm finished this washing.'

'It's definitely working,' pronounced Alma, 'yer fading away – tae an elephant!'

'Cheeky bizzum, so ye are,' replied Miss Colbert.

Ma returned from the spinners, having survived the attentions of Wee Wullie.

'Right, son, that's us.' She folded up the sheets and shirts and placed them in the tin bath. 'It'll be heavier mind, now that everything's damp.'

'Ah'll still be able tae carry it, Ma.'

She smiled. 'Aye, of course ye will, son. You're ma big strong laddie.' We lifted the bath. 'Cheerio, girls.'

'Cheerio, Netty. Cheerio, son – whit a good help ye are tae yer mammy.' I tingled with pride.

We emerged from the tunnel into the street. It was now light. As we set off on the few hundred yards back home, the metal handle was already cutting into my fingers as the bath bobbed up and down between us.

'Are ye wantin' a wee rest, or will we swap sides?'

'Naw, ah'm awright,' I lied. I moved my fingers to let the handle start cutting into a new bit. I wondered if I'd make it all the way home without dropping it. It was getting to be painful.

'Oh!' said Ma. 'Well, *ah'm* gonny have tae swap sides, it's cutting intae me. Ah don't know how you can carry that without having' tae change hands.'

I gratefully laid the bath down and we swapped over. As we set away again I flexed my aching hand. I'd make it now.

The Baker's Roof

'We cannae play in this. It's still too cauld, and mair slippery than ever.' As if to prove it, Tommy Hope dug the heel of his tackety boot into the frozen surface.

'Ah think this is the cauldest day yet.' John Purden pulled his long woollen socks up as high as he could, to try and narrow the gap between them and the legs of his short trousers.

'Gonny hurry up and decide whit we're gonny dae – before ma willy drops aff!' Billy Brittain stood shivering.

'Well, if we havnae enough money for the pictures there's only wan thing we can dae,' John finished his sentence on the run, 'make for the Baker's Roof – and ah'm gonny get there first!'

We all took off in pursuit, slipping and sliding on the hard-packed icy snow whilst pushing and pulling at one another to try and gain an advantage, all the while killing ourselves laughing. Through the close into the back court, up onto the wash house, along the top of a short wall on all fours because it was icy, and onto the Baker's Roof. The flattened cardboard boxes still lay where we'd left them. We rearranged them on the flat concrete roof then sat on them and leaned back against the red-brick chimney stack.

'Ahhh! This is better, in't it?' I said. I placed the palm of my hand on the surface – and quickly withdrew it. 'They must be baking at the minute, it's red hot.'

'Nae running aboot, mind. Otherwise the two Johns'll chase us. They'll no bother us if we sit quietly.'

Donny May leaned back and stretched his legs out. *'Ooyah!'*

He quickly drew them back and rubbed his calves vigorously. 'It's no half hot.' He placed a piece of cardboard on the concrete and rested his legs on top of it.

The six of us looked around. It was early 1947 and the city, along with the whole country, was in the grip of the worst winter ever. It seemed like it would never end. At first we had thought it was great; we'd never seen so much snow. But that had been months ago. The novelty had long worn off. The tenements stood grey and sombre, their roan pipes hanging with ice. On the roofs, the short-lived thaw of a few days ago had caused the snow to slide to the edge, where it had been refrozen by the next cold snap. It now hung menacingly over the eaves, sixty feet up. From the gutters hung dozens of icicles, some six feet long, waiting for the next thaw when they would drop like lances in the middle of the avalanche of snow which would suddenly rumble off the roofs without warning. Over this already miserable scene hung a freezing fog.

Inside the tenements, families, rationed to just one bag of coal a week, fought a losing battle to keep warm. Sometimes their hearts would lift when from the street would come the cry, 'Coal briquettes! Coal briquettes!' Some enterprising lads would have bought a pile of coal dust and dross from a coal yard, mixed it with their 'secret ingredient', and compressed it in moulds to produce the small, hard briquettes. Their pony and cart would be besieged and, in minutes, the entire load sold – with customers rationed to one bag each. With briquettes to mix in with it, the coal ration could be eked out for another couple of days. Eventually, still a day or two short of the coalman's next visit, the bunker would be empty. It was now a losing battle to stay warm; everything that could be burnt, had been burnt. Many just took to their beds for most of the day.

On the Baker's Roof we were impervious to all this. It was always summer up there. Sometimes we'd catch sight of adults enviously looking down at us from their windows. For six feet on either side of the chimney the concrete was always dry and warm. Viewed from a distance on even the coldest day, the eddies of warm air rose like a mirage. Ice and snow were held at bay and formed a threatening ring around us. Freezing fog evaporated in the rising heat before it could reach us. As long as we stayed in our enchanted circle we were protected; balaclavas were taken off, scarves discarded, socks rolled down. As we sat there blethering we would often forget that winter waited jut six feet away.

'Jeez, what would we dae withoot the Baker's Roof?' said Donny.

'Be found deid up a close somewhere,' I suggested.

We heard the bakehouse door open, and all looked to our left. A cloud of blue smoke spiralled up; 'young' John was out for a smoke. We could just see the top of his head.

'Hiyah, John.'

He took a few steps away from the door and looked up onto the roof. 'By, youse are quiet the day. We never knew ye's were there.'

'We're feart tea move, John. This is the warmest place in Maryhill.'

He laughed; little clouds of flour fell from him. 'There's a couple of empty boards tae be collected from yon wee cooked meat shop up near Wilton Street. If wan o' ye's goes and gets them, there might be a cream cookie in it for each of ye's.'

'You go, Tommy. You're the warmest dressed,' suggested John.

'Okay.' Tommy rose. 'Ah'll get them, John.'

Ten minutes later he was back, the empty boards with COLMAN'S BAKERY stamped on their sides balanced on his head. He emerged from the bakehouse carrying a white cardboard cake box. 'Here ye are, boys.' He reached it up onto the roof, then climbed up and regained his place against the chimney back. 'Ah'll tell ye's what, ah'm glad tae be back. It's bitter cauld. Worse than it was when we first came up.' We let Tommy open the box and distribute the cookies.

Two minutes later we wiped the excess cream from our lips and sighed contentedly. Colman's were well known for their cream cookies. The business was owned by Miss Colman, a spinster in her forties who lived in Hillhead – where all the toffs came from. She served behind the counter with her two female employees, but so as there would be no mistake as to who she was, Miss Colman *never* wore an overall. Like many of Glasgow's 'Ladies in Business' she always wore her hat when she was behind the counter. This was the 'guinea stamp'. It said quite clearly – in the "refained" tones of Kelvinside – 'As you can see, I am the proprietrix of this establishment and I just happen to have taken off my coat, but, heaven forfend, *not* my hat, to help out.' She was a nice soul, though, and a regular source of cream cookies and the occasional threepenny bit when we collected her boards. Miss Colman was the type of lady of whom it could be said, 'She thinks "sex" is what the coalman brings the coal in.'

Sometimes, after we'd brought the boards back we'd hang about in the bakehouse and watch the two Johns at work. 'Young' John was in his fifties, thin, and wore horn-rimmed specs. 'Auld' John was in his sixties, short and fat, with rosy red cheeks. They started work at four-thirty in the morning. Their first task on arrival, so they told us, was to kick the bakehouse door before opening it to make the cockroaches scatter. Otherwise, when they stepped inside to switch the lights on they would stand on them. It also served notice on the rats.

We'd been up on the roof for over two hours. The latest films had been re-enacted for the benefit of those who hadn't yet seen them. Tommy had described, in salacious detail, what his sister and her boyfriend had been up to when he'd spied on them the other night. There was now a pause.

'What aboot a game of guesses?'

'Right.'

'CC,' said Billy.

Within minutes the limited number of CCs were exhausted.

'We give in.'

'Ye's aw give in?' Billy looked around to make sure.

'Aye.'

'Cat's ceech,' he said, triumphantly.

'Whit dae ye mean, cat's keech?' said Robert Walker. 'Ah cannae see any cat's keech.'

'It's under the snaw,' said Billy. 'Ah was trying tae make it hard.'

'It'll be hard awright if it's under the fuckin' snaw,' suggested Tommy.

'Naw, ah mean hard tae guess,' mumbled Billy.

'We're supposed tae be able tae see what we're trying tae guess,' I said. 'Anyway, diz "keech" no start wi' a "k"?'

'Naw, ah "C",' replied Billy.

'How dae ye *know* it starts wi' a "C"?' queried John.

' 'Cause it diz,' said Billy, defensively.

'Ah'll bet that ye couldnae show us it in a dictionary,' challenged Donny. 'It's just Glasgow slang.'

'Is it shite,' said Billy.

'We know it's shite,' agreed Tommy, 'and if ye'd used "shite" that would have been okay, but ye used "keech", and ye cannae spell it – never mind see it – so you're *doubly* oot of order!'

Billy tried hard to think of a reply, but couldn't. 'Anywye, it's only a game.' He paused. 'Och, ah'm hungry, ah think ah'll away hame for a piece.' He rose, and began to wrap up, ready to leave the protection of the roof. He sat on the edge of the concrete, about to drop into the back court. 'Right, ah'm away, boys.'

'Aye, cheerio, Billy.' We watched as he entered his close, then saw his figure appear briefly at the landing windows as he climbed the stairs to his top-floor flat.

'Jeez,' said Donny, 'it's only aboot three o'clock and it's nearly dark, already.'

We looked out. Everything was greyer than ever as the temperature dropped further with the coming darkness. The freezing fog hung even heavier round our haven. We were under siege.

'Have ye ever thought,' said Tommy, 'if Captain Scott and his mates had been lucky enough tae come across a baker's roof – they wid aw have survived, eh?' He looked around.

'Huv ye ever heard such a load of shite?' said Donny.

'Dae ye no mean keech?' queried Robert.

'Well, efter that ah think it's time for hame,' said John.

We all agreed, rose and began to get ready. Except for Donny.

'Ah'm staying for a while. We've ran oot o' coal in the house, so ah'm as well here.'

We said our cheerios to Donny and dropped off the roof.

Within a few steps of leaving our oasis, the cold, which had waited patiently all day, claimed us. As John and I walked toward a close to take us out to Trossachs Street, I glanced back. Donny leaned against the warm chimney. He was busy using some of the spare cardboard to cover his legs. He gave us a wave. John and I hunched our shoulders. In just ten yards all the warmth we had taken from the roof had gone. I stuck my hands deep into my pockets.

We stopped outside John's close. The lamplighter hadn't been round yet to light the gas lamps.

'See ye the morra, John.'

'Aye, see ye the morra, Robert.' He vanished into the gloom. I was about to walk away when his voice echoed down to me: 'Ah think it'll be the Baker's Roof again.'

Three Cheers for the Boiler Stick

I was sound asleep. That deep sleep that comes after playing out in the street all day with your pals and then, around nine p.m., so tired you can't keep your eyes open, your ma just undresses you and bundles you into bed, unwashed.

From far, far away there come unintelligible voices, loud voices. My bed-chair is bumped once, twice. Reluctantly I begin to head for the surface from the depths of that sleep tunnel. I keep my eyes tight shut but it is no good, I know it is happening again. I won't get the silence needed to sink back down into that lovely tunnel. There is the sound of the table scraping on the floor. A chair goes over with a bang – I recognised the sound of the Rexine-covered seat as it falls out and turns over a few times; the same sound it makes if I drop it when I'm making a den with the four chairs and a blanket. I can make out the voices now.

'You're nuthin' but a wee hoormaister, ya bastard!'

'Ah'm telling ye, if ye don't shut up ah'm gonny hit ye! Ah'm no gonny keep telling ye.'

I am now wide awake, but lie with my eyes closed. *Ma, don't say any mair.* Even though I'm just nine, already I know it won't make any difference. If she does keep quiet he will soon find something else to pick a fight over. Why couldn't he have stayed working up at Loch Sloy on the hydroelectric scheme? It's been great these last few months while he's been away.

'Why should I shut up? Ye'd like that, widn't ye? Jist shut up and let ye run aboot wi' aw yer hoors. Well, ye can think again.'

'Ah'll dae whitever the fuck ah want tae dae, so ye might as well save yer breath. Now, get me something made for ma supper.'

'If you want something, you get it made.'

'Dae ye hear whit ah'm fuckin' saying? Get me something tae eat.'

'Away an' get yer fancy wumman tae make ye something, 'cause ah'm no.' Aw, Ma.

Another chair goes over as he makes a lunge at her. I hear her draw in her breath in fright, the same fright that stabs my stomach as I picture what is happening. *Ma, why dae ye have tae be sae brave?* I sit up in bed and start crying as I watch him hitting her. I have a forlorn hope it might make him stop. It is always slaps when he goes for her face – he doesn't want her to be marked when she goes out into the street. But it's punches when he hits her in the body.

'LEAVE MA MAMMY ALANE!'

He has her in the corner by the press door. She covers up, but plenty are getting through. As he hits her he is continually effing and blinding.

She usually gets hit every second Saturday. She knows he is regularly seeing his fancy woman again. Ma won't stop getting onto him about Big Nell so he starts hitting her when he gets fed up with it. After a couple of minutes of being battered Ma starts banging the press door with her fist and screaming at the top of her voice, 'MRS McLEAN, MRS McLEAN, HE'S HITTIN' ME. SEND FUR THE POLIS! SEND FUR THE POLIS!' She repeats it three or four times.

'Ah'm no fuckin' bothered aboot the polis. S'no the first night ah'll huv spent in the cells.' In spite of the bravado he begins to ease up hitting her. He knows Mrs McLean will have sent one of the weans for the polis. He turns to me, still sitting up in bed crying.

'You fuckin' shut up and get doon under them covers and get tae sleep, otherwise you'll get it!'

I lie down and pull the covers up over my face, but continue to give big, dry sobs now and again. I have my eyes open under the sheet, and spend most of the time willing the policeman to arrive soon. My father has stopped hitting Ma. He fills the kettle and puts it on the gas. At last we hear heavy footsteps in the close; please God, make it the polis. There are a couple of loud bangs on the knocker. GREAT! That's a polis's knock. Ma lets him in. He stands just inside the room, Ma beside him. I sit up in bed. My father looks at me but says nothing. He is standing by the fireplace, not looking at the policeman.

'Has he been hitting you again, hen?' Ma nods her head. He turns to my father. 'Whit is the matter wi' you? You've a nice wee wife and son; can ye no behave yerself?'

My father half-turns, but still doesn't look the policeman in the eye.

'It's her, too much bloody lip.'

'He's no content wi' what he's got,' says Ma, 'thinks he should jist be allowed tae run aboot wi' his fancy bits and ah should say nothing.'

'So, what's he been doing to ye?'

'Slapping me roond the face and punching ma arms and side.' As she speaks she shows the bruises on her upper arms then lifts her blouse to show those on her sides.

'Do ye want him lifted?'

'Aye. He's no stayin' here the night.' My father scowls at her. I am delighted.

'Right, c'mon, you're up the road wi' me.' The policeman turns to Ma. 'If you want to prefer charges you'll have tae be up the station before nine-thirty in the morning – otherwise we'll let him oot.'

They exit, and we hear their somehow companionable footsteps receding as they leave the close and set off into the quiet night to walk the half-mile to Camperdown Street Police Station.

*

Ma begins to tidy up.

'Are ye gonny charge him, Ma?' I feel my spirits rising now that he's away.

'Ah'll make ma mind up in the morning.' I know she won't. She never does. He'll arrive back in the morning about ten, unshaven, slightly hungover, tired from an uncomfortable night in the cells, and in a foul mood. No matter what I do, within the hour I'll get at least one 'bat on the lug', if not more.

They had married in March 1938. I don't know whether he'd been hitting Ma before he went abroad in 1942; he'd certainly been seeing other women before then. It wasn't too long after his demob in late '45 when he took up with Big Nell again. He had returned from his two years in Italy not only a heavier drinker, but a mean drunk. His habit of drinking cheap red wine – Red Biddy – and chasing it with pints of McEwan's Pale Ale made him more aggressive, and put his normal bad temper on a hair trigger. By 1948 he had been hitting Ma for the last two years or more. The incidents had increased in frequency and Ma was being knocked around at least twice a month, sometimes more. She decided to do something about it.

It was, of course, a Saturday night. He had come in very drunk. So drunk, he didn't even bother to find an excuse, just started hitting her because he felt like it. After a few minutes he tired of this, got undressed and went to bed. He ordered her to turn the radio off and come to bed as he wanted the light out because he was tired. He fell asleep very quickly with Ma lying trapped behind him in the recess bed.

By two a.m. he was deep in a drunken sleep, lying on his stomach. Ma had been lying awake all this time. She now gingerly climbed over him and out of bed, put her coat and shoes on and, brandishing the key for the communal wash house, made her way out to it by moonlight. Minutes later she returned to the house with the white boiler stick in her hand. Made of pine and over a foot long, it was used by the women of our close to stir and prod their whites as they bubbled in the large copper boiler. My father was still, obligingly, lying on his stomach. Carefully lifting back the covers, and with just the light from the dying fire to see by, she proceeded to lay into him with the boiler stick from the nape of his neck to his buttocks. She must have felt that this white wooden baton was just the right length and weight to do the job without causing too much damage. There was the poker at the fireplace, but she must have considered that as too heavy.

For two or three minutes, until her anger was spent – or perhaps her arm became tired – she laid into him. By the time he began to come out of his drunken stupor, it was too late. He couldn't move as the blows rained down, and lay helpless until she was finished with him. She then spent the rest of the long night sitting on the chair by the fire. I slept through it all.

When morning came he still lay on his face, unable to move. His entire back and buttocks were covered in enormous black, blue – and even green – contusions. It was three days before he could get out of bed.

Although the arguments continued just as bitter as ever, from that day on, no matter how drunk he was, he never lifted his hand to her again. Sometimes he would move toward her in a threatening manner, barely able to contain himself. She would stand her ground and say, 'Remember, if ye do, ah'll get ye when yer sleepin'.'

Ex Libris

'Kids can join the library, ye know,' said Robert Walker.

'Ah thought it wiz jist for big people.'

'Naw, they huv a children's section. Next time yer going tae the Woodside Baths jist nip doon tae the library an' tell them ye want tae join. It's nae bother.'

At nine, I was already an avid reader, mainly of the *Dandy* and *Beano*, but I was now at the stage of reading everything in sight, from cornflakes boxes to *Wide World* magazines. Robert had an ancient set of encyclopedias in the house, and every time I called for him I'd hope he was having his tea so as I could say, 'I'll jist have a wee look at wan of the encyclopedias while ah'm waiting.' I'd then sit myself in a corner and hope he'd take ages with his tea while I immersed myself in the *Bec to Dat* volume. I found them fascinating.

The idea of joining the library filled my mind. Was it really as easy as that? Did they really let ye borrow books for nothing *and* keep them in the house for up to a fortnight? But first I had a decision to make: which library should I join, Maryhill or Woodside? Maryhill was furthest away and entailed a tram ride. If I was broke it would be too far to walk. Woodside was the nearer, and could always be reached by shanks's pony if I had no money. Woodside was the one for me.

I'd been standing across the road from the Woodside for twenty minutes or more. It was an imposing, late Victorian structure, built to impress. I was so impressed I was feart to go near it. Eventually I crossed the road, climbed the steps and peered through the glass of one of its grand outer doors. The vestibule – it was certainly *not* a lobby – gave further evidence of Glasgow's love affair with *la belle époque*. I gazed at the art-nouveau tiles, door plates and balustrades. Jesusjonny! Surely Robert huznae got it right? They're no gonny let me become a member of a place like this; only toffs would be allowed in here. I looked on past the shadowy vestibule and through the glass panel on another door into a brightly lit room. *Books!* Shelves and shelves of hardback books. The occasional figure flitted past. One of them was a wee boy! He didnae look any better dressed than me. Mibbe it was really true. C'mon, ya big fearty. I took hold of the beautiful, big bronze door handle and pushed; it barely moved. I put both hands on it, braced my legs and pushed again; it opened about a foot. On the other side, unseen by me, a woman approached and yanked the door open – I went flying past her and came to a halt in the middle of the Hall of the Mountain King! I was in.

I looked at the signs: LIBRARY. READING ROOM. I was there because I wanted tae read. I headed for the Reading Room. Pushing the door open, I entered a large, almost silent room. There were rows of sloping, desk-like structures with a dozen or more men, mostly scruffy, leaning against them reading newspapers opened wide in front of them. Now and again the turning of a page, a muttered aside or a hacking cough broke the silence. I was immediately reminded of a scene set in a workshop in the penitentiary. I looked around to see if I could spot Cagney or Edward G. talking to one another out of the side of their mouths. As I tiptoed self-consciously through the stillness toward the desk I wondered why they let these scruffy old men into their grand building. I also noticed there weren't any chairs for them to sit on. Was this to let them know they weren't welcome? It reminded me of Granny Douglas and my father.

A frosty-faced woman peered over the desk at me. It looked as though I wasn't very welcome either. She never spoke. I cleared my throat. Surely everybody could hear my heart pounding.

'I'd like tae join the library, please.'

It came out all squeaky. I felt myself blush. The Ice Queen sighed and shook her head.

'You'll have to go back downstairs and through the doors with LIBRARY above them,' she intoned. '*This* is the Reading Room.'

I felt my face burn. I wanted to say, Look, this is ma first time in the library, I'm only nine ye know. Instead, I said, 'Oh, sorry, aye, right, thanks very much, doonstairs is where ah should go.'

I skulked off toward the door, my face burning. I sneaked a quick look at the assorted inmates. They had all stopped planning the big break for the minute and were watching me – except for one old soul who was losing the battle to stay awake in the warmth. Knees bent, head nodding, held up by a dusty shaft of sunlight, he balanced precariously on folded arms as he leaned on the wooden slope.

Out of the Reading Room, I resolved that I might as well persevere in my bid to become a member. If I decided to go home I probably wouldn't be able to open the main door anyway. I entered the door marked LIBRARY and found myself in an enormous room. The first thing to hit me was the smell; no, it wasn't a smell – it was an aroma. A mixture of floor polish, beeswax, wood and leather bindings, it was wonderful, heady. The Reading Room had been stale, but this was full of promise; the smell of learning, of pleasures to come. It would be worth joining the library just for the smell alone.

'Hello, can I help you?' A young woman had appeared behind the desk just by the door. She gave me a smile. I was still dizzy from the atmosphere. Please God, gonny let me join this library? Don't let them say naw. Ah really, really want to be a member.

'Ah'd like tae join the library, please.'

She reached under the desk. 'Here you are.' She handed me a pencil and a card about the size of a postcard. 'Fill that in with your name, address and age, and what school you go to.'

I was back in a couple of minutes with it filled in. I wanted to impress her that I was as sharp as a tack and would *obviously* be a valuable addition to the membership.

'Thank you. Right, you'll hear from us by letter in about a week, then you can come and collect your tickets and that will be you a member.' This was a disappointment.

'Eh, can ah no go in and jist have a look round the children's section, even though ah cannae take a book out?' I just wanted to be near the books, and smell the smell.

'Sorry, not until you're a proper member.'

I looked past her at the myriad aisles and shelves. It was like a maze. I was longing to be able to walk amongst them. I was bad at waiting. For a moment I toyed with asking if I could maybe come down every day till my tickets came and just sit somewhere out the road and smell the place. But you can't ask for something as daft as that. So I just said, 'Right, thanks very much. Cheerio.'

'Ma, ah've been doon and joined the Woodside Library the day.'

'Have ye, that's good. They might be able tae keep ye gawn in reading material fur a while.' She carried on peeling potatoes.

'Ah had a look in the Reading Room, Ma. It wiz full of auld men leaning against these big desks, reading newspapers. There wiznae stools or chairs for them tae sit doon. It wiz sort of funny-looking. How come they don't let them sit doon, Ma?'

'Aye, well, ye see nearly aw they auld men are unemployed, or even worse, homeless. They go intae the Reading Room because they've naewhere else tae go, just tae pass the time away. In the winter maist o' them go in because it's warm. That's why the library disnae put chairs in, so as no tae encourage them. Maist of them would jist sit there dozing the day away.

I thought it over. 'Well, ah don't think it would dae any harm. They're gonny be in there anywye so they might as well huv a wee seat.'

'Well, you would think so, but libraries never put chairs in reading rooms.'

I crossed the room and sat up on the coal bunker next to the sink. She continued peeling potatoes. 'That's a shame, in't it?'

'Aye, so it is, but that's the way things are.'

With much less trepidation than the previous week, I forced an entry through the Woodside's front entrance and headed for the library.

'Ah've got ma letter tae say ma tickets are ready.' I watched as the nice girl from last week riffled through a box.

'Ah, here they are.' She handed me four, heavy card tickets. I looked at them. They each had 'Glasgow Corporation Libraries Department' printed in black ink on the green cards – and my name! I felt a tingle up the back of my neck. The girl spoke.

'You can take up to four books. Two fiction and two non-fiction.'

Two what? I didn't want to show my ignorance. Ma mammy'll know. I'll just take one book out today, and let the lassie take whichever ticket she wants. I stepped through the barrier, then stood for a moment, aglow with anticipation. I looked at what seemed to be miles of shelves; books towered above me to the left, right and centre, but I didn't feel intimidated. This was a new world and it was up to me to explore it. All I needed was my four tickets.

'See whit ah borrowed oot the library, Ma.' I held the spine of the book toward her.

'Mmmm, *Greek Myths and Legends*. Dae ye think ye'll like that? It's nearly all words, ye know; there are'nae many pictures.'

'Aye, ah know.' I did like it. In fact I loved it. Within a month

I'd devoured everything the library had on Greek mythology and was soon regaling my pals with the epic adventures of Ulysses (which I pronounced Usessless), Jason and the Argonauts, Perseus and Andromeda and the Spartans. Once I had exhausted that subject I prowled the children's section and was lucky enough to come across Arthur Ransome's *Swallows and Amazons.* The Ransome books hadn't been taken out for the last couple of years. I felt I was the only one who knew about them. I soon went through Mr Ransome's output and revelled in the adventures of his upper-middle-class children, as they sailed their boats on sunny lakes and confounded villains. During my 'Ransome period' I would frequently persuade my pals to go down to the Boating Loch on Great Western Road, Here, for a shilling an hour, we would hire skiffs and race all over the relatively small pond until, all too soon it seemed, a cry would echo over the water, 'Come in Number 6, your time's up,' and I would be brought back to reality – and the knowledge that I'd blown my cinema money for another week.

This was the start of my love for books, which easily rivalled my love for the pictures. I still continued to read my *Dandy* and *Beano* and, in due time, the *Hotspur*, *Rover*, *Wizard* and *Adventure* – the 'boy's papers'. These all quite happily coexisted with my library books. My reading life was up and running. When I came home from school, I'd quite happily spend the rest of the evening with, as Ma put it, my nose stuck in a book. Occasionally I'd need a bit of help.

'Ma?'

'Whit?'

'There's a bit here ah don't get.'

'Whit is it?'

'Sometimes they huv somebody saying "tisk, tisk". Whit diz that mean?'

'How dae they spell it?'

'T-S-K, then T-S-K again.'

'Let me see.' I showed her. She went into a kink of laughter.

'Whit are ye laughin' at?'

In between more laughing she explained, 'Ye know how if you do something stupid I cluck ma tongue and make that tut-tutting sound?'

'Aye.'

'Well, that's how ye show it when ye write. Ye put it oan the page as T-S-K, T-S-K. So when ye see that written doon in future, it's no "tisk, tisk", it's "tsk, tsk".' She made the actual sound.

'Ah!' Suddenly I got it. I also realised how silly it must have sounded when I'd said 'tisk, tisk'.

For the rest of the evening, whenever she got the chance she'd say things like, 'Oh, tisk, tisk, dae ye no think it's time ye were gettin' ready for yer bed?' And I'd reply, 'Tisk, tisk, you have jist interrupted me at an exciting bit in ma book, Mammy.' We spent a great couple of hours laughing until our sides were sore and the tears streamed down our faces. Then my father came in and, of course, didn't find it funny, so we had to stop as it was about to put him in a bad mood. Trouble was, I kept thinking about it and regularly got the giggles, until he gave me a belt on the lug. That soon stopped me.

The Great Midden-raking Expedition of 1948

'Whit'll we dae the day?'

There was a general shuffling and scliffing of sandshoes on the pavement. Two weeks into the school holidays and already we were bored.

'It's a while since we raked the middens,' I suggested half-heartedly. As one of the youngest in the gang, my contributions were normally automatically rejected.

'Good idea,' said John.

'Aye,' said Tommy, 'it's a long time since we went looking for "lucks".'

I felt myself glow.

'Ah cannae go roond the middens,' said Jim. 'If ah get these new claes dirty ah'll get murdert!'

'Tough,' said John, 'we're for the middens.'

Wee Hughie looked at Jim. 'Ye can still come wi' us, but keep back oot the road. We'll dae aw the raking.'

Jim though it over. 'Well, awright then. But ah'm keepin' well away fae the stoor, mind.'

'Whit's the plan, then?' asked Tommy. We never did anything without a plan of campaign.

John spoke. 'We'll no bother wi' oor ain middens; there's never anything in them but rubbish.'

'Zat no whit's shupposed tae be in them?' lisped Hughie.

John ignored him. 'We'll go straight ower tae the far end of Wilton Street and dae the toffs' middens. They're good for lucks.'

'We'll huv tae be quiet, boys,' I reminded them; 'the toffs

don't like us in their back courts. They think we make the place untidy.'

'Ach, ye don't bother aboot them,' said John. At eleven, John was a little tough nut, frightened of nobody. I was two years younger – and frightened of everybody. Especially when we left our own bit and entered the outlands. Apache Territory!

'Right, c'mon then, ower tae the toffs.'

Wilton Street lay on the other side of Maryhill Road from Doncaster Street, literally just a stone's throw, but in reality a million miles away. It consisted mainly of handsome, red sandstone tenements with bay windows. Each flat was self-contained, no shared toilets on the landings, and the closes were richly decorated with art-nouveau tiles: 'wally closes'. Wilton Street's residents gave their address as North Kelvinside. We lived in Maryhill.

We entered the first back court. The comparison with ours was striking. All was quiet. Railings divided the back courts into separate, lushly grassed back greens. We could hear birdsong. Our back courts were a mixture of wasteland and playground; nearly all our railings had gone. If you found a blade of grass you were in line for a prize. Most of our sparrows were down with emphysema. I found the silence unnerving as the rows of disapproving windows glowered at us.

'See, ah told ye, they're great, these middens,' said John, reaching in and pulling out a brass letter holder. 'They're alwiz throwing away good things, the toffs.'

As with our own middens, the main contents were ashes, tin cans, newspapers and vegetable peelings. We had just added a Bakelite radio with a cracked case to our haul when John and Tommy spotted something – a child's scooter, minus one wheel, behind the dustbins. They began pushing and pulling at one another, to see who could get to it first, laughing as they struggled. Jim, forgetting his vow of cleanliness, thought he saw a chance and attempted to slip past the two wrestlers and claim it. John spotted him and deftly pulled over a full dustbin into his path. For a moment Jim was lost to sight in a cloud of Cumulus Ashus.

'Yah rotten bastard, John!' Jim stood, covered from head to toe in fine ash, looking like an off-duty baker. 'Ah'll get spifflicated when ah get hame,' he wailed.

We were all helpless with laughter, then we heard a window go up.

'What are you boys doing round here?' A man, whose clipped moustache matched his speech, glared down from a second-storey window.

'Waiting fur a Number 18 tramcaur,' shouted John.

Once more I marvelled at John's nerve, but it also alarmed me.

'CLEAN THAT MESS UP, THEN GET OUT OF HERE!' the man bellowed, in his best military manner.

Ever willing to oblige and ready to keep the peace, I reached for the bin.

'UP YER PIPE!' shouted John, also giving him the V-sign with two fingers.

We watched the man's face turn purple.

'RIGHT! I'll sort you lot out. Stay where you are.'

'Like fuck!' said Tommy.

'C'mon,' I said, 'he's coming doon tae get us.'

We all made a run for the close, except John, who dived into the midden and grabbed the scooter, then ran. As we sprinted through the close we could hear the man pounding down the stairs, but when he reached the street we were a hundred yards away, and safe. We began to laugh, now full of bravado.

'Did ye see the stoor blawing aff Jim as he wiz running?'

'He wiz like the Flying Shcotshman at full shteam,' said Wee Hughie.

Jim beat his hands against his trousers and pullover; we

moved away as great gouts of ash swirled up and got in our eyes.

'It's awright fur youse,' he moaned. 'Ah'll get a good baiting aff ma faither; these were jist bought two days ago.'

'Och, don't worry,' said Tommy, 'ye can clean up at ma hoose before ye go hame.'

As we turned into Maryhill Road, John spoke: 'C'mon, we'll check oot R. S. McColl's midden.'

With sweets being rationed it was often the case that the cheaper ones sold well, but the expensive assortments didn't. If they began to deteriorate, the staff had no alternative but to throw them out. We were waiting.

'Aw look!' Two almost full display boxes lay on top of a bin, covered in a fine ash. We examined our booty. The chocolate on the unwrapped ones was turning a powdery white, the wrapped selection were less affected.

'Are the unwrapped onesh very fooshty?' enquired Hughie.

'Soon tell ye.' John chose one at random, blew the ash off it and popped it into his mouth.

Four pairs of eyes watched as he thoughtfully chewed and slurped for about half a minute.

'Bloody awful!' he said, then quickly grabbed two handfuls and stuffed them into his pockets. We all followed suit, then split up the wrapped chocolates in a more orderly manner.

Minutes later, carrying our 'lucks' and chewing sweeties two at a time, we trooped into Doncaster Street and the safety of our own territory. As we made our progress, like Roman legionaries returning from a successful campaign, we handed out favours – well, foosty sweeties – to those of our friends who, when they heard our tale, would curse themselves that they had not been part of – the Great Midden-raking Expedition of 1948!

*

It was sometime later that day. After the excitements of our morning foray to the toffs, boredom was setting in.

'What aboot a game of guesses in Lizzie's windae?' said Tommy Hope.

'Good idea!' We headed for the corner shop.

'Who's going first?' asked Robert Sommerville.

'Ah will,' said Tommy, 'seein' as it wiz me that suggested it.'

'Can ah play, tae?' We all turned – then looked down. It was Wee Hughie Sommerville, Robert's six-year-old brother.

'You're too wee,' said his big brother, before anyone else could.

'Och, we'll let him play,' said John Purden. He looked at the diminutive applicant with a benign eye. 'Can ye spell? Nae good trying tae play guesses if ye cannae spell.'

'Ah'm a good ssspheller,' lisped Wee Hughie, 'ask oor Robert.' *Sniff!* Two glistening snails shot back up his nostrils. Wee Hughie was known the length and breadth of the street for his permanently running nose. Big brother Robert duly confirmed his spelling prowess.

'Ye might not get a shot, mind,' said John, winking at the rest of us. 'Ye have tae guess one correctly, *then* it'll be your turn tae pick wan for us tae guess.' He smiled benevolently. The smile vanished from his face as Wee Hughie elbowed him, and Tommy, out of the way as he barged through to the front to make sure he got a good place. He stood, forehead touching the glass, his nose already leaving its signature on Lizzie's window.

'Right,' said Tommy, 'something beginning with "K".'

We all took turns in rotation, and failed to get it. Wee Hughie, as befitted his lowly status, was last.

'It's you, Hughie,' said Tommy, condescendingly.

Sniff! 'Kolynossh tooshpaste,' declared Hughie.

The grin vanished from Tommy's face. He shifted from foot to foot. He forced a smile. 'Aye, right enough,' he said, grudgingly. 'Yuv got it. It's Kolynosh, eh Kolynos. Whit a lucky guess.' He cleared his throat. 'Right, it's your turn noo.'

We all gave Hughie serious looks from the corners of our eyes as he scoured Lizzie's window for his selection – leaving the occasional trail when his nose made contact.

'You're smudging Lizzie's windae!' said Tommy, who'd never previously shown any concern for the welfare of the premises. Hughie wiped his offending nose along the sleeve of his jersey. *Sniff!* 'Something beginning wi' . . . "T",' he announced, after great deliberation.

'Toffee,' said John, casually.

'Nope,' replied Wee Hughie.

'Tide washing powder,' said I.

'Nope.'

'TCP,' guessed Robert.

'Nope.'

'Toni: Home permanent wave,' suggested Billy Burns.

'Nope,' responded Hughie.

'Typhoo Tea!' exclaimed Tommy, confidently.

'Nope,' said Wee Hughie. Tommy looked balefully at him.

'Are you any kin tae John Wayne?'

'Nope,' answered Hughie. *Sniff!*

We all stared intently at Lizzie's window display. With rationing still on, there wasn't that much to select from. This was getting serious. We were about to start a *second* round of guessing – against someone playing his first game with the 'big boys'. Reputations were at stake. It was Tommy's turn once more.

'Toblerone!' He looked around, a half-smile on his face, ready to accept the plaudits.

'Nope,' droned Wee Hughie. *Sniff!* Tommy visibly winced.

It was my turn again. I stared into the window for minutes, then announced, 'Ah cannae see anything else starting wi "T".' There was a chorus of 'neither can I' around me. But Tommy was loath to give in. His eyes darted all over the window in a last, desperate attempt to find the elusive 'T'.

Sniff!

Tommy looked scathingly at Wee Hughie, then at his big brother, Robert.

'Diz he ever blaw his nose? Every time ye see him the snotters are trippin' him!'

Silently, we all regarded the offending member. Already the two snail-like entities had re-emerged and were making a dash for Hughie's top lip.

'Here.' Robert dug into his pocket and handed his sibling a somewhat off-white handkerchief. Hughie blew and blew, then blew some more.

'Jeez! Will ye jist listen tae that,' exclaimed Tommy. 'Is there nae end tae it? That's coming aw the wye up fae 'is boots.'

'Zat no enough tae put ye aff yer dinner,' said Billy.

At last, probably through exhaustion, Wee Hughie stopped blowing. He offered the hankie back to Robert.

'Eh, naw. Jist keep it.'

'Ah shuffer fae catarrh, ye know,' beamed Hughie.

'Ah jist hope it's no contagious,' muttered John.

'Anywye, ur yeesh givin' in?' Hughie looked up at Tommy. As he did so, reinforcements put in an appearance from his right nostril.

'Aw, my God!' Tommy looked heavenward. 'Is thur nae end tae it? Ah give in, whit is it?'

Sniff! The advance scout wheeched back up Wee Hughie's nostril. He looked around triumphantly.

'TARAMELS!' he said.

There was a moment's silence.

'Whit?' croaked Tommy. 'Whit's buggerin' "taramels"?'

'Eh, he means "caramels",' explained an apologetic Robert. 'He's always called them "taramels" – so he thinks they start wi' a "T".'

From inside the shop we could hear auld Lizzie howling with laughter. She must have been sitting on her chair by the window and could hear us through the glass.

'Yah wee scunner!' raved Tommy, red in the face. 'Jist wasting oor time. Nae wonder we couldnae get it. That round disnae count. And don't bother asking us for a game in future.'

Billy and me were frightened to look at one another in case we laughed. Tommy tried to regain his composure – and dignity.

'C'mon, boys, let's go roond tae the cafe.' He pointed at Hughie. 'And *you're* no coming.'

'Away you go hame,' said Robert to his brother, who wasn't quite sure exactly what he had done. Reluctantly he began to walk away.

'HERE!' We all turned. Lizzie was standing at the shop door, a couple of Penny Dainties in her outstretched hand. 'Here, Hughie, here's a couple of "taramels" for ye. Ah've never laughed so much in ma life!'

'Oh thanksh, Lizzie,' exclaimed Hughie, his face lighting up.

'Straight hame, mind,' said Robert. 'Ah'll see ye later.'

'Okay,' said Wee Hughie. 'Ah'll keep ye a taramel.'

Scared Stiff on a Saturday Night

'Will we have some toast?'

'Oooh aye.' It was just after eight o'clock, only two hours since we'd had our dinner. But I could always manage some toast.

'Gie me a hand,' said Ma. 'Put two plates and a knife oot, and the butter and jam.'

As I laid the table Ma cut two thick slices off a plain loaf.

'Here.' She handed me the first slice with the fork already stuck in it. 'Don't hold it too near the bars or you'll burn it. Ah'll make the tea.'

The blackened iron kettle sat on top of the range gently singing. Ma reached up to the mantelpiece for the red tin caddy, put three spoonfuls of dry tea into the aluminium teapot, poured hot water in from the kettle and gave it a good stir.

'We'll jist let it mask for a wee minute.' She crossed over to the sideboard and switched on the big, wooden-cased Pye radio. I watched the warm light glow behind the glass with all the station names, then, as the valves warmed up, the sound floated into the room. 'That's *Variety Bandbox* that's on at the minute.' She turned to me. 'Dae ye know what's oan next?'

'Aye.' I gave a nervous laugh. 'It's *The Man in Black*.'

In the late 1940s, still the heyday of the radio, *The Man in Black* took the country by storm. Every Saturday night more than half the population tuned in to the Light Programme for their weekly dose of terror. Next morning, the previous night's episode was the main talking point.

'When it comes on, will we listen tae it wi' the light oot?'

I thought back to last Saturday's episode. For a bet, a young man had agreed to be locked up for the night, alone, in an undertaker's salon. Unknown to him, one of his friends had secreted himself in a coffin, intending to play a trick on him. In the morning when the group gathered for the unlocking of the shop, they found that overnight the young man's hair had turned white and he had become a gibbering wreck. The one who had hidden in the coffin was found to be dead!

'Well, will we have the light off?'

'Aye, awright then.' I felt a delicious frisson of fear.

By nine we had finished our tea and toast and were sitting on either side of the range when the deep, sepulchral tones of the host, Valentine Dyall – *the* Man in Black – welcomed us to tonight's episode.

Ma said, 'Away and switch the light oot, then.'

'Och, mibbe we should jist listen tae it with it on,' I suggested.

'Naw, it's nae good, it's no scary enough. Ye need tae listen in the dark.'

'Awright then.'

I ambled over to the far corner of the room by the door, switched the light off and ran back to my chair. Ma laughed. The flickering flames from the fire were now our only light source. From the blackness on the far side of the room the disembodied voices of the actors, aided by sound effects, began to unfold tonight's descent into terror. Within five minutes we knew it had been a mistake to put the light out.

The story, set in late-Victorian London, concerned an impoverished young medical student who had obtained rooms, in an otherwise unoccupied large house. Earlier that day, as an aid to his studies, he had managed to buy a skeleton at a bargain price from a rather shady character. Unknown to the student the skeleton was grave-robbed. Also unknown to him was the fact that, in life, the deceased had been a murderer!

'Ah wish we hudnae put the light oot.' I pulled my chair closer to the fireplace.

'Me tae,' answered Ma. We both giggled nervously. 'Away and put it on if ye want,' she said.

I looked over to the blackness where the light switch – and the outside door – lay. In the moving shadows caused by the glowing coals, anything could be lurking there. My ten-year-old imagination was too fertile.

'Naw, we'll jist leave it,' I said.

'Ah'll give ye thruppence if ye go and switch it oan.'

'Ah widnae go ower there if ye gave me two bob!'

We both began to laugh; the laughs dried in our throats as the drama reached a higher level of fear. From out of the dark on the other side of our room we could hear the young man's pen scrape on the paper as he sat writing, by candlelight, alone in the large house. Outside the window we could hear the wind moan through the eaves; the BBC sound effects department were giving it their all. Slowly, the handle on the only door to his room began to turn. We all knew that the room on the other side was empty – except for the newly purchased skeleton! As the handle turned we heard boney, scrapey sounds. I could feel the hair begin to stand on my head and the back of my neck.

'Ah really will give ye two bob if ye go and put that light oan.' Ma paused. 'Can ye remember if ye locked the ootside door when ye came in?'

'Ah cannae remember.'

I pulled my chair even closer to the fireplace. One leg of it was now on the other side of the fender, resting on the hearth. Ma reached for the poker and sat brandishing it in case the skeleton went for us when it was done with the student. We looked at each other in the fire's glow, giggling and laughing in a mixture of fear and pleasure.

'You'll be in that fire in a minute,' said Ma.

'If ah hear somebody come in that door ah'll be up the chimney.'

At last the drama reached its climax. Valentine Dyall closed proceedings with his usual 'Goodnight. Pleasant dreams.'

Ma and me sat there, spent.

'Pleasant dreams, is it? Ah'll give him pleasant dreams. Ah'll never sleep a wink the night efter that. Jist aboot frichted the wits oot o' us.'

A music programme came on; we began to relax.

'Aw, Ma, that wiz even scarier than last week, wizn't it?'

'No half. Away and put the light oan, son.'

I looked over to the dark corner by the door. I *knew* if I went over there, just as I reached for the light switch the door would fly open and a boney hand would reach in and grab my wrist!

'You go, Ma.'

She tutted. I watched as she went over, switched the light on and returned unscathed. The skeleton must be busy going for somebody else in oor close! Probably auld Mrs Kinsella.

'Dae ye want a wee cup of tea afore ye go tae yer bed?'

'Aye. That's still a good fire for making toast, Ma. Can ah have another slice?'

'Aye, but go easy on the butter. That's aw we have till ah get the rations oan Monday.'

Soon I was, yet again, sitting drinking hot, sweet tea and devouring another slice of toast with butter and raspberry jam.

'That wiz great the night, wizn't it, Ma?' I was beginning to feel brave again now that the light was on.

'Wiznae half. Ah wonder whit next week's story will be.' She smiled. 'Will we listen wi' the light oot, again?'

'Oh aye, definitely,' I said. And tried to look like I meant it.

Does This Tram Go Tae the Orinoco?

'Mammy! Mammy!' I came galloping into the house all excited. Ma was silhouetted against the window as she stood at the sink washing dishes. 'Aw the boys are gettin' the tram oot tae Mulguy for the day and they're taking pieces and boatles o' ginger an' things an' Robert Purden's going an' he says he'll be keeping an eye oan his young brother John so if ye let me go he'll keep an eye oan me tae an' he'll no let us go near the watter or anything.' I had to stop and gulp a breath. 'Can ah go, ma, eh? Ah've never been tae Mulguy and if ah cannae go ah'll be left wi' naebody tae play wi' 'cause they're aw going, Robert and John an' Tommy Hope an' Billy Burns . . .' I was running out of momentum, as well as breath. 'Ah'll no dae anything dangerous, honest. Gonny let me go, Ma?'

She looked out the window into the back court. It was just after ten on an April morning and the sun, unseasonably, was blazing down into the tenement canyons. Overnight, winter had gone. Peggy Jarvie's cat, Darkie, lay in the shade of a wash-house chimney, eyes almost shut, indolently grooming himself now and again. Mr Lockerbie's big dog, Bruce, lay on his side in the shade of our midden, his tongue lolling, panting heavily. Aw the neighbours were saying they couldnae remember an April like it.

'Gonny let me go, Ma? Please?'

My hopes began to rise. She hadn't said no right away – that meant she was thinking about it. I decided not to say any more, just 'will' her to make the right decision.

'Gie me ma purse ower. Much'll ye need?' She was gonny let me go!

'Jist a boatle o' ginger and a sannie. Oh, and ma tram fare.'

'Jesusjonny! Dae ye think ah'm made of money?'

'Naw, Ma.' I tried to sound sympathetic without going over the top. Negotiations were at a delicate stage.

'Here.' She gave me a two-shilling piece. 'Away tae Lizzie's and get a wee jar of meat paste and yer ginger.' She paused, the open purse still in her hand. 'Much'll ye need for the tram?' This was a crucial moment. I wish she'd waited until I got my rations, then she would have been committed.

'Oh, fourpence. Tuppence each way.' I braced myself.

'My God! If ah'd known it wiz gonny be this dear ah'd huv said naw. Noo mind, don't you be bothering me later in the week for any mair money; this is yer lot, dae ye hear?'

'Aye, ah'll no, Ma.' I tried to look solemn as I lied. Solemn was good. Come this Thursday *Samson and Delilah* starring Victor Mature was on at the Blythsie. They said it was great when he knocked doon the temple. I was dying to see it. Anyway, I'd worry about that later in the week. Let's get to Mulguy first. Ma started to cut two slices of bread for my sandwich. 'And don't you go near that river up therr. Jist remember Wee Drew that droont doon the Kelvin yon day. Wee sowel. If you faw' in that river and survive ah'll kill ye when ye come hame. Go on, away doon tae Lizzie's and get yer stuff.'

I raced the fifty yards down to the corner shop. As I clicked the catch and entered, the bell above the door announced me. There was a slight pause, then Lizzie ponderously began to emerge from the back shop. She was so fat she could only make it by leaning on things as she advanced. She was called Lizzie Douglas, but was no relation to us. Her brown Chow dog, Chang, wandered out from the back shop, saw it was me and went back to his bed.

Lizzie let herself fall into the sturdy wooden chair behind the counter. The floorboards vibrated slightly through my feet and the pointer on the Avery scales flickered alarmingly. Her six chins wobbled, then settled.

'Yes, Robert?'

'Could ah have a wee jar of meat paste, please, Lizzie.'

'What flavour, son?'

'Ahhh, beef.' With a great effort Lizzie reached for the small, ribbed jar with its shiny, brass lid and placed it on the counter.

'And a bottle of American Cream Soda, please.' Right. That's my rations bought.

The five of us stood at the tram stop on the Maryhill Road, laden with an assortment of school bags and ex-army small packs. Here and there the top of a ginger bottle stuck its head out like a cat going to the vets. A tram glided into view down by the Seamore.

'Is it a Number 4?' Eyes were strained.

'Aye, it definitely is.'

The tram climbed up the slight incline until we all could see the '4' and the legend on the destination board: 'Milngavie'. I couldn't have been more excited if it had said 'Samarkand'. At last I was getting to go to Mulguy!

We clambered aboard and made our way up the spiral stairs to the top deck. The little separate compartment at the front was occupied. We took the nearest seats to it and hoped it would soon be vacated.

The conductor surveyed us. 'Youse aw the gether?'

'Aye.'

'Are ye's aw fur Mulguy?'

'Aye.' He counted us, then dialled the fare on the telephone-like dial on top of his ticket machine. We watched with great interest as he turned the handle until five long white tickets, with red printing, hung from it. He tore them off and handed them to Robert.

'Right, five tuppences, boys.' We handed over our money and

he turned to leave, then stopped. 'Remember, if ye's get that front compartment don't make too much noise. And nae banging feet; ma driver disnae like it.'

'We'll no, mister. Honest.' He went on his way.

'Robert?' I said. 'How come everybody says "Mulguy", yet, if ye see it written doon it should be said "Millengavie"?'

'Don't know. Naebody knows.'

We had been travelling half an hour or so when John, Robert's young brother, nudged me. 'See the sign, "Glasgow City Boundary"? That's us leaving the city. We're in the country noo.' Five minutes later he nudged me again, and pointed.

'WOW!' I gazed in wonder. Two hundred yards off to the right, in mysterious isolation in the middle of a green field, was a gantry-like construction, built from girders and perhaps some four hundred yards long. Suspended underneath the gantry was a silver, cigar-shaped machine with a propeller at each end. It just stood, alone, surrounded by railings. 'Whit is it?'

'That's whit they call the George Bennie Railplane,' said Robert. 'It wiz built around 1930 and should huv been able tae take ye from Glasgow tae Edinburgh in thirty minutes. They only raised enough money tae build this test track.' He looked at me. 'It's great, in't it?'

'No half. Whit a shame they couldnae finish it.' I had been immediately taken with this beautiful, futuristic machine, straight out of Fritz Lang's *Metropolis*. Even though it was twenty years old, it still looked ultra-modern. How could they not have raised the money?

The tram made its lazy way in the hot sun out into the country. The top deck, with all its windows, became a travelling greenhouse. Dust motes danced in the beams. The tram gave off its usual aroma of hot oil and metal and people; the woodwork

The George Bennie Railplane, a source of wonder to us boys. The test track was built in 1930, the world's first monorail. Bennie couldn't get finance. It lay marooned in a field until being scrapped in 1956. Nobody had the sense to save it.

creaked; leather hand straps squeaked when someone swayed their way along the aisle. We blethered away about stuff that was important only to us.

'Ah'm dying o' thirst,' announced Tommy Hope. 'Ah'll huv tae huv a drink o' ginger.'

'Me tae,' said Billy Burns. Soon we were all into our bags.

'Ah think ah'll huv a sannie as well,' said John.

Minutes later we were all devouring sandwiches and washing them down with mouthfuls of Lemonade, Irn Bru and Cream Soda. With each swig the amount of crumbs swirling about in the bottles increased. By the time we reached Mulguy half the day's rations had gone.

We trooped off the tram. At last I was setting foot in the legendary village of Mulguy, Glasgow's answer to Brigadoon! I was the only one who hadn't been there before. I gazed with great interest at the end of the tramlines. They just stopped. So this was a terminus. Somehow I thought it would have been a little grander than just a dead end. The word 'terminus' seemed to promise more.

There was a noise; I looked up. The conductor was leaning out of the front, upstairs window energetically turning the handle to wind on the destination blind. I watched as the names sped past: Airdrie, Auchenshuggle, Carntyne, Dalmarnock, Elderslie, Finnieston . . . I lost interest in the vicinity of Partick. The driver now took my attention. Using a long pole, he swung the roof-top 'collector' round to face the opposite way, ready for the trip back – after they'd had a smoke and a quick read at the paper.

I looked around the small Main Street. There was not a tenement to be seen. The stone-built buildings were all one- and two-storey. There were just a few shops. The air smelled different.

Robert gathered us all together.

'C'mon, boys, *forward yo*!' There had been a cavalry-versus-Indians film on at the Blythsie the week before; its influence hadn't worn off yet.

As we set away, I turned to Billy. 'Is Mulguy like the park?'

'Whit dae ye mean "like the park"?'

'Diz it huv railings and paths and flooer beds?'

'Naw, it's jist aw natural and open. If we come near a farm ye might see stane walls or fences. Farmers are allowed tae own big dawds of the countryside, so they usually build stone walls roond it and put up signs saying "Keep Aff!" If ye trespass oan thur farm they usually start shootin' at ye wi' shotguns an' that.'

'Fuck me! We're no crossin' ower any farms the day, ur we?'

'Naw. It's jist aw countryside.'

This was a relief. I'd had a momentary flash of me limping

into the house tonight with the arse blasted oot ma troosers and a bum full of buckshot for ma Mammy tae extricate with her tweezers!

We soon left Mulguy village behind and took a well-trodden path that ran alongside a dense wood.

'This is Mugdock Wood,' said Robert, 'but everybody calls it "The Bluebell Woods". It's only April so they should still be oot.'

We approached the edge of the trees and took a few steps into them. That half-dozen paces brought us from open, sun-drenched grassland into a cool, shady wood. Light hardly penetrated the closely planted trees. My eyes and ears began to accustom themselves to this new environment. At first it seemed not only cool but quiet; yet it wasn't. High up in the trees birds sang to one another constantly.

'See, the bluebells are still oot,' somebody said.

I looked down for the first time, and found we were knee-deep amongst them. As my eyes got used to the shadows, I caught my breath. Bluebells, seemingly a foot above the ground, floated away from me and filled the space between the trees. I could make out individual bluebells near me, but from about ten feet away they just became a blue haze drifting off into the dark depths of the wood. It was the most beautiful thing I'd ever seen. I wanted to say, 'Jeez, that's lovely, in't it?' But of course, I didn't.

Even though the boys had seen them before, we all stood for a few minutes just drinking it. Nobody spoke. It was obvious they thought it was as wonderful a sight as I did, but there was no way anyone would say so.

We screwed our eyes into slits as we stumbled out of the dark wood into the twice-as-bright sun. A few minutes later the track brought us to the side of a small, gurgling river. The sparkling, brown water tumbled and fell over rocky outcrops, in other places it lay in still, dark pools. It was mostly about thirty feet wide and two to sometimes three feet deep.

'Whit dae ye call this river?'

'This is the Allender Water,' said Robert.

'The Allender Water.' Its name suited it. It sounded like the sort of name Robert Louis Stevenson would have made up. As we walked along the side of the river we frequently came across families out for the day, picnicking.

'Look! There's the McLeans.' The McLeans stayed through the wall from us, in the next close. When my father got violent, it was to the McLeans' that Ma 'knocked through the wall' and shouted for them to fetch the police. Mr McLean had a motorbike and sidecar, and on good days would pack the wife and weans onto it and off they would go for a day in the country. 'Hello, Mr McLean, Mrs McLean,' we chorused as we passed. They were sitting on the banks of the Allender with a couple of blankets spread out, eating their picnic. Nearby a Primus stove boiled a kettle for the adults to brew tea. The kids gulped Irn Bru. A few yards away stood the old black Triumph bike and sidecar which brought them more pleasure than some folks got from a Rolls Royce.

'Hello, boys, is that you oot for a day's camping?' asked Mr McLean.

'Aye, might as well when the weather's good,' said Robert.

'See ya.' We trudged onwards.

'Is it much further?'

'Naw, it's no far noo. Mibbe another five minutes.'

We seemed to have been walking for ages, and had left the Allender behind. We crested a small rise. Robert stopped, and pointed.

'See where those two two stane dykes meet, and that funny tree's in the corner?'

'Aye.'

'Well, that's oor tree. We always camp there.'

We walked the last few yards to the little nook where the walls met. I looked at the tree. It had five equal-sized trunks curving gently outwards from its base. Just the sort of tree you'd find in a Disney cartoon. The boys took their bags and satchels off their backs and placed them in the welcoming embrace of the five trunks. I followed suit, then looked around. The area was lushly grassed with springy turf. There was a round bare patch on the ground; even to a 'tenderfoot' like me that was obviously the spot where fires had been lit. Robert started to organise us.

'John and Billy.' He looked at me. 'And you tae, Robert. Go looking for twigs and branches for the fire – and bring any dry grass or straw as well. Tommy, you take the tinnies doon the river and fill them.'

Ten minutes later the three of us returned with armfuls of fuel. Robert had the fire going from what had been lying around.

'Did ye use two sticks?' I asked, even at that age a romantic.

'Naw, just wan.' He held out a box of Bluebell matches.

I watched as he went over to a niche in the wall and returned with a number of sturdy, scorched branches which had been hidden there. He made a frame over the campfire. Tommy appeared with the tinnies and they were suspended from the centre stick. Robert and Tommy both produced well-used tea-and-sugar tins from their bags.

'Have ye ever hud tea brewed oan a campfire, Robert?'

'Naw.'

'Cannae beat it,' said Tommy, 'in't that right, boys?' He received a unanimous vote.

I'd already eaten half my rations on the tram. Now, with all the walking and gallons of fresh air, I was more than ready for my last sannie. As we sat around the fire waiting for the tinnies to boil, the older boys regaled us with tales of derring-do and expeditions to far-flung destinations within twenty miles of

Glasgow. It appeared you didn't earn your spurs until you'd spent a night sleeping in the bothy up the Whangie. I didn't reveal my ignorance by enquiring where, or what, the Whangie was. I soon deduced it was a hill, or, if Tommy Hope was to be believed, a mountain some three feet shorter than Everest. I looked over at some distant hills.

'Whit dae they call those hills?'

'That's the Campsie Fells,' said Robert. I wondered how he could remember all these things.

'The water's startin' tae bile.'

Dry tea was measured out and delicately stirred into the cheerfully bubbling water. The aroma of woodsmoke, newly familiar from the riverside picnickers, filled the air. Tommy placed a small twig on the surface of each tinnie.

'Keeps the ash from the fire from getting into the tea,' he said, mysteriously.

Last sandwich eaten, fingertips and lips burnt from the tinnie, the rest of the afternoon flashed by as we played sodjers and, to nobody's surprise, football. Robert Purden was 'fitba' mad' and had produced a leather football and bladder from his bag – complete with bike pump to inflate them. By late afternoon, as the sun began to go down, we lay in the lush grass, tired, faces smarting from sunburn – and starving!

'Jeez! It's nearly an 'oor's walk back tae Mulguy, forty-five minutes on the tram, and it's already three 'oors since ah ate ma last sannie.' I looked at Billy. 'Ah'll be deid by the time ah get hame.'

We tidied up the site, put the fire out and returned the sticks to their hideout. In the rapidly descending gloaming we set off on the return journey along the banks of the now-deserted Allender, the families all gone home with tired weans ready for their beds. We came across just two young men who remained from all those we had passed hours earlier. In a hollow on the opposite bank they had pitched their ex-army tent, and were obviously there for the night. The smell of frying bacon and eggs drifted across from their fire to torment us. They gave us a wave as we passed.

'Ye's have got it all tae yoorselves now, boys,' called Robert.

'Aye, this is what we've been waiting for,' said one.

'Ye's huvnae got a spare plate of bacon and eggs, huv ye?' shouted John.

'Sorry, boys.' We trekked on, the tantalising smell following us.

'Will ye smell that ham and eggs. Ah'm slaverin' at the mooth,' said Billy.

'That's nuthin' new,' stated Tommy.

We began to pass the Bluebell Woods.

'Ah'm gonny pick a bunch of bluebells tae take hame for ma ma,' said Tommy.

'So am ah.' 'Me tae.' 'Ah think ah will.'

Minutes later the five of us emerged from the ever-darkening wood with freshly picked bunches. Though I couldn't see as far as on my earlier visit and didn't get the effect of the blue haze going off into the distance, it had still been a chance to see again this natural beauty. En route we found some abandoned newspapers and shared them out to wrap our bluebells in.

At last, tired and bedraggled, we arrived in Main Street, Mulguy. A tram stood, in solitary splendour, at the terminus. It was now getting darker by the minute. The local chip shop had opened for the evening and the smell of fish and chips drifted over.

'Oh my God! Ah cannae stand it.' Billy slumped down onto the pavement. 'First it wiz bacon an' eggs, noo it's fish and chips. Dae ye think it's a test?' I joined him, sitting on the kerb.

'Ah've jist got enough for a bag of chips,' said Robert.

'So have ah,' echoed Tommy.

'Lucky bastards!'

'Ah'd better ask if we've got time.' The rest of us penniless vagrants watched as Robert spoke to the tram's crew, then returned. 'The driver says he'll wait for us.' The two millionaires vanished into the shop. Billy lay back on the pavement, arms outstretched.

'Ah'd gie a hundred pounds – for thruppence worth o' chips.'

Robert and Tommy emerged from the shop, already eating their portions. We scrambled up and surrounded them.

'You're gonny gie us a chip, in't ye?'

'Ye can huv wan each,' said Robert.

'Same here,' said Tommy.

I took my allotted two chips. They didn't even dent my hunger. I watched as John, Robert's young brother, reached for his ration.

'Take a few,' said Robert. Jeez, I wish I had a big brother.

The tram began its long journey back to Maryhill. Conversation was more subdued than on the trip out. Now and again I buried my nose into the bluebells and was instantly transported back to Mugdock Wood. At long last we came to 'our' stretch of Maryhill Road. We gathered on the platform, the conductor rang his bell and the tram stopped at the post office stop. Empty bags and haversacks flapping against our sides, we jumped off.

'Well, that wiz a smashin' day oot, wizn't it, boys?' said Robert.

'It wiz great,' I said, 'but next time ah'm taking *three times* as many sannies – and money for chips. Ah wiz seriously thinking of eatin' these bluebells.'

'Ah tried some,' said Billy. 'They don't taste as good as they look!'

I staggered into the house.

'Ma, ah'm starvin' o' hunger. Can ah huv a piece?'

She looked at me. 'Whit a state. Huv ye been doon the pit?'

I was too far gone to laugh. Then I remembered. 'Oh, ah've brought these for ye, Ma.' I swung my bag round from behind me, the heads of the bluebells stuck out from the top. 'They're fae the Bluebell Woods.' I held up the bunch of bright blue flowers, wrapped in the *Evening Citizen*. Some had lost their heads, there were one or two broken stalks, but the majority were still as fresh and bright as when they'd been picked. 'Smell them, Ma. That's whit the wood smelled like.'

She buried her nose into them. Her eyes seemed to glisten. 'Did ye bring them aw the wye fae Mulguy for yer mammy, son?'

'Aye.'

She took a newly washed milk bottle from the draining board, half-filled it from the tap and arranged the bluebells in it. She placed it in the middle of the table and looked at it for a few seconds. The embossed 'Co-operative Dairies' didn't seem to distract from their beauty. She reached for the bread knife and began cutting a thick slice of bread.

'Ah'll dae ye a piece, son.'

Sex, Tits and Other Dinky Toys

It was the summer of 1949. Definitely!

I hurried through the close, anxious to get back to playing 'motors' with my pals in the back court. Donny May stood talking to someone, unseen in the recess at the bottom of the stairs. He held out his hand to stop me.

'Hiyah, Robert.'

'Hello, Donny.' I looked to my right. Margaret Milson was leaning, casually, against the wall.

'Huv ye ever seen a pair of tits, Robert?' I wondered if I'd heard right, felt myself redden. They were both about thirteen, some three years older than me.

'Eh, naw, ah huvnae.'

'Show him yer tits, Margaret!' Without a word Margaret un-leaned herself from the wall, and with both hands lifted her pale blue knitted jumper to reveal two small, pert breasts. Donny reached over and played with one, as if tuning a wireless. He took his hand away.

'Dae ye want a feel?' I wasn't sure what I should say, in case I offended them.

'Oh, aye, ah widnae mind.' I'd never had a conversation like this before.

'Go on, then.'

Donny was a bit of a wild bugger. I hoped this wasn't some sort of trick which would finish up with him hitting me. I tentatively reached out and touched, then gently fondled Margaret's left breast. Donny had been playing with her right one so I thought I'd give it a wee rest. It felt nice. Firm and warm.

Margaret stood with a beatific smile on her face during proceedings.

'Whit dae ye think?' enquired Donny. As he posed the question Margaret pulled down her jersey.

'It's really nice.' I thought I'd better be complimentary. Anyway, it had been.

'It is, in't it,' said Donny.

'Anywye, ah'd better be going, the boys are waiting oan me.' I pulled my Dinky Toys 'Foden Lorry' out of my pocket as proof. I edged away.

'Right then. See ya, Donny.'

'Aye, cheerio.'

'Cheerio, Margaret. Aaah, thanks.'

She gave me a nice smile. I wondered if this now meant that in future I could see them on demand, even if Donny wasn't there.

The hot sun, shining into the rectangle between the tenements, had turned the back courts into a dustbowl. I was glad to see my pals were still playing. We had scraped 'roads' into the dust with a piece of cardboard. Various toy garages, houses and railway stations were dotted around to make up a town. I knelt down and began driving my lorry along the roads, making engine noises and frequent 'beep beeps'. The other boys drove an assortment of cars, lorries and military vehicles, all to a symphony of sound effects.

'Donny May jist got Margaret Milson tae show me her tits and let me feel them!' Immediately all the vehicles hit their brakes, and there was a major pile-up at the crossroads.

'Yur kiddin'.'

'Ah'm no.' I told them the tale, keeping an eye on the close in case Donny appeared.

'Yah lucky bastard!' Tommy and John, who were around Donny's age, found it very interesting. 'Wur they nice?'

'Aye, they were awright.'

'Ah might see if ah can get her on her own sometime,' said Tommy, 'see if she'll let me huv a feel.'

'Ah've noticed this last wee while she's beginning tae get tits,' said John. The traffic was now moving again, but the conversation on sexual matters was taking precedence. Now and again a car would run off the road. 'Dae you ever get tae see your Betty's tits, Tommy?' asked John.

'Aye, noo and again. Sometimes ah catch her washin' herself at the sink. Ach! But it's no the same when it's yer sister.'

'Naw. Better when it's somebody else's,' agreed John.

I lay down flat on the dirt so as I was at eye level with my lorry. It made it seem more real. A lot of the conversation washed over me. I wished I hadn't told them; it was beginning to spoil the game.

'Tommy and me wiz lying nice and quiet on the wash-house roof the other night, spying on John Anderson and Rita Mulcahy doing a bit of winching in her back close,' said John.

'Did ye's see anything good?'

'It wiz a rerr laugh. He kept trying tae get his hand up her skirt, and she kept stoaping him. Then at last, jist as she wiz letting him huv a wee feel, this rotten bastard here' – he pointed to Tommy – 'shouts, "Stop that ya dirty bastard!" and Rita lets oot a squeal. So we duck down so as John cannae see us, and we're nearly bursting, trying no tae laugh. Hey, it wiz great, wizn't it?'

'Aye,' said Tommy. 'And John's going mad trying tae spot us. He would huv killed us if he'd caught us. So he shouts, "Ah know who ye's are." But he didnae, he'd huv shouted oor names if he had. Anywye, this maddy here bawls, "Away and fuck yerself!" and we slipped aff the roof intae the Maryhill Road back courts and got away. Nae kidding, oor sides wur sore laughing.'

'Beep beep! Can ye move yer car while yer talking?' Once more the traffic began to flow.

'Huv ye ever caught yer mammy and daddy daein' it?'

'Ah sometimes hear them daein' it ben the room,' said Malcolm.

'Mine like tae dae it oan a Sunday efternoon,' said Jim. 'They always gie us money tae go tae the matinee. Don't they?' Billy, his wee brother nodded in agreement. 'But wan day he was sick aw ower himself so we had tae come hame early, and we caught them in bed. Ye should huv seen the pair o' them. Ma mammy wiz aw red in the face . . . "We were feeling a wee bit tired efter oor dinner, so seeing as the hoose wiz quiet, we thought we'd go for a wee snooze." Hah! Thought they'd go fur a wee shag seein' as they'd got rid of us, mair like.' Jim looked at me. 'Dae ye ever hear your two at it, Robert, wi' you living in the single-end?'

'No really. Ah think they must alwiz wait till ah'm asleep. Anywye, they dae mair fightin' than shaggin'. Ma ma's alwiz accusing him of daein' aw his shaggin' wi' other wimmen. That's whit aw their rows are aboot.' I deliberately crashed my lorry into cars waiting at a junction.

The sun sank behind the roofs of Hinshaw Street's tenements. The heat of the day soon vanished and it grew cool and grey. We still lay beside the roads we'd made, but there were only three of us left and there was little activity. I tried to think of something to say or do to keep them from losing interest and going home. It had been great fun today. I didn't want it to end; I wanted to stay out as long as I could. There had been a big row on Saturday night and things were still bad. I knew that when I went home he'd be picking on me the rest of the evening to try and goad Ma, then he'd have an excuse to start again. The wee bastard. The longer I was out the better.

We heard a window go up. 'Tommy! C'mon, son, yer dinner'll be ready in ten minutes.'

'Ah well, ah'd better away in. Anywye, ah'm starvin'. See ya, boys.'

'Aye, see ya the morra.' Tommy dusted himself down, stuffed his lorry and armoured car into his pockets then made his way down the back courts. Only two left.

Minutes later came the sound of footsteps coming through one of the closes from Doncaster Street. I looked up; my heart jumped. It was my father. He scowled as he saw me.

'C'mon, you, you should huv been in for your dinner half an hour ago. Dae you not know whit time it is?'

'Naw, ah didnae know it was late.' I tried to keep my voice steady. I didn't want Malcolm to know how scared I was of my father.

'You never know fuck all, you. Get a move on.'

As he spoke he placed himself to one side of the close entrance. I knew why. I picked up my lorry and looked at Malcolm. I could see sympathy in his eyes. I hated that. I was ten, but already I hated that. Amongst all my pals I was the only one who needed sympathy. Why did I have to be the unlucky one who got a father like mine?

'See ye the morra, Malcolm.'

'Ye might see him the morra, if you're allowed oot.' He has to say that, hasn't he.

'See ya, Robert.'

I could picture what would happen when Malcolm went home: his dad would look up and say, 'Hiyah, pal! What've you been doing the day?'

I braced myself as I passed him. I wasn't disappointed: I received my usual 'belt oan the lug'. My eyes filled with tears, not so much because it was sore, but because I was sick of it. He loved it when he could tell me off in front of my pals. He liked to show he was the big man. I knew I had years of it in front of me. I longed to be grown-up so as I could get away from him.

As we headed for our close I knew that I'd spend the rest of the evening wondering what to do to avoid him getting onto me. If I sat quietly, it would be, 'Whit's yer face trippin' ye for? Dae ye think ye shouldnae be telt aff for being late?'

If I sat in a corner and read: 'That's aw you ever dae, sit wi' yer face buried in a fuckin' book.' The book would then be snatched out of my hand. He liked that.

If I got on with some homework: 'Get that put away! You should have been in early if ye knew ye had homework. Ye can go tae school the morra withoot it done. If ye get the belt you've naebody tae blame but yourself.'

If I dropped or spilt something at the dinner table he'd immediately reach over and clout me – 'Yah handless fucker!'

At last bedtime would come and I'd climb into the bed-chair. I'd start to read a comic, and he'd maybe let me have five minutes. As usual I'd quickly become absorbed in a story . . . *Snatch!*

'Never mind lying therr reading. Turn your face tae the wall and get tae sleep.'

I'd turn and face the wall and pull the covers up as though trying to block out the light. With my head under the covers I'd suddenly have the idea: maybe I should try a prayer, again: Dear Lord Jesus. Ah've almost had a really nice day the day, until ah had to come in. Ah hope you'll look after ma mammy and me. But if you *really* want tae look after us it would be best if ma faither wisnae here. Could ye no get him tae take another job like when he was workin' away fae hame up at Loch Sloy? Something like that would be smashing. That would really be great for ma mammy and me. Amen.

Eat Your Heart Out, James Brown

My father's youngest brother, Jack, was a calming influence on him most of the time. When he called for him on a Saturday night, as he often did in the late forties, early fifties, Ma and I knew the odds were in our favour that he'd return from the pub, with Jack, in a reasonable mood. Occasionally we would have quite an enjoyable evening.

Uncle Jack was skinny, angular, and had lost the sight of one eye while serving with the Highland Light Infantry in the Western Desert in 1943, a fact he regularly bemoaned when in his cups. Then there was his habit of not *quite* swearing, especially in mixed company. He always substituted 'P' for 'F' in the F-word. When he'd had a lot to drink – or, as he called it, 'A good bucket!' – he'd regale us once more with the story of his eye.

'Fifty miles behind the puckin' front line, jist making a brew for the boys, and whit happens, eh? Ah'll tell ye's. RAF chasing this puckin' Jerry, so whit diz he dae? Jettisons his bombs tae try and get away, dizn't he. And where dae they land? Right oan tap o' ma puckin' cookhoose! Two years in the desert, never seen an angry German.' He'd look around in righteous indignation, then take another swig of beer. 'Pucker!' Sand had blasted into his right eye and taken its sight.

Jack was a window cleaner with a choice pitch in the city centre. He also had a lucrative sideline, washing and polishing businessmen's cars, which earned him as much as his window cleaner's wages. Whenever he visited he was always a regular source of two-bob bits and half-crowns for me. How often, with a child's simple logic, I wished Ma had married the good-natured Jack instead of his brother. Jack was a bachelor, but had a long-running on/off relationship with 'Aunty' Alice from Rutherglen. They even lived together for a year or so. In her late thirties, Aunty Alice was Catholic and appeared to run her own order, the Little Sisters of Perpetual Mourning. She was always in black. Her father had died some years previously. Alice had gone into mourning, found she had a knack for it, and never came out of it again. She always looked as if she'd just came back from a funeral where she had missed the 'ham tea'.

Like Jack, Alice was thin and angular. There was also an estranged husband somewhere. Because of her religion, divorce was impossible, therefore she couldn't marry Uncle Jack. He didn't seem unduly depressed about this.

Mostly Jack and my father went out on a Saturday night together. If he turned up with Alice on his arm, Ma would get dressed and the foursome would head for a pub with a lounge bar. The majority of local pubs had just one bar, and that was strictly men-only. On their return, with the obligatory carry-oot, the next item on the agenda was, 'Who's going roon tae Bundoni's for the fish suppers?'

My father would usually volunteer. During the war he had spent almost two years with the Royal Engineers in Bari, a large port in southern Italy. He had returned home speaking almost fluent Italian. Southern Italian. Mrs Bundoni's Italian. Although we knew it would take him ages to return with the fish suppers, it was agreed that letting him go was a wise move. He enjoyed speaking Italian and would always return in a good mood. Sometimes I would go with him.

As my father and I ambled round to Trossachs Street where the fish and chip shop lay, I'd think how strange it was that two Italian families, the Cocozzas and the Bundonis, seemed to play such a part in our lives. I imagined it must be the same in other areas of the city. Travelling on the tram through various districts, I'd regularly see Italian names like Capaldi and Renucci above cafes and fish and chip shops. Many had the frontage of their premises decorated in what I later came to know as art-deco style. I wondered if the folk in those districts called them 'oor Tallies' like we did.

Mrs Bundoni was a large, dark-complexioned widow woman in her sixties. Very southern Italian. She understood English, but preferred to speak Italian to her son and two daughters who worked with her in the shop. They had been brought up in Glasgow, understood Italian, but would rather speak English. Each evening, as the four of them busied themselves in the shop, she spoke to them in Italian and they replied in English. It worked.

On Saturday nights as the pubs emptied, there was always a growing queue for their wonderful fish and chips; always fresh and fried in the best beef dripping. My father would join the queue, which usually stretched out onto the pavement. Eventually, once we got into the shop, Mrs Bundoni would spot him. She'd give a big smile, put down the chip basket and:

'Buona sera, Roberto, come stai?'

'Molto bene, signora Bundoni, grazie,' he'd reply.

She'd wave him over to the far side of the counter where, her leaning on one side, him on the other, they'd enjoy a good 'conversazione' for the next quarter of an hour or so. Eventually, as the queue grew while Mrs Bundoni neglected her duties on the fryer, one of her kids would plaintively cry, 'Mamma, prego, assistere!' She would then, reluctantly, take my father's order and come back to the counter with enough fish, chips, pickled onions and Irn Bru to feed half of Doncaster Street. The fish suppers would be well wrapped in sheets of newspaper to keep them hot.

'Quanto costa, signora?'

She'd shrug her shoulders. 'Ohhh, due sheelings.' Two shillings!

'The waiting queue would look on as he took his leave.

'Mille grazie, signora Bundoni.'

'Prego, Roberto.'

'Ciao.'

'Ciao Roberto, buona notte.'

At last he'd return to the house.

'Where the puck have ye been, Govan Cross? We're aw starvin'.'

'Now ye know ah cannae get oot the shop withoot a wee blether in Italian wi' Mrs Bundoni. It's the only chance the poor sowel gets for a good auld parliamo.'

After a repast fit for a king, the next item on the agenda would be – Cabaret Time! The pint bottles of McEwan's Pale Ale would be opened and glasses filled.

Ma loved this part of the evening. 'Who's gonny gie us a wee song?'

Each member of the company would sing a song or two. I always looked forward to Uncle Jack's performance. He was unique. The James Brown of Glasgow 'soul', except he wasn't aware of it. This was long before the estimable Mr Brown had ever been heard of! Jack's repertoire consisted of just two songs: 'Nellie Dean' and 'When You Were Sweet Sixteen'.

After much persuasion – and pale ale – he would rise to his feet, stand unsteadily with his back to the range and compose himself. I would sit, ready to sing the song silently to myself to see if, in spite of his long pauses, he would keep the beat. He never failed.

He would sing, perhaps, the first two words of the chorus. Then there would be silence. He would jerk and sway, his arms would flail spasmodically, his mouth twitch, but not a sound would pass his lips. Meanwhile, after his opening two words I would silently sing the rest of the line to myself. Then *perfectly* on time, on the beat, Uncle Jack would come in with a strangulated version of the last word. He'd then start the second line . . . First two words then Silence, twitch, sway: Arms outstretched. Again, I would silently mouth the words until, once more spot on, Jack would come in with his heart-rending, audible, last word.

So it would go on. We only ever got the first word, or two, of each line then the 'Glasgow Soul' would take over and he'd emote the rest – only to burst out, heart breaking with emotion, with the last word of the line, perfectly in tune and on the beat thanks to his built-in metronome.

When he finished, he'd open his eyes, look around and say, 'Whit the puck are ye's laughing at? Ye's don't know good singin' when ye's hear it.' He'd resume his seat. 'Puck me!' he'd say.

Wee McGree-gor Sells Fish

WHAMMmmmm! He lunges over the table and hits me hard on the side of the head. Maybe I should have expected it.

'Get that fuckin' fish ettin'.'

'Ah don't like it.' I felt the tears well up in my eyes. I don't look at Ma. If I draw her into it it will just grow into a big row and he will start on her.

'Ye huvnae tasted the fuckin' thing, so how can ye say ye don't like it?'

'Ah jist don't.'

'Well, you'll jist sit therr till ye do.'

I sit. I looked down at my dinner. Ma has done a piece of cod in butter and milk with boiled potatoes. I like it when she fries a piece of haddock, that is okay, and best of all I love Bundoni's fish and chips. I don't like the look of this. As the two of them eat theirs they occasionally stop and take a bone out of their mouths. That's what I hate. I know there will be bones in mine. Just the thought is enough to put me off.

They both finish eating. 'Smashing!' says my father. 'Lovely grub!' All for my benefit. He is watching me as he speaks. He sits facing me; Ma is in between us. I sit quietly, staring at my plate.

'Ye'd better make a start oan that, it's gettin' caulder by the minute.'

I don't move. He carefully places his two clenched hands on the table, between dishes, then leans forward, his neck jutting out.

'Dae ye hear whit ah'm saying tae ye?'

'Ah don't want it.' My voice comes out as a frightened squeak.

WHAMMmmmm! For a second or two my brains are scrambled, I sway on the chair.

'Start eating yer dinner, NOW!'

I reach for my fork, break off a piece of cod and put it in my mouth. It is almost cold. I try to chew it. My mouth is dry. I attempt to swallow it but instead begin to boke. I lean over the plate and bring up a mixture of fish, milk and bile onto its rim. He reaches over and turns the plate round to a clean side.

'You're sitting there till you fuckin' eat some of that.'

Ma and he rise from the table. I make my mind up. I might only be ten but even if he hits me again I'm not going to have another mouthful.

Time seems to go into slow motion as I sit at the table. My father occasionally rustles his newspaper as he sits reading. Ma washes the dishes, the soapy water deadening the sound of the plates sliding over one another. The green, tinplate Smith's alarm clock on the mantelpiece sounds annoyingly loud at times, then it seems to stop ticking. I look at it, feeling certain it has stopped. Back comes the tick, seemingly louder than ever! I can hear voices of kids playing out in our back courts. I listen and try to identify some of them. I wish I was out there with them. I wonder if he'll hit me again. The yellow ring of melted butter and milk round the rim of my plate isn't liquid and bubbly anymore; it has dried into wrinkly waves. The fish looks cold and even more unappetising. I try not to look at the top edge where I was sick.

It seems ages since Ma and I went into McGregor's fish shop on the Maryhill Road to buy this fish. It was just this afternoon. The middle window of the shop opens upward so as passers-by can see the various fish and crabs as they lie on beds of ice on the marble slabs. On one of the side walls of the window hangs a large, framed print: a short-trousered, cloth-capped delivery boy sits reading a copy of *Tit-Bits*. Behind him, unseen, a tabby cat is making off with a whole fish from his board. I've known this picture since I was an infant and never fail to study it intently.

'What can ah dae for ye, Mrs Douglas?' Mr McGregor vigorously rubbed his hands together. 'Ah've got some lovely cod, fresh in jist an hour ago.' He continued to rub his hands. This was no Scottish Uriah McHeep; the shop was always cold. In summer the staff's hands were red; in winter, in spite of wearing mittens, they are purple. While Ma was being served I enjoyed myself looking for deep drifts in the generous amounts of sawdust covering the floor. When I found one I brought my foot down almost vertically, stubbing my toe hard into the drift. Done correctly it made the sawdust spray out in a satisfying explosion. I made sure none of it sprayed over Ma's shoes or there'd be another explosion – when she clouted me.

As I sit at the table I begin to feel drowsy. Jeez! If he sees me dozing off that'll be another fault. To try and keep awake I start running Ma's wee 'fishy song' through my mind. Nearly every time we go to McGregor's she sings it either going or coming:

Wee McGree-gor sells fish
Tuppence ha'penny a dish.
Cut the heids aff,
Cut the tails aff,
Wee McGree-gor sells fish.

'Ye don't know when you're fuckin' well aff, you.' From his chair by the range my father has decided to start again. A stab of fear as he speaks brings me wide awake. 'There's lots of wee darkie weans wid snaffle that dinner in a minute if they'd half a chance.'

I'd love to say, 'Well ye can parcel it up and send it tae them.'

'Go on, get up fae that table and get yerself ootside, oot o' ma fucking sight.'

Great! I get up quickly in case he changes his mind.

'Be back here in *exactly* one hour. Don't be one minute late. And, ye'll be going tae bed withoot any supper the night. If ye cannae eat yer dinner, ye can go tae bed hungry. Go on, bugger off. And remember, in here fur half past eight.'

I try not to hurry too much, but it's wonderful to shut the door behind me and run out the close into the street. It feels like I'm breathing pure oxygen. There are three boys kicking a ball around. Even though I don't like football I join in enthusiastically. As we play, I look at them: Jim Loan, Tommy Finegan and Billy Holland. I bet you boys didnae huv all the trouble I had before you came oot, and ah'll bet youse won't be dreading going back in like ah am.

We play for a while, then I wonder – what time is it? Nobody I know has a watch, so there's no good asking them.

'Ah'll be back in a minute, boys.'

'Where ur ye gawn?'

'Ah'll no be long.' I speed off round into Trossachs Street to Cocozza's and stand outside the corner door to the shop. I can see their red and white electric clock high on the wall above the wooden display shelves. Ten past eight. I race back round to Doncaster Street and rejoin the game.

'Where wur ye?'

'Ah forgot ah hud tae go a wee message.'

We play for another spell, then I spot a man coming down the street.

'Mister, could ye tell me the time, please?'

'Nearly twenty-five past eight, son.'

'Thanks, mister. Ah huv tae go in boys. Ah wiz telt tae be in for half eight oan the dot. See ye's the morra.'

'Aye, see ye the morra, Robert.'

*

As I approach my close I can see it's dark and gloomy inside. It's almost dusk but the gas lamps aren't lit yet. A few minutes ago I'd caught sight of the 'leerie' going in and out the closes further up the street lighting the lamps. He won't be down here for twenty minutes yet. As I walked toward the back close, where our door is, I begin to feel apprehensive about what sort of welcome I'll get. As the shadows swallow me up I start to sing under my breath to keep my spirits up . . .

Wee McGree-gor sells fish
Tuppence ha'penny a dish.
Cut the heids aff,
Cut the tails aff.
Wee McGree-gor sells fish.

Brushes With Death

'Dae any of ye's want tae see a deid body?'

We stopped the game we were playing. Joe went to our school, so we knew him.

'Is that the boy who died in the fire roon in Maltbarn Street?'

'Aye,' said Joe.

'Will it be awright tae go in and see him; we hardly know him?' asked Tommy Dunn.

'Aye, he's jist lying in the living room; people are in and oot aw the time.'

'Whit! Is he jist lying oan the floor?' said Ally McLean.

'Naw, ye daft get, he's in a coffin.'

The four of us looked at one another.

'Should we go?'

'Aye. Ah've never seen a deid body. C'mon, let's go.' I didn't count seeing Granny McIntosh in her coffin. I was too little then for it to make an impact on me.

We'd heard there had been a fire in a house in Maltbarn Street and a fifteen-year-old laddie had died. I had an idea who the boy was, but he was fifteen, four years older than me, and anyway, we hardly ever played with anybody from round there.

We followed Joe round to the street and into the close. Maltbarn Street consisted of the grey stone modern tenements built in the mid-1930s. They were self-contained flats with bathrooms and 'scullery' kitchens. It was always a funny feeling going into strange closes. We climbed up to the second landing and stood by the open house door.

'Go on; it'll be awright. Ah've already been in,' said Joe.

As we entered the lobby I could hear Joe going back down the stairs. In the living room the boy's mother and a young girl sat at the window. They barely looked at us. Quietly, rather nervously, we approached the coffin and all looked into it at the same time – and the four of us got the fright of our lives! We recoiled in horror, turned and ran as fast as we could from the house, down the stairs two at a time, and didn't stop until we reached Doncaster Street and safety.

The boy's face had been white. Pure white like chalk. The lips were very red and open in a sort of leer with the teeth showing. But it had been his eyes. They were wide open and green. Pure green. No pupils, no white. Just green.

We sat in a row at the edge of the pavement, pale and shaken.

'Jeez, that wiz horrible. Ah feel sick.'

'Me tae.'

'So dae ah.'

'Did ye see that pig's melt, Joe?'

'Naw.'

'He wiz oan the other side of the street laughing, when we came runnin' oot the close. He knew we'd get a fright, rotten bastard!'

'Ah wiz last coming oot the hoose,' I said. 'Ah wiz sure it would be oot the boax and grab me halfwye doon the stairs. Ah thought ah could hear it behind me, nae kiddin', ma hair wiz standin' oan end.'

'Ah'm never gonny look at another deid body again,' vowed Tommy.

'Me neither,' we all said.

The boy's face never left me. Death was now something to be frightened of.

*

It was just weeks after the 'dead boy' incident. Still the summer of 1950. Tommy Dunn and I were best pals. We went everywhere together. There was also a bonus to being Tommy's pal: his da, Andy Dunn, was a taxi driver. Often, if they were going on a Sunday drive out to the coast, Tommy would insist that I come too. We would pile into the roomy, pre-war blue and black hackney cab, with its lovely smell of leather upholstery. Tommy, his wee sister Jeanette, their ma, Annie, and me. Annie Dunn was the mainstay of Doncaster Street. If anyone needed help or advice they'd be told, 'Ask Annie, she'll know.' She took in dressmaking and alterations, helped with confinements, organised street parties, door-to-door collections if someone had died and if needs be, would lay someone out. Tommy and Jeanette were doted on by their parents. Tommy, with his red, short hair was a stocky, strong wee boy. Streetwise beyond his years, there was nothing that frightened him. If someone was about to lift their hand to me all I had to do was shout on Tommy.

Tommy Dunn and me were playing with another three or four boys 'ower the wa'' in our secluded little spot. It had been a dry summer and the Kelvin was well down. Taking our shoes and socks off, we decided to wade the forty feet or so to the other side. That day, the river was no more than two feet deep. By pulling our short trousers up we would easily do it. The rest had already made it to the other side and I was halfway across when:

'Hurry up, the big wave's coming!' Tommy shouted.

I looked. Once, sometimes twice, a day, further up the river they would open up the sluices and let dammed-up water flood into the Kelvin. It came down the river as a bore, two feet or more high and travelling fast.

'C'mon,' yelled Tommy, 'you've still got time.'

'Ah cannae,' I said. I was rooted to the spot with fear. Tommy had been in the group with little Drew when he'd drowned near here.

'Fuckin' hell!' he said. He ran, splashing toward me. When he reached me he turned round. 'Jump oan ma back.' I jumped on, my arms round his neck. He put his hands under my knees and shrugged me up higher. He ran, somehow keeping his balance on the slippery stones of the riverbed. We clambered up onto the dry, grassy bank. Seconds later the bore sped past.

'Thanks, Tommy, ah wiz too feart tae move.'

'Ach, it's awright.' We were both ten.

A couple of months later, Ma and me got off a tram in the Maryhill Road and turned the corner into Trossachs Street. There was a large crowd standing outside Rossleigh's garage. We could see the top of an ambulance in the middle of them. It was late afternoon. Ma spoke to the first person she knew.

'Whit's the matter?'

'Wee Tommy Dunn wiz up oan the garage roof after a ball and he's fell through wan o' the skylights! He's still in therr. They're trying tae find somebody wi' a key. They say he's no moving.'

'Oh, Jesus God!' said Ma. 'If anything happens tae him Annie will be demented.'

Rossleigh's had been requisitioned during the war and used by the Army. The glass skylights had been painted black as part of the air-raid precautions. It gave them a false look of solidity. Tommy had climbed up a roan pipe onto the roof after a mis-hit tennis ball and stepped onto one of the skylights. The glass had immediately shattered and he'd fallen twenty feet. His head struck the sharp, upper edge of a pre-war car's bumper and it had sliced into his skull like an axe. By the time the key-holder was located and the large doors slid open, Tommy was dead. The floor round the car was a pool of dark, red blood. I had lost my pal.

*

The Dunns lived in a ground-floor flat. That evening forty to fifty neighbours, Ma included, stood in the street outside their window, not knowing what to do. Just wanting to be there. Andy's taxi stood, somehow forlorn, parked at the pavement. All would be quiet for a while, then Annie would try again to get her grief out. She'd cry, and sob, then when sobbing was not enough it would become a wail like a wounded animal, as she tried to get it out. The women in the street, and some men, wept silently, unable to help Annie, who was always so ready to help them. We could hear Andy trying, in vain, to comfort her.

Three days later came the funeral. In 1949 there were only about fifty taxis in Glasgow and a great camaraderie amongst the drivers. Every taxi-cab in the city lined our streets. As the hearse and family cars pulled away the taxis followed in convoy. Neighbours and folk from nearby streets who knew the family filled the pavements.

Annie was never quite the same woman again. Andy pined quietly for his son.

I was ten years old and suddenly knew what death was. It was part of life.

A Good Teacher

'Good morning, children. I'm Miss Ross.'

'Good morning, Miss Ross,' we chanted.

It was in your last year at Springbank, before you went on to the 'Big School', that you got Miss Ivy Ross. You had heard about her from the older kids as you slowly wended your way from year to year; you passed her in the corridors or playground now and again, you sometimes listened to tales from those in her class. I could hardly wait for it to be my turn. And now it was. I sat at my desk and looked closely at her. Tall, slim and in her late fifties, she had a shock of white hair cut in a tousled style that wouldn't be popular for another twenty years. She wore a bright, almost gaudy, buttoned smock. And, she had the most striking, patrician, Roman nose this side of the Tiber. You paid attention to a nose like that. She'd married late in life, but still continued to be known as Miss Ivy Ross. She was also one of the world's best teachers.

It's difficult to pin down what made her such a wonderful teacher. It wasn't so much the way she taught her subject. In fact, it was her unfailing habit of going off the subject, that was when she cast her spell on us and took us out of the classroom – and ourselves.

It could be any day of the week. She is, supposedly, taking us for English. We all sit reading this chapter of a book she has told us to. It has been quiet for the last ten minutes.

'Oh, children, I've just remembered. I've brought David Stephen's article to read to you.'

David Stephen is a naturalist, with a column in the *Weekly News*. His pieces follow the seasons and Miss Ross is a devotee. Every week she reads his article to us and tries, if possible, to illustrate it with articles brought from home or garden. She'll reach into her copious bag and produce abandoned birds' nests; feathers from jays, thrushes or blackbirds; a piece of budding oak or willow branch. If she can lay her hands on anything which will help bring his tales alive, she will do so. These exhibits are passed amongst us and, as we listen to her and examine them we suddenly see the beauty and wonder of them.

I especially loved her geography lessons. During the 1930s, and resuming again after the war, Miss Ross would regularly take passage on tramp steamers during the long summer holidays. She'd often sailed the banana boats to South America; leaned on a ship's rail under a velvet, star-studded sky in the Med; sweltered down the west coast of Africa and 'crossed the Line' once more. She preferred the working ships, steamers which only had room for ten or twelve passengers. Where every night you dined with the Captain and his officers. Years later, when I read Somerset Maugham's short stories – some of them set on tramp steamers – always in my imagination I would see Miss Ivy Ross amongst Maugham's disparate passengers. I don't think the author would even have had to change her name.

We would sit at our desks and listen, goggle-eyed, as she made her adventures come alive – the ports, the storms, steamy tropical jungles, dry arid deserts. Then there were the markets. Souks where you could buy live parrots and monkeys or, if Madam desired, gold, silver and diamonds. We had only glimpsed these worlds in the cinema. Miss Ross had been there.

'Did you know that every year a snake grows a new skin, and leaves the old one behind, children?'

'No, miss,' we answer in unison. She delves into her bag of wonders and produces a large section of snakeskin.

'Do you know why the armadillo gets its name?'

'No, miss.' A stuffed armadillo emerges from the bag.

'Aw, miss, is it deid? Well, ah don't want tae touch it anywye, ah'll jist look at it.'

'Did you know, children, that silk comes from threads spun by little worms?'

'No, miss.' We look at one another. 'Huv you got worms, miss?'

'No, I haven't got worms' – she hides a smile – 'but I've brought you this.' With a flourish she whisks a beautiful, brightly coloured scarf from 'the bag'. 'This is pure silk, children. Just think, it all started with little worms who spin very fine thread.' The scarf is passed from hand to hand.

'Hey, miss. This is nearly as good as nylon, in't it!'

All too soon the bell would ring and we'd, reluctantly, troop out for playtime or head for another classroom. We'd rather have remained under the spell that Miss Ivy Ross had, once more, cast over us. Her routine never seemed to vary. On a daily basis she would start her lesson then, almost without fail, go off at a tangent and take us happy kidnap victims with her. As we broke off at midday she'd say, 'Now, children, after lunch we really must get back to the lesson.'

We seldom did, yet somehow we learned a lot as pupils of Miss Ivy Ross.

There was one more thing I was to learn at Springbank before I left for the 'big school'. How it felt to be in love! My first crush.

Miss Olive Welsh arrived at Springbank straight from training college and was placed with Miss Ross. She walked into the classroom, all tartan skirt and navy blue twinset, and I was immediately smitten. I took one look at her blue eyes, dark hair and Knight's Castile complexion and fell in love. Suddenly, I had no trouble getting out of bed in the morning; I would rise like a lintie, get ready and cheerfully set off to school with only one thought in mind – how I could attract the heavenly Miss Welsh to my desk, even for just a moment. Whenever she took over the class I'd be in my seventh heaven. I could then look at her for as long as I wanted.

I constantly schemed and plotted to think of a reason which would make her come to my side and give me personal tuition. If we were drawing, or practising writing, I would feign difficulty. 'Aw, miss, ah cannae dae this, it's too hard.' I always said the same thing. It worked. She'd come over and kneel beside my desk. Deep down inside I'd feel the first of the day's hot flushes start to simmer.

'Now then, what is the trouble, Robert?'

I wanted to say, 'You Miss. I'm just daft about ye.' In reality I'd say, 'Ah cannae seem tae get these curves right.'

She would lean nearer and place her hand over the top of mine. I could feel her closeness like magnetic waves passing through me; smell her perfume; then the underlying scent of the soap she had used that morning. I could have given Black Bob, the wonder sheepdog, a run for his money at the smelling stakes!

Using the hand on mine, she'd start to guide me into drawing a fairly acceptable arc. The effect on me was approaching terminal. I would tingle and pulse all over. I could feel my face prickle – from *under* the skin. The blood would pound so hard in my head I'd feel certain that any second it would burst and make an awful mess of her twinset. Surely she'd be bound to notice the effect she was having on me. She would lift our joined hands and, together, they glided over to the inkwell, dipped the pen in, gently shook it and made the return trip to the paper. By now I was so light-headed with ecstasy I was ready for passing out.

'There you are.' She began to rise. 'Is that all right, Robert?'

I looked at her through glazed eyes. 'Urghsnarfgurgle,' I said.

Perhaps she had finally seen the state I was in and thought it best she withdraw, before I became the school's first junior coronary case.

Sadly, I only had a few, short, months of my femme fatale before I had to leave Springbank. In spite of my crush on Miss Welsh, I knew that the teacher I'd never forget, and maybe never replace, would be Miss Ivy Ross.

What was her magic? She most certainly had the gift of expanding the horizons and firing the imaginations of children who knew nothing other than tenements and back courts. Boys who were troublemakers in other teachers' classes were like lambs in hers. Whenever a teacher left the classroom for a few minutes it was an invitation to start misbehaving. Not in Miss Ross's class. We knew she would have been disappointed to return and find a noisy rabble. So we didn't disappoint her. It was all quite remarkable. But so was she.

The Year When Christmas Fell in November

It really was a day to remember.

I came wandering down the street from Springbank School just after four o'clock and went into the house to leave my school bag, get a piece and come back out to play with my pals until dinner was ready. I came into the room and hung my bag over the back of a chair.

'Hiyah, Ma. Can ah huv a piece oan jam tae keep me going till ma dinner's ready?'

As was the norm at this time of day, she was preparing veg at the sink. She turned, a big smile on her face, took the towel from the hook behind the press door and dried her hands. Her smile got even wider.

'Whit? Whit ur ye laughing at?'

'You'll see. You'll be laughing in a minute, tae.' She hung the towel back up, took a few steps over to the range and brought down a letter from the mantelpiece. 'We were wondering where yer faither was, weren't we?'

'Aye. Is that fae him?'

'It is. Huv a look at the address.' She folded the letter in such a way that I could only see the address at the top of the page: '4051104, A/C Douglas, RAF Bridgnorth, Shropshire.'

'Eh?' I looked at her. 'What diz that mean?'

Her smile got bigger. 'Yer faither has signed himself up in the RAF for five years!'

'He huznae!'

'He huz!'

It was the first week in November 1950. Christmas was early this year.

I had felt that something *must* happen. I had been frightened in case it would be something really bad. The rows between my ma and da had been escalating; no longer just Saturday nights after he'd been drinking, but during the week as well. Even I could feel that it couldn't go on like this; it was becoming too intense. Then, the previous week, he just hadn't come home. We thought maybe he was staying at Uncle Jack's, though Ma never made any enquiries. The longer he stayed away, the better.

I had been increasing my prayers, hoping he would maybe take another job away from home, such as when he'd worked on the hydroelectric scheme at Loch Sloy. This was wonderful. Jeez! This was the first time I'd had a prayer answered. Thanks a lot, God. I'll be in touch.

'Aw, Ma. In't that jist great.' My mind ran on: nae mair belts oan the lug for nuthin'; nae mair huvin' tae eat things ah don't like; nae mair comics snatched oot ma hands; nae mair gettin' sworn at aw' the time and told ah'm stupid. I wondered if I should say to Ma, 'Don't bother getting me any Christmas presents this year. This'll dae fine!' I gave it some more thought.

'Will he still be coming hame noo and again? They get what's called "leave", dain't they?'

'Aye.' She held up the letter. 'He says he'll still be coming hame when he gets leave. He's joined up because we're jist fighting aw the time when he's at hame, so this might be better.'

'Ah thought he would be too auld tae join up, Ma.'

'It's a surprise tae me, tae.' She did a quick sum, out loud. 'Born 1911, this is 1950. He's thirty-nine now. Aye, ah would have thought that wiz too auld tae join up.' She paused. 'Mibbe he's lied aboot his age!'

My heart fell. 'Ah hope they don't find oot. You're no gonny tell them, urr ye?'

'Ah'm bloody sure ah'm no,' she said. We both started to kill ourselves laughing at the vehemence of her reply, tears running down our faces. She then tried to say something else: 'If they ask me how auld he is . . .' She couldn't finish for laughing. She tried again – three times. Then finally, 'If they ask me how auld he is . . . ah'll tell them – nineteen! Then they'll no throw him oot.' The two of us had to sit down, we were weak with laughter.

For the rest of the night, every now and again one of us would spontaneously start laughing – and set the other off.

That night as I lay in my bed-chair I found it difficult to concentrate on my comic. My head was full of thoughts on how good the future was going to be. I began to try and work out how little I would see his scowling face from now on. Ma had said he would get about six weeks' leave a year. Six weeks' leave; fifty-two weeks in a year. Jeez! That meant he'd be *away* forty-six weeks of the year. If he took his leave a week at a time he'd only be home every two months or so. That's just great! He signed on the last week of October 1950. He shouldn't be out until October 1955. That's terrific. I'd be sixteen and a half by then.

The next five years looked really good, now. Things should be great. Thanks a lot, God.

Linlithgow

At the age of eleven I sat the Scottish version of the eleven-plus – the Qualifying exam – and scraped through with an S3 pass. I would be going to North Kelvinside Senior Secondary School. Those who had failed were doomed to attend East Park Junior Secondary, the academic equivalent of Barlinnie Prison.

Before we left Springbank a treat was arranged for those of us in the leaving class. A bus trip to Edinburgh to visit the Zoo and the Castle, at a cost of five shillings. I was dying to go; Edinburgh was even further away than Mulguy.

'Aw, Ma, can ah go? It's jist five bob. Everybody in the class is going, ah'll be the only wan left behind. Gonny let me go, Ma, eh?'

My pleading eventually wore her down and, on a fine spring morning in March 1951, I gathered outside the school with the rest of my classmates and, under the envious gaze of the younger kids, we boarded a single-decker with Miss Ivy Ross and my first love, Miss Olive Welsh, as escorts. We set off full of excited chatter which soon died down as the bus left the city boundary and took us into uncharted territory: the countryside. The majority, like myself, had rarely left Glasgow. As we headed into the Lothians we contented ourselves by gazing at the green fields, some with cows and sheep in them. We regularly passed pit heaps and winding gear; in the early fifties this was still a busy mining area.

Believing we were going straight to Edinburgh – school trips at this time were on a 'need to know' basis – to our surprise we drove into a small town and found ourselves decanted onto its main street.

' 'Zis Edinburgh?'

'It's awfy wee, in't it?'

'Where urr we, miss?'

'This is Linlithgow.'

'Miss Ross says it's called Linlithgow.'

There was a chorus of 'Never heard of it.'

'Whit huv we stoaped here for, miss?'

'Because we're going to visit Linlithgow Palace, the birthplace of Mary, Queen of Scots.'

'Oh, we've heard of her, miss. She's the wan that got her heid chopped off, in't she?'

'Yes, that's her.'

We were herded through an impressive gateway with lots of carved stone coats of arms above it, then through the main entrance to the palace itself. Suddenly I found myself in a large courtyard. I was immediately struck by how cool and shady it was. And filled with a beautiful silence. We were too impressed to break it. In the centre stood an elaborately carved stone fountain. I had never seen, or been, anywhere like this. I looked around me. Although supposedly a ruin, Linlithgow Palace was fairly complete and it didn't take much imagination to picture it in its full glory. A lady guide joined us. It was our good luck that she happened to be on a par with Miss Ivy Ross when it came to telling tales. I was spellbound. Kings and queens appeared and disappeared; there were wars, plots and counter-plots and, of course, the birth of Mary, Queen of Scots, the most romantic, but ultimately doomed young queen. She described how, in times of celebration, the fountain in the centre of the courtyard would spout wine instead of water. I could see it all. I could see the lords, ladies and courtiers milling around, filling their glasses and goblets and chattering in French – the language of the Scottish Court. A few at a time, we climbed up Queen Margaret's Bower, where that queen had waited, in vain, for the return of her husband from battle. I felt a tingle to think I'd been sitting where a real, live queen had once sat. I gaped at the enormous fireplace in the Great Hall, and double-gaped when told it would burn a whole tree trunk for five days. It all came alive for me. I could easily imagine the hall, its floor covered in rushes, the walls hung with tapestries. We had been dipping into history at school and I quite liked it. But with this visit it all came alive. It was real. I would never forget Linlithgow Palace and its impact upon me and my imagination.

Reluctantly, I boarded the bus again and we travelled on to Edinburgh Castle. It made little impression on me. There were only two things I'd remember: Mons Meg, the giant siege cannon, and the Scottish Crown Jewels. Linlithgow Palace had got to me first.

Over the last half century I've made three well-spaced visits back to Linlithgow. Each time, without fail, she easily recaptures me. The last time was summer 2000. I walked into that shady courtyard, sat myself in a quiet corner . . . and became a schoolboy again.

Soon, the lords and ladies are milling around filling their goblets. I look up at the red sandstone walls, gaze at Queen Margaret's Bower. Let the stillness wrap itself around me. It's gone fifty years since I wandered into this courtyard – and was taken prisoner. It is still exactly as it was, nothing has changed. A time capsule.

After I've sat for a while I *know* that if I rise and hurry back through the main gate I'll find the Alexander's 'Bluebird' bus waiting to take me back to Glasgow. My ma will probably be starting to get the veg prepared for our dinner. She'll be looking forward to me bursting in tonight, all excited, dying to tell her where I've been and what I've seen.

I'll just sit for a few more minutes. The bus will wait for me.

Tuning In

'Can ah stay up tae hear the Top Twenty oan Luxembourg, Ma? Ah'll get up for school nae bother in the morning. Honest!'

It is 1951. Johnnie Ray is number one with 'Cry', the Best Record ever made in the History of the World! With my father away in the RAF, I know she'll let me. If he was around I wouldn't have wasted my time asking. The trouble with the Top Twenty is that it's on from eleven till midnight and the 'twenty' are played in reverse order – so it's five to twelve before the number one is played.

I get into my pyjamas, read and half-listen to the show until, at long last, the DJ has ploughed through the lesser hits. It's almost time. Up until now I've only had a passing interest in music. Ma always has the radio tuned into the Light Programme, which features lots of record shows or, usually of an evening, broadcasts by dance bands. She loves dance music and any records by the crooners, Crosby, Sinatra, Como et al. It all washes over me until Johnnie Ray, 'The New Singing Sensation', burst upon the scene. He is unique, quite different from his contemporaries, and aimed directly at a young audience. Although just short of being a teenager, I am really taken by Johnnie and all his gimmicks – me and a couple of million others. He cries and chokes with emotion when he sings, which soon garners him a host of nicknames: 'The Nabob of Sob', 'The Prince of Wails', 'The Cry Guy'. Whenever there is a record programme on I'm always hoping they'll play 'Cry'. Only by listening to the Top Twenty on a Sunday night am I guaranteed to hear it.

*

'It must be great tae huv a record player, eh? Imagine being able tae hear yer favourite record any time ye want.'

'Aye, it wid be smashing.' She continues darning my sock.

'Billy Rodger's ma and da huv goat wan. They like Frank Sinatra so they've goat a stack of 'is records, they play them aw the time. Whose records wid you buy, Ma, if we hud a record player?'

She stops darning for a minute. 'Ohhh, Vaughan Monroe and, mmm, Hutch.'

'It'll be oan in a minute, Ma.'

I go over to the large, wooden-cased set. As usual, reception isn't that good, the signal strength fluctuates; it's a long way from the small, European principality to a single-end in Doncaster Street. The piece of wire we have for an aerial isn't quite up to the job. I stand close to the set, literally hugging it, and reach round the back to touch the aerial lead. The signal improves; I don't mind having to stay here for the duration of the record.

'Watch you don't blaw yersel' up!'

'Ah'll no, Ma. SHHH! Here he's comin'. He's aboot tae come oan!' I feel a frisson of excitement; I turn the volume up.

'And now, still number one for the fifth week in a row, it's Johnnie Ray and . . .'

He doesn't finish the sentence, just plays the familiar opening bars as the backing singers come in with, '*Ooowah, ooowah, oo oo wah*.' Then Johnnie comes in with the song's first line.

The back of my neck has electric tingles running up and down it. I pretend to swoon.

'Yah daft bugger, ye.' Ma laughs and shakes her head.

'Aw, Ma, is that no the best record ever made?'

'If you say so.' The record finishes all too soon.

'They should play the number wan twice, shouldn't they? Ye stay up aw that time and ye only get tae hear it wance.'

*

I switch the radio off, make a lightning visit – candle in hand – to the outside lavvy, then climb into my bed-chair. I reach for the *Superman* comic I've saved for bed, having resisted all temptation to read it during the day.

'Eh, excuse me. How long dae ye think you're gonny be reading? It's efter midnight.'

'Ma, if ah jist lie here wi' ma eyes shut ah'll never get tae sleep. If ah huv a wee read ah'll be away in five minutes.'

'You'd better be, 'cause ah'll be switching the light off in aboot five minutes whether yer away or no.' She is already in bed, swotting up the *People's Friend* in case I ask for a story later in the week. 'And remember, nae shenanigans in the moarnin' or they'll be nae Jackie Ray next Sunday.'

'Aye, ferr enough, Ma. And it's *Johnnie* Ray.'

'Aye, him as well.'

Harry Forshaw

It was just after the Easter Holidays of 1951 when I started at North Kelvinside Senior Secondary School – mercifully known as NKS for short. It was a good school with a fine academic record. As I passed through its gates that first morning I felt very much a new, small, boy. There were 'kids' up to seventeen years of age stoating about the playground, with 'Tony Curtis' quiffs and drainpipe trousers. On that first day I would meet Sammy Johnson, who would become one of my great pals. He had already been at NKS for a year. It was from him that I would receive the bad news.

'You'll be awright for yer first year, but in yer last two years you'll get the worst teacher in the school, Harry Forshaw. He's a real pig's melt! Teaches maths.'

'Why? Whit diz he dae?'

'Whit diz he dae? Knocks fuck oot ye every chance he gets, that's whit he diz.'

'Fuck me!' Within my first hour at my new school I'd realised I'd have to up my swearing rate to increase my social acceptability. It was mandatory. 'Why diz he dae that?'

' 'Cause he's Radio Rental.'

'Radio Ren—' I was about to enquire.

'Mental – Radio Rental,' explained Sammy, impatient at my ignorance.

'Oh, aye, right.' Jeez, there was going to be a lot to learn at the big school.

'Gonny point him oot tae me when ye get the chance?'

'Aye, first time he's oan playground duty ah'll show ye him.'

*

My great pal, Sammy Johnson, in between Irene Maloney, on left, and Janette Dunn, on right, probably 1953.

I hadn't long to wait. A few days later during morning break – it wasn't 'playtime' anymore – Sammy sidled up. I had forgotten his dire warning of the other day. Hands in pockets, head down, Sammy leaned over to my ear, and in a manner reminiscent of Edward G. Robinson whispering into George Raft's lug in the yard at Sing Sing, mumbled from the corner of his mouth, 'Don't shlook, thatsh him ower therr!'

Caught off guard and thinking he'd maybe just been to the dentist, I could only say, 'Eh?'

Maintaining his 'penitentiary persona', Sammy tried again; 'Ye shaid ye wanted tae shee Harry Forshaw. Thatsh him ower therr. Don't look!'

'How can ah shee him, see him, if ah don't look?'

'Well, jisht wait a minute, then look ower – dead casual.'

Sammy whistled tunelessly as he made a pretence of examining the brickwork of the boys' toilet. I glanced over. Everything about the man was brown. He was in his late thirties, around five foot eight, wore a brown, three-piece suit, brown boots, was quite bald on top with brown hair round the sides and sported a dark brown, heavy moustache. His skin was a sallow, pale brown.

'So that's him.'

'Aye, thatsh the bastard. You should start praying that he's mibbe away tae another school, or drapped deid, by next year.' I had no such luck.

In April '52 I moved into my second year at NKS. I looked at my new timetable. Maths: Mr Forshaw. I had him for three one-hour periods a week. My class, 2C, and I would be getting him for Arithmetic, Geometry and a new subject to us – Algebra. I would quickly discover that algebra was, and would remain, a total mystery to me; as obscure as the most unbreakable Russian code. I soon settled into a routine of knowing that three times a week I would have to face this man for Maths. And on every occasion I would enter his class in a state of fear.

We come in from the yard and stream upstairs. The next period is maths.

'The next hour is gonny seem like two, in't it?' says Billy.

'Seem like two? Mair like a week wi' this get.'

'Ah always bless maself before ah go in,' says T. H. Docherty.

'Ah didnae know you wiz Catholic,' I say.

'Ah'm no, but ah'll try anything.'

'Diz it work?'

'Diz it fuck. Ah got four o' the belt last Thursday.'

We file in like condemned men and sit at our desks. Forshaw

isn't yet in the classroom. In any other class this would be a chance for banter, for throwing things. But there is little noise, only whispered words as we await the moment when he appears amongst us and our hearts sink. He is often a few minutes late; we are thankful for small mercies. As ever, I wonder if I'll get the belt today. Depends on what subject he chooses. I'm quite good at arithmetic, not bad at geometry. Then there's algebra. The door opens and he comes striding in, his boots sounding loudly on the wooden floor. He looks around at us as he heads for his tall, solitary desk, which stands four-square in front of the blackboard. He opens its lid; we wait with bated breath.

'Right, get out your algebra books.'

Fuck. That's me for the belt unless I'm lucky. There are audible sighs of apprehension all round me.

We are half an hour into the period. By mentally wishing myself invisible I have, so far, escaped his attention. If only my powers of concentration will hold up for another thirty minutes.

Mr Forshaw stands at the blackboard, chalking as he speaks.

'Right, *x* squared plus *b* minus *c* equals 10. If *x* is 3 and *c* is 4, what does *b* equal?'

He looks around, seeking a victim. I hunch down and look at my desk; I concentrate on my lucky knothole, hoping to keep up my screen of invisibility.

'Douglas?'

Oh Jesus! He's penetrated my force-field. I stand up and look at the totally unintelligible shite on the blackboard. God's curse on the ancient Greek bastard who invented poxy algebra.

'Ehhh, *b* is 5, sir.'

'Correct. Very good.'

Fuck me! Imagine that. That was lucky. I look round at the incredulous faces of my classmates. A wee round of applause wouldn't be out of order. I start to sit down.

'Now.' Harry holds out a piece of chalk. 'Come up to the board and show us how you worked that out.'

Oh, mammydaddy! The fly bastard knows it was just a lucky guess. Like a prisoner setting out for the scaffold, I leave my desk. This is a short trip that will have only one ending. The belt. My mind races, trying to think of something I could do that will extend the time before the inevitable happens. Bump my knee? Trip and fall down? Faint? I tamely walk down to the front of the class and take the proffered chalk. I look at the equation as though working it out; in reality I'm sending 'thought messages' to the headmaster that now would be a good time to press the bell for a practice fire-drill. He isn't receiving. I clear my throat.

'Well, actually, sir, it wiz jist a guess.' There is a titter from the class. Bastards!

'Yes, knowing your ability with algebra, I thought it might be. So, can you work it out?'

'Eh, no, sir.'

'Well, I'll show you.' He takes the chalk back and proceeds to work out the problem, at the same time explaining it to me before starting on another example. Trouble is, he seems to be speaking in Serbo-Croat. I'm doomed. I know exactly the scenario that is about to unfold. I make one last try to get in touch with the headmaster . . .

'Therefore, what does *c* equal in this case?' He is warming to his task.

'I don't know, sir.'

He visibly stiffens. 'Right, *I'll try again*!' He runs through it once more, this time in Latvian. None of it registers. As ever, when he reaches this stage in his routine I am so rigid with fear that I probably would have difficulty spelling my name. I begin to wonder how many of the belt I'll get. It was four last week. My thoughts wander; there is no point in even trying to understand what he's saying.

'So, what does *c* equal?' He puts his face close to mine, his voice gets even more threatening. I feel my sphincter grow weak. I know I'm for it now. 'Go and stand on the other side of my desk, I'll deal with you shortly.'

That's all you ever hear out of him. He turns toward the rest of the class; their smiles at my discomfort vanish. He is now in a bad mood. I won't be alone for long. He starts picking on those he knows have trouble with algebra. There are plenty to choose from. Five minutes later I have another four for company. Then, by accident, he chooses someone who manages to work it out. That means he is now free to indulge in his hobby. Belting kids.

'Right, line up. I'll show you what happens to people who waste my precious time. You're first, Douglas.' He opens his desk and brings out the thick, coiled-up, brown leather tawse. He elaborately straightens it out then takes a few practice swings. It swishes through the air. I watch in fascinated interest.

'Hold out your hand.'

While waiting I've been trying to pull down my shirt cuff as far as I can. Most teachers try to hit you fair and square on the fingers and palm. Not Forshaw. He always stands at a bit of an angle and nearer to you than other teachers. His intention is to hit you on the ball of the thumb and have the 'fringes' on the end of the tawse just catch you on the inside of the wrist; the soft area where the pulse is taken. Both very tender spots.

The pulling at my shirt cuffs has been in vain. As I hold out my hand my cuff, disobligingly, draws back to reveal my wrist. He brings the belt down with a vicious swipe.

'Oh!' Yah bastard. He'll be pleased with that one, got me just where he wanted to. It stings like buggery. I fold my hand into a ball and blow inside it.

'Again,' he says. Huh, there's a surprise. I hold out my left this time. For some reason I dislike the belt on my left even more than my right. He comes down with another full-strength stroke. Again, bang on target.

'Ohhh!' I put my hand, palm open, underneath my right armpit and press tightly to try and ease the stinging. Maybe he'll be satisfied with two; he knows he's hit two beauties.

'Again.' Pig's bastard, dae ye never think of jist givin' somebody two? I hold out my still-stinging right palm again. *Whoosh!* Just as hard and accurate as the first one, but it hurts even more because it's already had one.

'*Ooooooyah!*' I double up; tears sting my eye. I blow urgently on my clenched hand to try and cool it somehow. I hold out my left without being asked. He's never been known to give three; it's always even numbers. I might as well get my fourth over and done with. He unleashes another corker. Instinctively I withdraw my hand. The belt flashes by, unhindered, and hits him on the right shin. Some in the class laugh. He glares them into silence then gives his shin a quick rub. Oh God, ah wish ah hadnae done that. He looks like my father when he scowls.

'HOLD YOUR HAND OUT!' I hold it out and shut my eyes so as I won't see it coming.

'Oh yah, oh yah, oh yah!' This is the hardest one yet. I don't mind letting him know he's hurting me; that'll please him. Some boys try not to flinch or make a sound. He just takes that as defiance and really lays into them. I turn to go.

'Where do you think you're going, Douglas? I never said you could go.'

Jesus wept, the evil bastard is gonny gie me six! Ah've never, ever had six. Tears trickle down my cheeks. As in a dream, I hold each throbbing hand out for the remaining two strokes, both deadly accurate. The pain is excruciating. When I'm finally allowed to go back to my desk I glance at the four who are waiting. They are whey-faced.

Back at my desk, I look at my hands. The palms and fingers are red and tender; the balls of my thumbs are turning black and blue. As usual, and as he intended, the inside of my wrists are the worst. Both are up in welts: red on the edges and green, like a blister, in the middle.

Over the years, on visits to Glasgow I sometimes see those I went to school with. Ask the question, 'Did you get Miss Ivy Ross at Springbank?' and, even after more than fifty years, the answer is always along the lines of, 'Aw, wizn't she jist great, ah loved being in her class. Ah often tell ma grandweans aboot her.' Mention Harry Forshaw at NKS and the reply, invariably, is something like, 'Wasn't yon a bad bastard? Should never have been allowed near weans, that yin.'

Two epitaphs.

She Could Have Been a Contender

Annie Dunn stopped Ma and me in the Maryhill Road.

'Did ye hear, Big Mrs Broon's away?'

'She's no, is she?' said Ma.

'Aye. Funeral's oan Wednesday.'

'For goodness sake, that wiz awfy quick.'

'Aye, especially for her!' The two of them avoided each other's eyes and parted quickly. As Annie went on her way I looked at Ma.

'Whose funeral's oan Wednesday?'

'Big Mrs Broon's – wur ye no listening?'

'Naw.' I paused. 'Huz Big Mrs Broon died?' Ma cast her eyes heavenward.

'Naw, she's only kidding. She's jist lying in the boax daeing impressions!'

We both tried hard not to laugh after this tirade.

'Aw, that's a shame.'

'Aye, poor big sowel.'

So, Big Mrs Broon was deid. I felt sorry, and quite sad. Jeez, ah hope she'd forgiven me. Och, she must have done after aw this time. It wiz ten years ago; ah wiz only three.

It was almost certainly the summer of 1942. A really hot, sunny day. The heat stoated back up off the warm cement of the pavement, the tar on the road was melting. I lay on my stomach, at eye level with my few toy soldiers, in a world of my own. Suddenly there was a slight vibration in the ground and the sun was blotted out. I looked up in fright and found my eyes scaling a sheer, brown cliff – broken only by four cloth buttons. I craned my neck further back. A little head, wearing a littler hat, looked down at me from the summit.

'Hellooooh, son, are ye playinnnn' wi' yer soldyeeeers?'

Letting out a yell of terror, in one movement I got to my feet and fled into my close, abandoning my platoon to their fate. Not hearing any pursuit, I stopped at a safe distance and looked back. This giant figure, holding a patent leather handbag, had her head turned toward me. She stared for a few seconds, then forlornly went on her way, walking on what looked like two whisky kegs. This was my first encounter with Big Mrs Broon.

She really was big. Very big. Over six feet tall and weighing more than twenty stones. If that wasn't enough, the poor soul also suffered from elephantitis. Her enormous legs always held a special fascination for me as I grew up and never failed to draw my eyes. They seemed to be the same thickness all the way down to where her ankles, or what should have been her ankles, hung over her shoes. How did she get her shoes on and off? On top of her small head she always wore a little pointed hat with a long feather, just like Errol Flynn in *Robin Hood*. From then on down she got wider and wider to the bottom of her bespoke, long brown coat. Seen from a distance she appeared conical. She walked slowly and ponderously. And talked in the same manner.

I soon got used to her and, even though I was very young, I felt a bit guilty about taking fright that day and obviously hurting her feelings. From then on, as I grew up, I always made a point of thinking of something to say when she came down the street. Trouble was, once you did speak to her it would be ages before she'd move on. She also had an effect on Ma whenever they met. Something Ma called 'the coincidences'.

Ma and me were heading for the shops.

'Oh God, here's Big Elsie!'

I looked up. Mrs Broon had just come out of her close and was gliding – the long coat seemed to give this effect – relentlessly toward us. She stopped directly in front of us, blocking our way.

'Helloooh, Misssess Douglasss, how are ye the daaaay?'

Ma gave a wee, choking cough. 'Fine, Mrs Broon, how are ye yerself?'

'Och well, no saaaay baaad under the circuuumstaaances.'

Forty minutes later we were still there. She stood, immobile, only her lips moving, deflecting every attempt by Ma to bring the one-sided conversation to an end. I had lost the will to live. At last Mrs Broon swayed a little – this was a good sign – Ma's grip tightened on my hand. My eyes began to unglaze. We could soon be free.

'Och wellllll, ah'll have tae ruuuun.'

Ma's grip tightened even further at this, and she seemed to have developed a tickly cough.

'Ah'll see ye agaaain, Misssess Douglasss.'

'Right, cheerio then, Mrs Broon.' We set off to trek round her.

'Aye, the shoappps will soon be shuttt. Ah'ddd better hurrrry.'

Ma let out a wee squeak and just nodded her head. We had barely taken half a dozen steps when she dragged me into the nearest close. She leaned against the wall, holding her side while she reached for a hankie to dab her eyes.

'Whit's the matter, Ma? Are ye awright?'

'Aye,' she gasped. 'God! Ah wish she widnae always say "Ah'll have tae run."'

'How come you nearly always go like this efter ye've spoke tae Big Mrs Broon?'

'Aw, it's jist a coincidence.' She shook her head. 'The poor sowel couldnae run tae save herself.'

As I grew up, Mrs Broon continued to be a source of fascination for my pals and me. There was the time when one of our gang, who lived up her close, reported that, 'Wee Mr Broon's alwiz shouting at her, ye know!'

'You're joking. The size of him?'

'Aye.'

'And diz she let him away wi' it?'

'Seems tae.'

With the collected wisdom of seven-year-olds we couldn't figure this out. Mr Broon was a wee skelf of a man; maybe eight stones – wet through. How come Big Mrs Broon put up with this? We reasoned that all she had to do was get the wee nyaff in a corner, lean on him and that would soon knock the cheek out of him. In fact, after further debate it was unanimously agreed that if Big Mrs Broon could just get Joe Louis, the World Heavyweight Champion, in a corner of the ring and lean on him she'd easily have his title off him!

And now Big Mrs Broon was dead. Never got a shot at the title. I was thirteen now, well used to seeing her and talking to her – even if she did take some getting away from. Later that day a few of us gathered at Lizzie's corner.

'Did ye hear aboot Big Mrs Broon?'

'Aye, the auld soul's died.'

There was a silence. A pregnant silence. Tommy broke it.

'They're gonny huv an awful joab gettin' her doon the stairs, in't they?'

There now followed a certain amount of not looking at one another.

'They stay two up, dain't they?'

'Aye.'

'Four flights of stairs and tight bends, eh?'

'Might be easier lowering her oot the windae,' said John. One or two walked to the edge of the pavement and stood, backs to the rest of us, their shoulders shaking.

'That wiz a genuine suggestion,' said John; he was having difficulty keeping his face straight.

'Lying bastard!' said Robert Walker.

'Anywye,' said Tommy, 'ah think that oot o' respect—' He stopped to compose himself. 'Ah think that oot o' respect –' he had to pause again – 'we should aw gather oan Wednesday – tae see how the fuck they're gonny get her doon them stairs!'

The hearse, its back open, stood at the pavement outside Number 20, two cars for mourners parked behind. As was the custom, most of the neighbours had gathered in the street at a respectful distance. We had positioned ourselves fairly near the close. We strained our ears and discreetly nudged one another as, faintly at first, we listened to the bearer party begin to negotiate the stairs and landings. Like scaling Mount Everest – in reverse!

'Tilt a bit your end, Erchie.'

'Carefy, carefy!'

'Take the wecht a minute. MIND MA FINGERS!'

'Huv a blaw. Rest it oan the windae sill.'

All this was accompanied by a chorus of gasps, groans, muffled curses and the shuffling of overloaded feet. Finally, the first two red-faced bearers appeared. For a second it looked like they were carrying a large wardrobe, then the brass handles came into view. There were *eight* bearers instead of the customary six.

'Jeez!' said Wee Hughie. 'Dae ye think they've knocked two coffins intae wan?'

'Huv a bit of respect,' said Tommy.

'Listen tae who's talking.'

'Watch it,' warned John, 'some of oor mothers are beginning tae look at us.'

The bearer party teetered out into the road and, with a last major effort, lowered the head of the coffin onto the rollers at the back of the hearse, which immediately sank down onto its springs with a grinding noise. With much heaving and pushing, the coffin was slowly slid into the hearse and, at last, Big Mrs Broon was ready for the journey to Lambhill.

The mourners boarded the cars, engines were started and dignity seemed to have been restored. Then the hearse proved unequal to the task of moving off sedately up the slight incline of Doncaster Street. Clutch slipping, engine racing, it rolled back some two yards and hit the funeral car behind with a loud crunch. This proved too much for even the most sympathetic of onlookers who began to disperse, eyes averted, frightened to look at one another. It was too much for us. We began to laugh and pummel each other until, in a fine example of 'synchronised clouting', Jim and I felt our ears ring as our mothers reached over from behind and simultaneously belted us.

Suitably chastised, I contented myself with watching the hearse, at last, make its way slowly up the street. Just as it began to turn left into Hinshaw Street it suddenly dawned on me – Big Mrs Broon was in there, I'd never see her again. I hoped that the last ten years of always saying hello to her first had made up for the day I ran away and hurt her feelings. She always gave me a big smile. I think it had.

A Day in the Life of . . .

Jim McDonald and I lean against the wall in the warm sun. Parked at the pavement in front of us is John the carter's horse and cart. We are looking at everything through squinty eyes, the sun is very bright. John has left the Clydesdale, Benny, with his feed bag on. Every now and again the horse lowers his head to the ground so as the bag lies slack, then gives a couple of big snorts and the chaff comes flying out the sides. He raises his head and resumes eating.

'Where is John?' I ask.

'He knows somebody that lives up Davy Sim's close, so when he makes a delivery tae the Fairy Dyes (a factory making coloured dyes for clothing) he sometimes goes up and has his piece wi' them. He'll no be long.'

We lean back against the warm sandstone for another few minutes. I have my eyes shut, face turned up to the sun.

'Look!' Jim nudges me. 'Benny's gettin' a hard-on. It'll be the sun oan his back making him radgie.' We watch with interest until the horse's penis hangs down in a gentle curve.

'Some tadger that, in't it?'

'S'fuckin' beauty,' I say.

'Jist think o' they poor auld lassie horses huvin' tae take that.' We start to giggle.

'Ah bet they don't half limp the next mornin'.' He can hardly finish the sentence.

It takes me three attempts to say, 'It'll no half make their eyes watter!'

'Listen, listen,' says Jim, trying to regain control. 'Let's go and stand in your close mouth and watch any wimmen that go past Benny. If they don't think they're being watched ah bet ye they'll aw' be huvin' a fly keek at his dick.'

We stand just inside the entrance to my close. Minutes later a woman, perhaps thirty, walks up the street. As she passes the horse she takes a good look.

'See,' says Jim. 'Ah told ye.'

Two 'big girls' of about fourteen turn the corner. As they approach Benny one nudges the other and draws her attention to the display. They have a quick look round, don't spot us and decide the street is empty. They walk *very* slowly past Benny, having a whispered conversation as they do, which ends with then convulsed in laughter. As they near our hideout Jim steps forward with a big smile on his face.

'Awright, girls?'

They realise we have been watching them, and hurry on with faces red as beetroot.

'Didn't ah tell ye?' says Jim. 'The buggers are as bad as us – if ye can catch them.'

'Here's John coming!'

He is carrying the galvanised bucket that usually hangs from a hook under the body of the flat-bed cart. Water slops over its brim. He throws his 'piece bag' up onto the cart and takes Benny's feed bag off, fondly stroking the great horse's muzzle and talking to him. He puts the bucket down for him to slake his thirst.

John wears the carter's 'uniform' – cloth bunnet, old make-shift apron of a heavy canvas sack tied round his waist with a piece of rope and moleskin trousers. On his feet are a pair of ex-army tackety boots.

'John, can we huv a wee hurl oan the cart jist doon as far as the Seamore, then we'll get aff?'

'Aye, on ye's get.' John throws the last of the water into the gutter then hangs the bucket under the rear of the cart. Benny starts peeing.

'Will ye look at that,' says Jim. 'Ye'd think somebody had turned a tap oan, widn't ye?'

We lean over the edge of the cart and watch, with envy, as the great stream gurgles along the gutter and vanishes down the cast-iron stank at the bottom of the street.

'Imagine being able tae pee like that.'

'Ye could put small hoose fires oot, couldn't ye?' says Jim.

John puts a foot on the shaft and heaves himself up onto the cart. He sits on an old potato sack stuffed with straw. 'Hup lad, hup!' Benny sets away.

The cart rumbles down our street, right into Trossachs Street, then left onto Maryhill Road. John turns his head.

'You'll no be gettin' many mair hurls in future, boys.' He speaks loudly to overcome the noise of the cart's steel-rimmed wheels.

'How no, John?'

'The railway is daeing away wi' the horses and cairts next year. Aw the local deliveries is gonny be motorised. They're bringing in mair of yon three-wheelers that hitch on tae a flat-bed cairt instead of horses.'

'Are you no gonny get wan, John?'

'You'll no see me in a lorry, boys. Ah cannae drive, and ah've nae intention o' learnin'. Ah've been a horse-man aw ma life. Ah'll jist be retiring.'

'Whit'll happen tae Benny and aw the hoarses?'

He pauses for a moment. 'Ehh, we don't know yet.'

When the cart turns into the Maryhill Road the noise trebles as the steel rattles off the granite setts. The flat surface of the cart vibrates and I watch, fascinated, as the small pieces of straw and other debris seem to go into a frenzied dance. Jim and I are also being shook up, so we crawl over and sit on the folded-up tarpaulin that lies behind John. All too soon our short trip is over and we jump off the cart to walk back home again.

'Cheerio, John.'

Without turning he waves his hand and Benny plods on toward College Goods Station with no guidance needed from John.

'Whit'll we dae noo?'

'Whit about goin' tae the Book Store and huvin' a look in the windae, eh?'

'Aye. Good idea, there might be something new.'

The Book Store is a toyshop on the Maryhill Road, owned by two elderly sisters. Soon, we are standing with our noses pressed against the wire-mesh shutters which permanently cover the windows. Behind them lies an Aladdin's Cave of toys and books. I've never had a present bought at the Book Store, they are always too dear. We survey the cornucopia of children's dreams for a silent minute or two, then Jim speaks.

'If somebody granted ye a wish and ye could huv jist wan thing oot the whole windae, whit wid ye pick?'

After a good look, I decide. 'That blue six-shooter. It's got a revolving barrel, ye know.' I look at Jim. 'Whit wid you huv?'

He answers without hesitation, 'That train set wi' the station, signal box, people, cars and aw that.'

I look at Jim, then at the large train-set lay-out, then back at Jim. 'Ye said only *wan* thing. That's no *wan* thing!'

'Aye it is. Train set: it's jist the wan thing.'

'Is it shite, it's aboot twenty things – engine, coaches, village, cars, people. It's mair than wan thing, it's a *stack* o' things!'

Jim shakes his head in dissent. 'Train set. *Wan* thing.'

'Okay then, if that's how yer gonny dae it, ah'm changing ma mind. Ah'm no gonny huv the revolver noo, ah'm gonny huv something else.'

'Aye, that's fair enough,' says Jim, 'as long as ah can huv ma train set you can huv whit ye want.'

'Aye, nae bother. You can huv aw they bits and pieces.' I pretend to study the window, but I've already made my decision.

After a minute or so, Jim enquires, 'Ye made yer mind up yet?'

'Aye.'

'Well, whit are ye gonny huv?'

'Shop windae!' I try to keep my face straight.

'Eh?'

'Shop windae. You can huv yer train set and stuff – ah'll huv the rest.'

'Ye cannae huv the whole fuckin' shop windae!' splutters Jim.

'Aye ah can. You jist saying "train set" covered ye for aw they things, so me jist saying "shop windae" is exactly the same. It's only wan thing, but it covers me for aw the stuff in the windae.'

Jim's mouth opens, but no sound comes out. I can't keep it up any longer and burst out laughing. Jim joins in.

'We're standing here arguing about who's huvin' what,' says Jim. 'Ah huvnae even got enough in ma pocket for a penny caramel.'

'Me neether. Ach, let's go back roond tae the street.'

As we enter Doncaster Street, Billy Morrison runs up.

'Yon fella's roond singin' in the back courts again. Are we gonny dae it this time?' He looks from one to the other.

'Should we?' Jim laughs in anticipation.

'We said we would definitely dae it next time,' I remind him.

'Right! C'mon then. Och, wait a minute, we'll need a penny. Robert and me urr skint.'

'Ah can wangle a penny oot of oor Jim's bank,' says Billy. We all three laugh at the thought of adding 'bank robbery' to the bit of devilment we have in mind. We set off for Billy's close, then on up to their house which is two-up.

'Is there naebody in?'

'It's awright, ma ma and da are at work and Jim's at the matinee at the Blythsie.'

'Perfect!'

First thing we do on entering the house is to look out the window to check how far the 'back-court maestro' has got. Billy peers through his mother's nets.

'We've plenty time, he's still two backs away.' He reaches up and undoes the snib then raises the window six inches. We can now hear the troubador as well as see him. The man is one of two or three who regularly come round the streets, going from back court to back court, singing a limited repertoire of old music hall songs – badly. Folk open their windows and throw down a coin or two, for which they are always profusely thanked.

While Billy, using a table knife with practised skill, makes a withdrawal from brother Jim's bank, I look down at the singer. About sixty years old, he wears an old, badly stained gabardine mac and, of course, the statutory bunnet. He sports a few days' growth of beard. The thought enters my head that he probably is a regular at some library's reading room. As the occasional coin stoats off the tarmac he breaks off the refrain to pick it up. 'Thank you very much, missis. God bless, thanks very much; much obliged.' Most of the time he is not quite sure from which window this manna has come, so his thanks are shouted in all directions.

'Right, ye'd better start now,' says Jim, 'he's intae the next back.'

Billy grips the penny with a pair of pliers while Jim lights a gas ring. We watch as the blue flame caresses the coin. The three of us cackle in anticipation, like the witches in *Macbeth*. All the while the plaintive strains of our intended victim drift up to the window. Billy reaches down toward the companion set in the hearth.

'Ah'm gonny put it oan the shovel for throwing, jist in case ah let go the pliers and mibbe split the poor bugger wide open.' We go into further paroxysms at the thought.

'How will ye know when it's hoat enough?' I enquire.

Billy takes the coin away from the flame, holds it under his chin and lets a spitball fall on it; it immediately sizzles and bounces off the coin. 'Ah'll know,' he says. He puts the penny back over the flame, laughing away to himself like a mad scientist.

'Right! He's intae oor back now.'

The man begins emoting an atrocious version of 'If You Were the Only Girl in the World'.

'Are ye's ready?'

'Aye.'

Billy drops the coin, which must be approaching meltdown, onto the shovel and heads for the window. Jim stands on one side, me on the other. We peer through the pattern of the net curtains.

'Right, he's lookin' the other way.'

Billy flicks the shovel and the penny wheeches down in a graceful arc toward the back court just as the minstrel is hitting his peak.

Jim and I quickly close the window as the penny hits the ground. The three of us watch through the nets as the man breaks off and makes for the coin.

'Thank you very much, missis.' He looks all around, but cannot spot his assumed benefactress. He reaches down for the coin. 'Thank you very mu . . . OHYAHFUGGINBASSA!' The penny goes flying through the air. He sticks his fingers in his mouth. 'Yah fuggin bassa!' He looks wildly around but cannot spot us.

Two storeys up we three are in pain. Helpless. Billy has fallen on the floor; Jim and I hold our sides with the stitch and lean on the sink; we cannot get our laugh out and gasp for breath Jim manages to look out the window.

'He's had tae kick it intae a puddle tae cool it doon.'

We go helpless again. Billy just lies on the floor, gurgling, unable to rise. I join Jim at the window. We watch as the man retrieves his hard-earned penny. He is still looking up at the windows, looking for a sign. He pockets the coin and, muttering curses, slips through a gap in the railings into the next back.

Billy finally manages to rise. Jim and I get our breath back. Moments later 'Only a Bird in a Gilded Cage' fills the afternoon air.

The Man Who Made Shadows

John Purden put a pinch of carbide on the road and spat on it. We watched it begin to bubble and hiss and give off the sour-smelling acetylene gas. Robert Walker had already acquired an empty tin can from a midden and punched a small hole in its unopened end. He placed it over the bubbling carbide and John covered the hole with a finger.

'We'll gie it aboot three minutes, eh?'

'Aye, that should dae.'

Three or more minutes dragged by.

'Dae ye think that's long enough?' said John.

'Aye.' Robert struck a Bluebell match. John removed his finger.

'Stand by fur blastin'!'

The flame was applied to the hole. BAMM! With a satisfying explosion the gas ignited and the can, spinning all the while, rocketed thirty feet or more into the air. I retrieved the battered can, ready for a repeat performance.

'We huvnae got enough carbide.'

'It'll no be long till it's dark,' said John. 'The Wee News of the World should be roon any minute. Dae ye think he'll let us have some?'

I shook my head. 'Nae chance. Ah tried him a few weeks ago. Jist aboot bit the heid aff me.'

The memory of what happened ran through my mind again. Persuaded by Billy Ferrie and Jim Loan to approach our diminutive leerie – nicknamed the 'News of the World' because of his fondness for a good gossip – I should have known my quest was doomed as soon as he entered the street. He was obviously late, the wee legs were just a blur, *and* he was in the middle of an argument with himself – and losing. I smiled.

'Mister, dae ye think ye could mibbe let us huv a wee drop of carbide?' He whizzed on past me for about three yards, skidding to a halt on his tackety boots, then spun round. I got ready to run.

'Whit? Whit?'

You just knew he'd have a high-pitched voice. Suddenly it dawned on me I'd been conned by Billy and Jim. I shot a glance at them. They were hanging on to one another, wetting themselves. The Wee News of the World was now hitting his stride.

'Gie ye some carbide? Whit fur? So as ye can blaw the bloody street up, then ah'll get the blame!' His voice was now so high only Mr Lockerbie's dog, Bruce, caught the end of the sentence. 'You'll be gettin' nae carbide frae me. If the Lighting Department wiz tae find oot ah'd gave carbide away ah'd get ma jotters, so ah wid.' He spun round on his heel and shot off up Number 28.

'Well, if there's nae good asking him,' said John, 'we'll jist huv tae hang aboot till he finishes his shift.'

'Aye,' agreed Robert. 'Wi' a bit of luck we'll cop for some then.' We didn't have long to wait.

He came bustling out of Hinshaw Street into Doncaster Street. Around four feet six inches tall, with legs as short as his temper, the News of the World's fast walk gave the impression he was always busy as he made his twice-daily visits to our street – to turn the gas lamps on in the evening and off again in the morning. His peaked cap, with its 'Glasgow Corporation Lighting Department' badge, was perched precariously on the back of his head. A shammy leather hung from one jacket pocket, a yellow duster from the other. His short ladder was slung over a shoulder. In his right hand was his 'Field Marshal's Baton'

– the lamplighter's staff. The Eighth Wonder of the World!

About three feet long, the first two feet was just an unremarkable wooden pole, but the remaining foot was *Boy's Own* stuff; a beautifully engineered Aladdin's Lamp in shining brass. It consisted of two round compartments. The upper held water, the lower carbide. The turn of a finely machined knob allowed water to run into the lower compartment, mix with the carbide – and produce acetylene gas. A twist of a miniature tap let the gas run through a spigot where the lamplighter lit it. The resulting flame would burn all through his shift and be used to light the lamps.

In a routine unchanged since the reign of Queen Victoria, the wee leerie would enter a close, prop his short ladder against the wall underneath a lamp and climb up a couple of rungs. Using the small lug on the tip of the staff, he would open the metal, draught-proof flap on the bottom of the lamp. The same lug was then used to turn on the gas, the flame on his staff applied to the mantle and plop! the gas flowing through it was ignited. At first it glowed faintly then, after further adjustments with the lug, the gas would flow steadily with a soporific *hiss* and the delicate mantle pulse and grow brighter until it burned with a pale, greenish-white light. The News of the World would close the bottom flap – if a draught got in the flame would gutter and burn unevenly with a constant *phut-phut* sound. He'd shoulder his ladder, take a final glance at his handiwork then climb the stairs to the next landing.

Behind him – in stairwells, recesses and the imaginations of children – he left a world of shifting shadows.

'Here's the wee bugger at last. Jist keep on talking, don't let on we even know he's therr.'

Robert took a glance at him. 'He'd huv been ideal for midget submarines during the war, widn't he? Widnae huv bumped his heid wance.'

The News of the World was about to finish his shift, but would he head in the direction we wanted him to? We watched his every move, willing him to make for the end of our street.

'He's going tae the stank!' We elbowed each other. 'Don't look!'

He stood over the heavy iron drain at the bottom of the street, unscrewed the cap of the carbide compartment and, bending down, tapped the staff on the ground to expel the remaining carbide. We waited impatiently until he turned the corner into Trossachs Street, then made a dive for it.

'Be carefy,' warned Robert, 'don't get any oan ye. It disnae half burn when it's damp.'

Gingerly, John scraped a fair amount into a matchbox. Minutes later the tin can was once more attempting to go suborbital. As I returned with it, Robert began reciting one of our 'street poems'.

> Tomorrow night there's an old folks' meeting

We all joined in.

> Admission free – pay at the door,
> Cushion seats, sit on the floor,
> Electric lights, lit by candles –
> Don't stand up or you'll break the mantles!
> Moving pictures, stookie men.
> Hallelujah! Amen.

We proceeded to laugh ourselves silly.

Fresh carbide was put down.

'Whit about trying this, boys?'

We looked up. It was Donny May, carrying a full-size McVitie's biscuit tin. We looked at each other. Even though it had been three years, I often wondered if Donny was still getting to play with Margaret's tits. Or maybe a wee bit lower. Donny was the street 'maddy', ready to try anything once – then another fifteen times!

He held the tin out in front of him. 'This'll haud a lot of gas; mibbe go the height o' the tenement.'

'Mibbe fuckin' take us with it,' said Robert.

Donny laughed. 'Naw it'll no. It'll jist go higher than a wee can.' He paused. 'Youse urnae feart, ur ye's?'

He knew John and Robert would take the bait. I was glad I was younger; I wasn't under any pressure.

'Naw,' said John, 'we're no feart, but are *you* gonny light it, seein' as it's your idea?'

'Nae bother.' Donny smiled. 'Ah'll light it.' Thing was, the mad bugger meant it. He wasn't bothered.

A hole was punched in the bottom of the shiny foot-square tin and it was placed over *all* our remaining stock of hissing, bubbling carbide. It had been decided to make this an all-out effort.

'Better gie it aboot ten minutes,' suggested Robert; 'a tin as big as this will take some filling.'

As the countdown dragged by we all grew increasingly nervous, though no one would have admitted it. I heard a window go up.

'That's wee Mrs Docherty leaning oot her windae. She'll be wondering whit we're daeing,' I said.

'She spends aw day wondering whit we're daeing,' said John.

'When this goes aff she'll probably shite herself,' said Donny. We began to giggle at the thought.

'Right, ah think it's time,' stated John. He was lying, rather dramatically, flat on the ground with his arm outstretched, finger over the hole. Donny lay in the same position, matches at the ready.

'Aye,' said Robert, 'if we put any mair gas intae it they'll fin nuthin' but two pairs of smoking boots either side of a hole in the road.'

John removed his finger, Donny struck a match and reached out to the hole. KABOOM! It was the loudest explosion I'd ever heard, and it was accompanied by the loudest scream I'd ever heard – from wee Mrs Docherty! The tin, instantly mangled, catapulted out of a great cloud of smoke and went whirling up in a graceful parabola, a vapour trail behind it. It soared to about fifty feet, then began re-entry, in the general direction of wee Mrs Docherty. As she saw McVitie's 'V-1' heading toward her she let out another scream, slightly lower in the decibel scale, and jerked herself back in from the danger zone, dunting the back of her head on the bottom of the raised window as she did. The cushion she'd been leaning on fell off the sill and landed on the pavement below.

We watched, open-mouthed, as the tin hit the wall near her window and noisily crash-landed a few feet from her cushion. She reappeared at the window, holding the back of her head.

'Yah bad buggers, ye's. Ah could huv split ma skull wide open. Ye's should aw be loaked up in Borstal, every wan o' ye's! Just wait till ma son, John, comes hame fae his work.'

We made a hurried, but dignified, exit into the nearest close, taking the remains of our embryo space capsule with us, after obligingly throwing Mrs Docherty's cushion back up to her in the hope of mollifying her.

Once in the back court and well out of earshot, we started laughing.

'Whit wiz it like when it went aff?' I asked.

'It fuckin' stunned me when it went,' said John. 'Ma ears are still dingling.'

'When ah lit it,' said Donny, 'it didnae half throw ma arm back.' He held out his hand. 'Look, the bugger's aw bruised!' They both laughed, united for the moment by a shared danger.

'Mind, ah think ah'll stick tae Heinz beans tins in future,' said John.

'Me tae,' agreed Donny. A dreamy look came over his face. 'Ah'll tell ye what, mind. Jist think what we could dae wi' an oil drum!'

Out of the Blue

It had been another rotten day at NKS. I'd had Harry Rotten Forshaw for rotten algebra and, as usual, got the rotten belt. When I came home a man was sitting facing me, his back to the window, almost in silhouette. It looked like Uncle James, the oldest of Ma's three brothers.

'Hiyah, Uncle James.'

He laughed. So did Ma. I took a closer look, my heart leapt with pleasure.

'UNCLE GEORGE! Aw, ah havnae seen you for ages, for years.' I went over and laid my hand on his forearm. I'd have been quite happy if he'd kissed me, but I was thirteen; only aunties kissed you at that age, not uncles.

'Hello, pal, how're you doing?'

I was about to answer, but Ma spoke. 'There's not just your Uncle George here.' I looked to my left. A young woman was sitting by the fireside. 'This is your new aunty, Aunty Joan.'

'Hello,' she said. She was quite stunning. A beautiful nineteen-year-old whom George had been courting since she was seventeen. Yeah, I knew that when my Uncle George finally got himself married she would be something special. Plain Janes need not apply.

'Oh, hello.' I felt my face go red; it was like talking to a movie star. Even so, I wanted to talk to my Uncle George; it was so wonderful to see him again.

'Have ye any idea how long it is since ah last saw ye? It was during yon bad winter.'

1952. Aged thirteen.

'Aye, ah know. It was '47. Ah'd just signed up for another five years wi' the Marines. That was my first leave.' He smiled. 'And here we are, that's me finished ma time and Joan and I just got married a couple of weeks ago.' He sat back. 'And it's civvy street for me from now on.'

When he'd come on leave that winter, after joining up again, he'd seemed to be just about back to his old self. The war was finished, he was still only twenty-two, and was full of fun once more – though still drinking heavily. The moods seemed to have left him. The snow had lain four feet deep in Glasgow that winter and he'd spent lots of time out the back with me and my pals, having snowball fights, cutting ice bricks and showing us how to build walls. My pals thought he was wonderful and I revelled in the fact that he was *my* uncle. All mine. As usual, when his leave was up and he had to return to camp I was disconsolate and longed for his next leave. For the rest of this time he never came to us again. All Ma had during the ensuing long period were three or four letters. But now, at last, after five years, here he was.

'It's great tae see ye again, Uncle George.'

'And it's smashing tae see you, son. You're no half getting tae be a big laddie.'

We exchanged a few more words then Ma started to pour some tea. Soon the three of them began to blether. Ma was obviously delighted to see her 'wee' brother again and I could tell she was pleased he was married and, presumably, about to settle down. As they spoke, as usual I couldn't take my eyes off him. He looked well. He wore a nice, pale blue suit and a greenish gabardine mac. Yet, I was childishly disappointed. This was the first time I'd ever seen my Uncle George in civvies. He sort of – I couldn't keep the thought out of my head – looked ordinary. Just like any other fella. His dark blue Marines uniform enhanced his good looks and blond, wavy hair. Made him stand out: King of the World, Centre of Attraction. I wondered what his new wife thought of him in civvies. Over the last couple of years she had been courted by this handsome Royal Marine, still in his mid-twenties and with two rows of medal ribbons: Second World War and Korea – during his second stint he'd served on HMS *Belfast* in Korean waters. I bet she preferred him in uniform too.

I sat at the table, as always next to him, and hung on his every word. Joan was from Rochester in Kent. They had got married days after his demob. He'd brought her up to Scotland to meet his sister and two brothers, they were staying out at Blackburn, West Lothian, with Uncle James and Aunty Jenny. In a couple of days' time he was taking her to Edinburgh to meet Bill, the middle brother. Bill had stayed on in the Army after the war and was stationed at Redford Barracks in the capital.

They were having an extended honeymoon. George had

picked up a reasonable gratuity on discharge, but it was dwindling rapidly. Soon they would have to go back to Kent, where they were lodging with Joan's mother. They'd have to start looking for jobs and get their own place. It was quite obvious Joan adored him. She was a beauty in her own right; together they made a striking couple.

Much too soon, their fleeting visit was over. It was time for them to take a tram down town and get the bus out to West Lothian. As ever, he'd lit up our single-end for the few hours he'd been here. Yet, as I sadly watched him take his leave, I knew things had changed. I still loved him, idolised him. But, it was 1952. I was thirteen now and he was no longer a god. Not in civvies.

Big Deal at Dodge City

I entered the close at 375 Maryhill Road and went up the stairs two at a time until I reached the second landing. As I rang their bell for the thousandth time I looked again at the clear plastic nameplate with 'F. Johnson' printed on a tartan background. As ever on a Saturday night, I had that pleasurable feeling of anticipation. I knew the next few hours would be full of fun and laughter.

Since meeting Sammy on my first day at NKS, we had become great pals, almost inseparable. Sammy's ma, Lottie, opened the door. The familiar smell of their house slipped past her. I liked that as well.

'Hiyah, Lottie.'

'You're early again, eejit features! Dae ye ever think of givin' us time tae finish oor dinners?'

'Oh, sorry. Will ah come back in ten minutes?' I offered.

Lottie shook her head. 'Naw, yah silly bugger, come oan in.'

I smiled as I followed her along the lobby; she was always saying things like that.

As she entered the living room Lottie graciously announced me: 'It's yer daft pal,' she said to Sammy. 'Cannae wait tae lose his poaket money.'

Everybody said hello. I managed to find a seat and began to make a fuss of Sally, the cross-breed terrier, and Toby, the black and white cat. Sammy and his dad, Frank, were still at the table finishing their evening meal. Grandfather, Old Sam, was already sitting in his chair by the fire filling his pipe. He leaned forward.

'Sally, watch him, he's after Lottie's bag!'

Sally immediately ducked away from my fingers and ran over to where Lottie's well-worn message bag leaned against the leg of the sideboard. She turned to face us, ready to defend it. I took my cue. Without looking over at dog or bag, I began to slowly reach my hand out in their direction. The nearer I came, the louder Sally's growls became. Every twenty seconds or so Old Sam would mutter, 'The bag, Sal, the bag!' This would drive Sally even more frantic as she looked from Sam to me, her growls becoming half-yelps. Finally Lottie would intervene.

'Will youse stoap tormenting that dug!' She crossed over and lifted the bag to put it on top of the sideboard. 'Whit urr they daein' tae ye, hen?' Sally wagged her tail in pleasure at having her bravery recognised, then darted back to me, the attempted theft of Lottie's bag forgiven.

I went on to the next part of our routine. 'Has she been behaving herself, Sam?' I nodded in Sally's direction.

Sam took the pipe out of his mouth, an air of great seriousness came over him. 'She got out onto the stairs the other day as a woman was going down, and the coalman was coming up.' He gravely shook his head. 'Nothing left but heels of boots, torn shawls and lumps of coal strewn everywhere.' He gave a sigh. 'A terrible sight for a man to see. I couldn't do a thing, she's too powerful.'

As usual I went into fits of laughter at yet another of his surreal stories about the little black terrier. In his late seventies and a veteran of the Boer War, Samuel Montgomery, a Northern Irishman, was still a big, strapping man. To me, at fourteen, he seemed very old, but we got on well. I never tired of his stories of fighting the Boers, and we were also on the same wavelength with our sense of humour.

'Are we here tae play cards, or what?'

Sammy sat shuffling the cards at a newly cleared table. I took my usual place, facing Sammy. Lottie sat on my left, Frank on my right. Just before he started to deal, Sammy paused.

'Tell me, Robert, whit's the difference between Bing Crosby and Walt Disney?'

My mind raced, it's got to be a trick question. After a minute or so I gave in. 'Naw, Ah don't know. Whit's the difference?'

'Bing sings – but Walt disnae!'

It was around five minutes before I was ready to play cards. It's a very Glasgow joke. Alas, it doesn't travel.

Most days of the week I was in and out of Sammy's house, but Saturday nights were always the best. Sammy had introduced me to the delights of three-card brag and pontoon, and for months now it had been the same routine on Saturday evenings – up to the Johnsons' around seven with the prospect of three or four hours of fun and laughter.

Their three-room tenement flat was always comfortably untidy. Lottie would make a major effort to have it spick and span for Hogmanay, then the rest of the year it would be allowed to recover. I loved being up there.

It was 1953 and the Johnsons, like us, still depended on radio for entertainment. Without the distraction of TV, a game of cards was still a popular pastime. Although I very much enjoyed 'playing for coppers', what I really looked forward to was when Lottie had had a few whiskies and, hopefully, was losing. Preferably to Frank. That was when the fun started. There was no need for television. Lottie was a bad loser at the best of times. If she was losing to Frank she became an atrocious loser!

They were two opposites. Both in their late forties, Lottie was thin, round-shouldered and waspish, with a tongue that would make a Govan docker blush. It all hid a heart of gold. Frank, a gentle soul, didn't smoke, drink or swear. He'd served in the Royal Navy during the war as a Petty Officer sick-berth attendant, mostly on the escort carrier HMS *Vindex* on Russian convoys. He now worked as a male nurse at Ruchill Hospital. He was very like Stan Laurel, not just in appearance but also in manner. Never more so than when under pressure from Lottie.

It was sometime after nine p.m. Lottie was nine shillings and three whiskies down. Unfortunately for him, Frank was up. We were playing pontoon and Lottie was trying for a five-card trick. The four cards in her hand totalled fifteen. If Frank, the dealer, gave her a six or less she would be all right.

'Ah'll buy ma last card for sixpence,' said Lottie.

I tried not to laugh as I watched Frank, reluctantly, pass her a card face-down. Lottie lifted a corner of it. She glowered at Frank.

'Yah wee scunner, ye!' He'd given her a nine. Frank, apologetically, took the money.

'It's no ma fault, Lottie. It's the luck o' the draw.'

'Luck o' my arse!' snapped Lottie, winking at Sammy and me while Frank was absorbed getting the cards together. I stifled a giggle.

An hour or so later the game had changed. Lottie's luck hadn't. We were now playing three-card brag and she continued to lose consistently, needling Frank all the while. More and more he was turning into Stan Laurel. Eventually there was a big pot of almost a pound – with just Frank and Lottie playing for it. Frank sat, sweat beading his brow, as he and Lottie continued to bet. He began to crack under the tension.

'Ah hope ah don't win this,' he said, a sickly smile on his face. 'Ah'll never hear the end of it from her.'

Lottie sipped her whisky and put another shilling in. 'Stoap being such an auld fanny,' she hissed.

'Is that no terrible?' said Frank. 'Ah don't know why ah play cards wi' this wumman.' Then his nerve gave. 'In fact, ah'm gonny see ye.' He put another shilling in.

Lottie laid her cards face-up on the table. 'Seven, eight, nine,' she intoned, looking menacingly at her beloved.

Frank avoided her eyes, he swallowed hard. 'Eh, ten, jack, queen,' he murmured.

With a whine, Sally slunk away from the table and slipped under Old Sam's chair. Frank reached for the money.

'Yah wee shite!' snarled Lottie. 'That's the biggest pot o' the night.'

Frank tutted. 'Lotisha, mind the boys.'

'Fuck the boys!' said Lottie.

Frank now went into full Stan Laurel mode. 'Ah don't know why this wumman plays cards,' he said, his voice getting higher and higher. He was interrupted by me choking with laughter, holding my side as I tried to get my breath. 'Whit are you laughin' at?' he said, glad of the chance to escape Lottie's wrath. I pointed weakly at him. 'It's you, you're daein' it again. When you said "Ah don't know why this wumman plays cards" your voice got higher and higher jist like Stan Laurel's. Ah wiz waiting for ye tae start scratching yer heid the way he diz before he bursts oot crying.' I went into kinks of laughter again at the thought of it.

Frank laughed. 'Can ye blame me?' he said. 'Is this no the worst wumman in the world? She wiz thrown oot the SS for cruelty, this yin.'

I wiped my eyes. 'Ah cannae help it, Frank. You've nae idea how like him ye are when Lottie starts gettin' oan tae ye.'

Lottie looked at him. 'He's right, mind. Ah think Stan Laurel's faither must huv hud a bike and took a wee run up tae Glesga, and bumped intae your mother!'

Frank looked at me again, in mock severity. 'See whit you've started, Robert Douglas.' He turned to Sammy. 'Whit dae you think, son?'

Sammy took hold of his tie and waved it at his father, then did a fairly good Oliver Hardy: 'Just deal the cards, Stanley, deal the cards.'

Springer

Now and again he'd come and stand at Lizzie's corner, maybe once every two or three weeks.

'Look, therr's Springer. Let's go doon and listen tae his patter, he's a scream when he starts.'

As we head toward him we can see he's into his usual routine; he's on his toes, swaying from side to side like a boxer warming up. He's never still. That's how he got his nickname. He's twenty, maybe twenty-one. That makes him five or six years older than us.

'Hiyah, Springer.'

'Hello therr, boys.' He acts as if he hadn't seen us coming. He spots I have an American comic tucked under my arm.

'Whit's the comic? Gie's a look.'

Reluctantly I draw it out. 'It's *Superman* – but ah've no read it yet.'

'Don't worry, ah'm no wanting a lend of it. Jist haud it up and gie's a look at the cover.'

I hold it tightly between both hands so as he can see the artwork on the front.

'Och, yer awright, ah've read that wan. Anywye, ah've gone aff Superman. Ah'm no gonny read him again!'

One or two of us laugh.

'You've gone aff him. Why? Whit's the matter wi' him?'

He sways slightly, changes balance. 'Ah'm beginning tae huv ma doubts aboot him. Ah think he might be a bit of a nancy-boy!'

'SUPERMAN!' we chorus. 'You've got tae be joking.'

Springer tries to look serious. 'How auld would ye say Superman is?' After a quick discussion amongst the four of us, we agree on twenty-eight. Right, twenty-eight. Now, that Lois Lane, the wumman reporter oan the *Daily Planet*, she really fancies him, dizn't she?'

'Aye.' We know that we are about to be led off on a verbal goose chase, but it'll be fun.

'So, how come Superman huznae shagged her by now?'

We burst out laughing. 'It's a comic, ye cannae huv them shaggin' in a comic.'

'How no? It's obvious Lois Lane really goes for him, so, how come he's no intae her drawers? He diznae even seem interested.'

Even as we protest, we can't help laughing. 'Aw c'mon, Springer. Ye cannae get away wi' that.'

'Right, ah'll jist huv tae prove it tae ye's. Now, would ye's agree that Superman is a fine, big healthy fella?'

'Aye.'

'He's absolutely bursting wi' muscles and energy and aw the rest of it?'

'Aye.'

'So how come he's no shagging Lois?'

' 'Cause he isnae.'

As Springer talks, I take a close look at him. He is the double of a young Clark Gable. He knows it, so to heighten the effect has grown a moustache and taken to combing his hair straight back, Gable-style. But the double-breasted suit he wears has seen much better days. The cuffs are frayed, as is the material round the buttonholes. His shirt collar is worn and grubby. He wears a pair of crepe-soled brothel-creepers. Dressed up in a smart suit and using his quick wit to amuse, Springer could easily be devastating with the girls. Sadly, he has two serious faults which ensure the girls give him a wide berth – he is workshy and whatever money he gets, he drinks.

At fourteen, I am just a year away from leaving school and I m looking forward to getting into the world of work, smart clothes – and girls. I cannot understand why a good-looking guy like Springer is just wasting himself. He interrupts my train of thought . . .

'Right, let's take a look at who Superman is when he's *not* being Superman. Clark Kent, mild-mannered reporter oan the *Daily Planet*, and well-known eejit! As everybody knows, Clark huz a big crush oan Lois when he's Clark. But when he's Superman he's got nae time for her. Is that right?' He looks around for confirmation. He gets it. 'Now, Clark is really just Superman wi' a suit oan and a perr of horn-rimmed specs, yet we're supposed tae believe that naebody ever recognises him, eh? Cummonnnnn! Anywye, as ye know, Clark's in love wi' Lois, but she'll huv nothing tae dae wi' him 'cause she's in love wi' Superman – who is really Clark withoot the specs.' Springer stops and dramatically claps a hand to his forehead. 'Awww! Ah'm beginning tae get a fuckin' heidache wi' aw this!' He does some more footwork, then resumes. 'How come we never see Clark Kent taking Lois tae the movies, or oot for dinner, eh?'

''Cause she disnae fancy him.'

'Naw.'

''Cause she's waiting fur Superman tae ask her oot?'

'Naw. There's a reason why she never goes oot wi' Clark. What is it?'

We fail to come up with an answer.

'Right, ah'm gonny huv tae tell ye's. It's very simple. If ye's hud gave it a bit of thought when ye's were reading the comic ye would huv spotted it years ago. Clark cannae afford tae take her oot – he's always skint!'

Between laughs we try and remonstrate with him. 'Gie us a

break, Springer, he cannae be skint. He's a reporter fur the newspaper, he'll huv his wages.'

Springer shakes his head, saddened by our collective ignorance. 'Well, once again ah'm gonny huv tae explain. But first tell me something. After years of reading the comic, how many times a week wid ye say Clark has tae change intae Superman and fly aff somewhere tae dae a rescue or battle criminals?'

After thirty seconds' debate we announce our decision: 'At *least* two or three times a week.'

'Just remind me,' says Springer, 'whit diz Clark Kent dae, *every time*, when he wants tae change intae the Big Fella?'

I take it upon myself to describe Clark's routine: 'He finds the nearest phoneboax, dives inside, birls roon that quick ye cannae see him, and seconds later steps oot intae the street as Superman.'

'Couldnae huv put it better maself,' says Springer. 'Now, whit diz he dae wi' his suit while he's away daein' aw these great things?'

'Jist leaves it in the phoneboax 'till he comes back.'

'Exactly!' says Springer. He sounds triumphant. We still can't figure where he's taking us. 'And am ah right in saying they live in a big city jist like New York?'

'Aye.'

'So, jist like any other big city, it's bound tae huv its share o' dossers and winos, won't it?' He doesn't wait for an answer. 'And ye know whit they'll be daeing, don't ye?'

'Naw.'

'Well, ah'll tell ye. They'll spend a lot of their time stoating about the city centre in the vicinity of the *Daily Planet* building, keeping their eyes oan the phoneboaxes! And we know why, daint we?' Again he doesn't wait for an answer. 'Because they know that two or three times a week they always find a nice suit – complete wi' wallet – lying in wan o' the local phoneboaxes. This huz been going on for years. The dossers ur intae a routine: One: Take wallet oot of jaiket pocket. Two: Transfer donation tae the Tramps Benvolent Fund intae their pockets. Three: Fold up suit ready for trip tae pawnshop. En route sling empty wallet intae trashcan. Four: After visit tae pawnshop, make straight for nearest off-licence tae buy the carry-oot. And finally, Five: Head for the park wi' the clinking, broon paper carrier bags whilst singing a chorus of 'Isn't This a Lovely Day Tae be Caught in the Rain'.'

As he lists these events Springer rhythmically sways on the balls of his feet. We are in stitches. He holds his arms out wide in an appeal for order.

'So, jist picture the scene twenty minutes later. Superman flies back hame, having jist saved 314 people doon in Brazil or somewhere. He's wondering whit he should make for his dinner the night, lands in front o' the phoneboax, opens the door. "Bastards!" He looks aroon', hears singin' coming fae the park, so he flies ower, "Excuse me interrupting your wee celebration, boys. But did ye happen tae see anybody near the phoneboax in the last half 'oor?" The dossers obligingly stoap singing while halfway through a rendition of 'Misty'. "Naw, Superman, we've been here fur ages but we didnae see anybody near that phoneboax. Did we, boys? If we'd seen anybody we wid tell ye, widn't we, boys? Sorry we cannae be any mair helpful. Huv ye loast something, Big Man?" "Oh, it's awright," says Superman. "Anywye, ah'll huv tae be going, ah'll huv tae get doon tae Hepworth's before they shut and get measured fur a new suit – that's the second this week!" So he zooms away up in the air like he always diz, and the dossers are aw shouting, "All the best, Superman" and "Sorry aboot yer suit" and they're aw dying tae laugh, but they huv tae wait until he's well oot the road in case he hears them wi' his super hearing. Finally, when he's well oot o' sight they start saying things like, "Is he thick or whit, eh?" and, "Huv ye ever met such a numpty-heided bugger in yer life?" and, "When is he gonny take a tumble tae himself? That's aboot twenty-five suits this year – and it's only February!"'

By now we are all hanging onto one another, laughing.

'Well, there ye's are, boys. Now ye know why Clark Kent and Lois Lane are never gonny get the gether. He's always skint and can hardly keep the payments going at Hepworth's, never mind being able tae take her oot.'

All four of us are wiping our eyes. 'Aye, awright, Springer, we give in. We believe ye.'

'It's aw true, boys. Ye know Springer widnae tell ye's lies. Anywye,' he shoots his frayed shirt cuffs out of his frayed jacket sleeves, 'it's time ah wiznae here.' He does a sort of shimmy like a boxer shadow-boxing. 'Ah'll see ye's another time. Cheerio, boys.'

'Aye, cheerio, Springer. See ye around.'

It's 1969. I've been a prisoner officer at Winson Green Prison, Birmingham, for the last seven years. Jimmy Wallace is a prisoner. He's a Glasgow man, and when he gets the chance he likes to have a wee blether. There are just five Scots officers on the staff. I'm the only one from Glasgow.

'Awright, boss?'

'Fine, Jimmy. How's yerself?'

'You're fae Maryhill, Mr Douglas, in't ye?'

'Aye, that's right.'

'There's a guy ah know, jist came in oan remand fur sentence, he's fae Maryhill. He's known as Springer. Did ye ever know a Springer?'

I smile. 'Aye, ah did know a Springer. Ah'll huv a look at him when ah get the chance. Where's he located?'

'He's in B3-24.'

'Ah'll huv a wee wander doon when ah get the time.'

*

About forty minutes later I have the time. When I come to the cell I flick back the spyhole cover and look in. It's a single-cell. The guy's lying on his bed. When he hears the spyhole cover rattle he looks round. Yeah, that's Springer. It's maybe sixteen years or so since I last saw him, he'll be about thirty-six now. The slim boy I knew is gone; he's now stocky. The hair is still combed back but is getting thin at the front. The Gable jaw-line could now best be described as 'jowly'. The moustache is still the same. Moustaches don't get fat. I open the cell door.

'So, how's Springer?'

He double-blinks at a screw using his nickname. 'Dae ah know ye?'

'You used tae. Last time I saw ye wid be the early fifties. Ah'd be aboot fourteen or so. Ah don't think you'll recognise me. Ah lived in Doncaster Street, and ye often used tae come and gie us yer patter when we were standing ootside Lizzie's shop at the bottom of the street. Ye used tae huv us in stitches.' Springer smiles at the memory I've just evoked, or is it the compliment? 'How did ye finish up doon in the Midlands, Springer?'

'Ach, ah wiz supposed tae be gonny make a new start. Ah got fixed up wi' a joab in Coventry, in the car industry.' He shook his head. 'It didnae last long. As usual ah fucked it up!'

I don't bother to ask how. 'Well, ah'd better be going, ah'm no on this wing. It wiz Jimmy Wallace that telt me ye were in. Ah'll see ye around.'

'Aye, cheerio.' I lock him up.

Next morning, when I have a few minutes to spare I wander round and open his door. He is sitting on his bed reading a library book. I place a half ounce of Old Holborn, a packet of Rizla cigarette papers and a box of matches on his bed. He looks surprised.

'There's a wee smoke fur ye, jist fur auld times' sake.'

It's the first time I've known Springer to be stuck for words. I almost have the cell door shut.

'Thanks a lot, boss.' He pauses. 'Sorry ah don't remember ye.'

'Och, it's awright, Springer. Ah remember you.'

Getting the Big Picture

As the queue shuffled toward the kiosk, the more my apprehension grew. Now I knew how an escaped POW felt as he approached the ticket window in a German railway station. I was one of a large crowd lined up outside the Regal Cinema in Sauchiehall Street waiting to get in to see *The House of Wax* starring Vincent Price. The first film to be shot in 3-D. My problem was it was rated 'X' certificate, no one under sixteen allowed in. I was fourteen.

I had queued for over an hour in a fine drizzle, to ensure I'd get into the second house. I confided my guilty secret to a young couple next to me.

'Och, you'll get in nae bother,' they assured me, 'you'll easily pass for sixteen.'

I wasn't so sure. The nearer I came to the window the more convinced I became that I'd be spotted and humiliatingly ejected from the foyer. I could see it all, everybody looking at me as the manager berated me and banned me for life from the Regal; maybe even sent for the polis! Finally, there was just one person between me and discovery. The man moved away, I stepped up to the grille and held out a ten-shilling note. In as deep a voice as possible I said, 'One please.'

Without even a glance the girl issued me a ticket and handed me a pair of cardboard-framed spectacles with red and green cellophane lenses. I was through. I'd made it! All I had to do now was get across the Swiss Border.

*

The Blythswood cinema, in 1967.

Once in my seat, as my mac slowly dried out, I endured an interminable hour or more of shorts – newsreel, cartoon, travelogue and 'coming attractions' – until, at last, on came the main feature. There was an outburst of embarrassed laughing and giggling as, in unison, the audience donned their flimsy specs. Immediately the double-image on the screen sharpened up – and had depth! I thought it was just wonderful. Soon we were all oohing and aahing as, at regular intervals, knives, clubs and assorted weaponry came flying out of the screen toward us, making us flinch and blink. Halfway through, there was a dull thud and a howl from a few rows away as some man, ducking to avoid a dagger thrown by mad Vince, bumped his forehead off the man in front!

Sometime after ten p.m. I staggered out into a still-damp Sauchiehall Street, my head buzzing with the sights and sounds I'd just seen. I could hardly wait to get a tram home so as I could tell Ma all about it. I thought 3-D was terrific. Yet it was not to last.

*

In the history of cinema, 1953 has to have a chapter all to itself. Big things began to happen. Television, especially in America, was making major inroads into cinema audiences. The movie industry had to hit back. The day of the small, square screen was over. The movie studios had to entice people by giving them something that black and white TV couldn't compete with. Spectacle!

Just months later, *The Robe*, starring Richard Burton, was released. The first film to be shot in Cinemascope *and*, another innovation, stereophonic sound. 3-D movies were swept aside. Cinemas all over the country rushed to have their new wide screens and associated equipment fitted. The Seamore, just three hundred yards further down the Maryhill Road from the Blythswood, was the first cinema in our district to be converted. A large, fan-shaped hall, it was the ideal shape for the new medium and had installed one of the largest screens in the city. During the few weeks the Seamore had been 'closed for conversion', Sammy and I had waited with great impatience.

A full hour before the Grand Opening we joined the queue for the matinee.

'Don't forget, Sammy, when we get in, make a dive for the middle of the stalls, that's the best area tae be in tae get the full effect. Ah read it in the paper.'

At last we were allowed through the doors, we bought our tickets and got seats exactly where the *Evening Citizen* columnist said you should. Once more there were an interminable number of shorts to endure until, unusually for the Seamore, there was an interval. The house lights were turned up. Sammy and I sat, with mounting excitement, looking at the enormous stretch of brand-new gold curtains, trying to imagine what wonders lay behind. When the shorts had been shown the curtains had only parted to the width of a normal-sized screen. Sammy was beside himself.

'When are they gonny start this scunnering picture? Dae they no know we're aw dying tae see it?'

Seconds later, as if in answer, the lights dimmed. The curtains opened, but once more just to the width of the old, square screen. Sammy looked at me, but said nothing. On came the usual 20th Century Fox logo and signature tune.

'That disnae look any bigger than the auld screen,' said a disappointed Samuel.

After the 20th Century Fox logo and music, the screen went blank – then the curtains closed! Sammy turned to me.

'Whit's going on, dae ye think we fell asleep and missed it?'

I was about to answer, but once more the curtains began to open, and open, and open until, revealed for the first time was a massive screen at least four times wider than the old one and half as tall again! There was a ripple of awed comments from the audience. From somewhere up above the blank screen came a God-like voice.

'Ladies and Gentlemen, THIS IS CINEMASCOPE!'

Immediately the giant screen was filled with the familiar 20th Century Fox logo, bigger than anyone had ever seen it. This was accompanied, in stereophonic sound, by a revamped version of the studio's signature tune specially written for Cinemascope productions and ending with a stirring flourish of three crescendos! I felt the hair stand on the back of my neck. I glanced at Sammy. He never took his eyes off the screen, never blinked. Just murmured, 'Fuck me!'

Wee Neugh Neugh

His name was Billy, and when he played out in the street with the rest of us he was called Billy. But when he wasn't around, amongst ourselves he was always 'Wee Neugh Neugh'. This was because he had a harelip and a habit of speaking so fast that that was how it sounded as it tumbled out, a sort of non-stop *neugh-neugh-neugh*. He didn't get called that for badness or anything, it was just that he was always making that sound.

What we also found strange was the fact that he was such a wee blether. I remember somebody saying, 'If ah spoke like Wee Neugh Neugh ah'd hardly speak at aw.' Really, you couldn't shut him up. He was a good-natured wee soul and nothing seemed to bother him.

There was the day nobody could get a word in for him. He'd been blethering away for a solid five minutes and finally Tommy says, 'Billy! Gonny gie us a break. Nae kiddin', ye could talk a gramophone tae scrap iron!' Billy just laughed with the rest of us.

Sometimes his handicap would come into the conversation as we stood at Lizzie's corner. Eventually we arrived at the conclusion that Billy mustn't be able to hear himself as we heard him. Maybe he thought he spoke all right.

Once we got into our early teens, I didn't mind being in a group with Billy. But, on reaching the constantly embarrassed age of fourteen, I used to hate being on my own with him, especially if we were amongst folk who didn't know us. He would be neugh-neughing away, people would be looking and I'd be thinking to myself, Ah bet aw these folk think we're huving a day oot fae the home. Terrible, I know, but that's how you are at fourteen.

There was the day I was in Cocozza's. I was sitting in a booth on my own, drinking a cup of Ovaltine and wondering if I should chance a letter to Debbie Reynolds, seeing as her and Eddie Fisher had just split up, when somebody slipped into the opposite seat.

'Nurr ye non yer own, Robert?'

'Oh, hello, Billy.' I put Debbie on the back burner and looked around to see if anybody was listening.

'Nurr ye wantin' a nuther Novaltine?'

'Eh, aye, thanks, Billy.'

He leaned out into the isle. 'Maria!' Maria Cocozza popped her head out of the kitchen door. 'Two Novaltines fur Robert nan me, Maria.'

Directly across the narrow aisle, in the opposite booth, sat a woman and two children: a wee boy and girl about five and six years of age. From the corner of my eye I saw the woman point the finger at the pair of them, giving them the 'gypsy's warning' about not laughing at those less fortunate than yourself. Billy, as usual, was totally oblivious. Or not bothered. He launched into the latest news.

'Did ye know the Sneamore's ngetting Cinemascope nin?'

'Aye, somebody telt me.' I knew it would make no difference. Billy would still tell me all about it, getting himself excited as he did. Like me, he loved going to the pictures.

'Billy Robertson's working noan ninstalling it.' He stretched his arms out wide. 'He says nits ntwo ana half times as wide as the nauld screen and nhalf as tall again!' As he became more and more enthusiastic he spoke too quickly and his words ran together and sounded, especially to the uninitiated, like an unbroken *neugh-neugh-neugh*.

A movement from the opposite booth caught my eye as the woman gave the two weans a clout. I took a quick glance. The two of them were red in the face trying not to laugh and frightened to look at one another in case they set each other off. Minutes later she gave them a sweet, probably to try and take their minds off Billy. All went well until Billy spotted John Purden come into the cafe.

'nJohn! nJohn! 'mon doon here. Robert nand me nurr doon here. Will ah norder ye a Novaltine?'

As John approached, the three of us were distracted by the bustle of activity in the nearby booth as the woman grabbed the wee boy, spun him round, and began to batter his back in an attempt to dislodge the boiled sweet stuck in his throat – caused by Billy shouting on John.

We watched with great interest until, at last, the sweetie came flying out the bairn's mouth, stoated twice down the aisle, and shot out the door into the Maryhill Road. A couple of minutes after that the woman left the cafe dragging her kids behind her.

Billy turned to us, totally unaware of his contribution to the drama. He shook his head. 'nYou huv tae be noffy careful when yer ngivin' nweans big sweeties!'

It wasn't too long after this that Billy's family moved. It would be twenty years before I ran into him again. I was on a rare visit to Glasgow, walking along Renfield Street. Coming toward me was the easily recognisable figure of Wee Billy. He had a little boy by the hand.

'Hello, Billy.'

He stopped. 'Aw nJesus, Robert! Nimagine that.'

'So, how's things?'

'Great! nthis is ma wee boy, nan the wife's nexpecting a nother wan.'

We blethered away for about twenty minutes, with Billy doing most of it, then:

'nHere, remember that nimpediment ah hud wi' ma nspeech?'

'Oh, aye, ye did.' I had to stop myself from saying, 'Ah see it still bothers ye.'

'nDid ye know, nooadays their daein' noperations at the Nuffield for it. Nonly five hundred pounds.' He paused. 'Nit wiz them that ncured me!'

Something of Value

Every week, for 3/6d, I bought the brown ticket with 'Glasgow Corporation Education Department – School Dinner Scheme' on it. The 'Dinner Ticket'. Along its bottom edge were five squares, which were punched each day as I collected my midday meal. I liked school dinners. There was always soup, followed by meat and two veg, or fish, then pudding. I normally scoffed my dinner without any problem. Puddings were the thing I sometimes had trouble with. Most of the time it was the standards, such as plum duff and custard or boiled rice with a spoonful of jam – 'Mmmm, lovely! Any extra, missis?' But, at least once a week, twice if I was unlucky, there would be either tapioca or sago – 'Yeeeugh'! Wallpaper paste and frog spawn. We also got our free little bottle of milk to drink every morning in class. Helping to make us fine, healthy, rickets-free children. Then, of course, when I went home from school I'd get another dinner from Ma around six o'clock. Even the Queen didnae get *two* dinners a day!

'Ah'll need ma dinner money the morra, Ma.'

She reached up and brought her purse down from the mantelpiece. Then stood looking into it.

' 'Much huv ye got, Ma?'

'Bugger aw! It's three and six, yer dinners, in't it?'

'Aye.'

She sighed. 'Ah weesh ah knew where the money goes, ah really dae.' She slipped her wedding ring off and held it up between finger and thumb. 'Right, it's up tae Uncle John's wi' you.' She placed it in her empty purse. 'Are ye coming up wi' me, pal?'

'Aye. Wait till ah put ma sandshoes oan.' I liked going up to the pawn with Ma. We always had a laugh. But, as I tied my laces, I thought back to just a few weeks ago. I still felt guilty.

Sammy and his cousin, Billy Rodgers, had sidled up to me in the playground.

'Dae ye want tae join oor scheme for skinning yer dinner money?'

'How can ye dae that?'

'We dae it regular.'

'But if we keep the three and six, whit urr we gonny eat? That's no enough tae get us pies and cakes every day.'

'Ah know,' said Billy, 'but we go tae ma hoose at dinnertime and ah get stuff oot the wee dairy oan tick oan ma Ma's line. So that leaves us oor dinner money fur oorselves. Dead brilliant, eh?'

I had the feeling Billy hadn't quite worked this out. Still, I allowed myself to be persuaded. Three and six bought a lot of sweeties *and* a couple of visits to the cinema – but it didn't bring much pleasure. As that first week went on I found I wasn't enjoying my ill-gotten gains as much as I thought. I knew I was cheating my ma. I resolved not to do it the next week. I didn't have to worry, the Great School Dinners Swindle fell apart. Sammy called round for me on the Wednesday evening.

'We cannae go tae Billy's the morra or Friday.'

'How no?'

'His ma went intae the dairy and the wumman said, "Dae ye know your Billy's coming in here every day and gettin' six rolls and two quarters of Spam and corned beef *and* three cream cookies – and getting them marked oan your line?" '

'Fuck me! Whit's happened tae Billy?'

'His faither's jist aboot murdert him!'

In a way I was glad. I'd been trying to think up a reason for not carrying on with the skinning. This saved me the bother. But now there was a problem.

'Whit ur we gonny dae for something tae eat? Ah've spent aw the money.'

'Me tae.'

For the next two days Sammy and I, stomachs churning, watched enviously as our more honest schoolmates queued for the dinner hall. The punishment fitted the crime.

We set off on our regular five-minute walk up to the Garscube Road. There were just two things in the house that were pawnable: Ma's wedding ring – and the wireless. We would have missed the wireless. For the past few years, as my father's behaviour worsened, I'm sure Ma looked on that nine-carat gold ring as a link in a chain shackling her to my father. When the money ran out in the middle of the week, as it often did, it was off with the ring and up to the pawn. As she once put it, 'Ah get mair pleasure oot o' the wireless than this ever gave me.' The ring usually went in on a Wednesday and was redeemed on the Friday. Maybe.

We climbed the stairs and entered the spartan, wood-panelled vestibule. I breathed in the familiar smell of mothballs and disinfectant. I liked it. As usual, we could hear the murmur of voices coming from some of the cubicles. The problem now was to choose an unoccupied one and save the embarrassing 'Oh, sorry' and 'Excuse me' that selecting one in use always entailed. Especially if you knew the folk. We looked at the eight wooden doors facing us.

'Whit dae ye think?' whispered Ma. For the duration of our visit she would speak in nothing but whispers. I moved nearer to the doors, trying to judge where the voices were coming from.

'That one!' I pointed to my selection.

Ma stepped forward and with an effort, pulled open the

heavily sprung door. Mrs Nelson and her daughter, Mary, glared at us!

'Oh sorry, sorry. Thought it was empty.' Ma went red and let the door go – forgetting how strong the springs were. *Bang!* Dust fell from the rafters, most of it into the cubicle. I heard Mrs Nelson mutter, 'Jesus wept!' and we could hear them coughing and dusting themselves off. I was dying to laugh.

'See you!' whispered Ma.

'Whit?' I said loudly.

'Shhh, shhh,' she said. 'Ah'll pick wan myself.' She tiptoed along the row of doors. 'This wan.' She forced the door open. It was empty. We squeezed into the narrow cubicle and managed to avoid getting fingers or legs caught as the door snapped shut like a trap. We leaned on the counter, half-facing one another in the narrow space. I beckoned to her to bend her head down toward me.

'Ah bet ye big Mrs Broon never ever pawned anything; she'd never have got intae a cubicle.'

Ma looked away quickly, the corners of her mouth twitched. There was something about the ultra-quietness of the pawn that made Ma and me prone to the giggles.

'Don't start.'

We listened to the discreet conversation going on just two doors away.

'Gonny jist gie us another ten bob on that, John?' requested the supplicant.

'No, I'm sorry. If I'm left with it, these are always very difficult to resell.'

'You'll no be left wi' it, John. Ah'll be back for it in less than a month.'

Ma leaned toward my ear. 'Lying bugger,' she whispered.

'Mmmmfff!' We both made noises as we tried not to laugh out loud.

'It's you that's startin' this time,' I managed to say after minute. I stretched up to her ear. 'Ah wonder whit they're trying tae pawn?'

Ma thought for a moment. 'A hand grenade – wi' the pin oot!' We immediately looked away from one another, funny noises coming out of us again.

After a struggle I said, 'That's jist stupid,' which set us off again. Then she spent the next few minutes trying to reply, but couldn't get it out, which made the two of us helpless. Finally, 'So why are we laughing?' that made us worse. By now we were into our usual 'pawnshop cycle' of finding everything hilarious, no matter how banal. Our sides ached, eyes ran with tears, and the close confines of the cubicle made us sweat. We attempted to calm ourselves down a bit by not looking at one another. That just set us off again.

As the disappointed customer left, John began to talk to another one in the next bay to us. Unfortunately, Ma recognised her voice. This meant she now went into her mime to try and inform me who it was. In the library-like silence, and severely constrained by the small cubicle, with a mixture of ventriloquism and an early form of the hand jive she endeavoured to inform me, 'That's Mrs McCaskill from up the tap of oor street.'

'Whit?'

This made her semaphore even more wildly. I tried to lip-read.

'Who?' I said loudly, screwing up my face in exasperation.

'Jeesusjonny! Never mind.' Her eyes gazed heavenward.

'Well, ah never know whit yer saying when ye dae that carry-oan.'

'Shh, shh!' We went into fits again, the quietness seeming to encourage us. Ma held her fingers to her lips, continually going 'shhh, shhh' until we finished up helpless and hardly able to get our breath. Eventually she said, 'Ah'm no bringing you up here again.'

'Ye said that last time,' I reminded her, and we went all useless again.

A loud bang signalled Mrs McCaskill's departure.

'Shh, behave yourself. Ah think it's us next.'

'It's no ma fault.'

John hove into view in front of us. For a moment he surveyed these two red-faced individuals, obviously having difficulty in looking serious. Ma cleared her throat. I looked at John. In his forties, with dark wavy hair and a fine, trimmed moustache, he always wore a grey buttoned overall just like my woodwork teacher at NKS. Ma held out her wedding ring in the palm of her hand.

'Can ah just huv the usual ten bob, John? It'll be oot again on Friday.'

'Yes, that'll be fine.'

He took the ring, wrote something on both halves of a buff-coloured ticket, tore it at the perforations and gave half to Ma. He didn't need to ask the name.

We made our spring-resisted exit from the cubicle with Ma gently cuffing me, as I still had the giggles. We trooped down the stairs and onto the Garscube Road. Ma put the ten-bob note into her purse as we stood on the pavement.

'Ehh, Ma. That wiz a good laugh, wizn't it?'

She smiled. 'How much dae ye need for yer dinner ticket?'

'Three and six.'

'Right. Will we huv a wee donner along tae Queen's Cross and huv an ice cream at Jaconelli's?'

'Oh aye, that wid be good.'

'C'mon then. Tae hell wi' poverty!'

Arm in arm, we set off along the Garscube Road.

Cancer is a Four-letter Word

'Dae ye remember that wee lump ah telt ye ah found on the side of ma chest?' 'Breast' wasn't a word a Glasgow mother would say to her son. Not in 1953.

'Aye.' I was reading and listening to *Take It From Here* on the radio at the same time.

'Dr McNicol's arranged for me tae go intae the Western tae get it cut oot. He says it's a cyst.'

I looked up. 'Intae the hospital? Tae stay in?'

Ma had never been in hospital. Not since she'd had me. She'd never been anywhere, without me.

'Ah'll jist be in a few days, less than a week. Yer faither's gettin' some leave tae come hame and look efter you while ah'm away.'

'Aww, diz he huv tae? Ah could look efter maself.'

Since he'd joined the RAF we'd hardly seen him. Now that he'd got himself a new fancy woman, down near Stranraer, he was home even less. It was great. For me, anyway.

'You cannae look efter yerself; you're only fourteen. I'd get hauled ower the coals if ah left ye tae fend for yerself.'

The thought of there being just him and me in the house for a few days was not a pleasant one. Even though we seldom saw him now, when he did come home for a week's leave or a long weekend, he still got drunk on a Saturday night and, most times, caused a row. I didn't fancy the idea of Ma not being there.

He arrived home in uniform. With his corporal's stripes and five colourful medal ribbons he always looked smart. Respectable.

Next day Ma went into the Western and the following day had her operation.

The couple of days since he'd come home had passed reasonably well. He was his normal sarcastic, scowling-faced self. When he'd spoken it had been, as usual, to tell me off or complain in general. So far I hadn't been hit, but I hadn't been allowed to stay out as long as my pals. I was sent to bed earlier than usual and, after ten minutes or so, he would tell me to, 'Put the comic doon and get tae sleep.'

As we were both in the same room, and he was listening to the radio with the main light on, this was a tall order. The programme was one of my favourites too, *Ray's a Laugh*. I just lay with my eyes shut, listening to it. After a few minutes I turned to face the wall and buried my face under the covers, as though hiding from the light. I was making sure he didn't see me smiling. If he thought I was enjoying the show, just for spite he would almost certainly switch it off.

The evening after Ma's wee op we went to see her. She was propped up by loads of pillows and was wearing a specially bought green nylon nightie with a lacy neck. I'd never seen her in a nightie before. At home she slept in her slip.

When she moved she seemed to be in pain. We were only in a few minutes when she called to a nurse that she felt sick. Just in time she was handed a fairly large, stainless-steel bowl. I watched as she repeatedly vomited into it, filling it right to the brim. It looked like soup. I didn't like this. I didn't like to see my ma not well, see her in pain, stuck in the hospital.

The smell of antiseptic and disinfectant and just having watched Ma being sick was making me feel queasy. I was only half-listening to their conversation – when something registered. I turned to Ma.

'Ah thought you were just gettin' a wee lump cut oot, Ma?'

She tried to smile. 'Ah, well, ye see, when they opened it up

. . . there wiz a bit more than they expected – so they had tae—' My father interrupted: 'They've hud tae take yer mother's right breast aff!'

The word 'cancer' wasn't mentioned. It wouldn't have made any difference if it had been. I barely knew the word. But I knew, somehow, that something bad was going on. At thirty-four Ma, or any other woman, shouldn't be having a breast cut off. As I sat at the side of her bed a feeling of dread came over me. I felt isolated. Powerless.

When, out of the blue, my father had joined the RAF for five years, I'd felt it was one of the best things that had ever happened to me. The future looked good. Now, in an instant, it had all turned to shite. I was in the middle of a bad dream – but I wasn't sleeping. A shaft of cold fear stabbed me in the stomach. I wasn't going to have my ma for much longer. With a terrible certainty I knew it. I looked at her. She knew it too. Already she looked different. Smaller. She knew she was going to die. I could tell she was filled with the same awful fear that had hit me. But worse for her.

I was going to lose my mammy. Why was God doing this?

As my father and I travelled home on the tram the optimism of youth began to reassert itself. Ma was really quite young, that's why they'd taken her into the hospital, to give her the treatment she needed to get better. She hadn't looked very well because it was so soon after her operation. As the tram wheels squealed their usual complaints as they went through the points at St George's Cross and we started up the Maryhill Road, I thought of a million reasons to convince myself Ma was going to get better. I'd even try praying – though why God had let her get sick in the first place was hard to understand. If He'd been doing the right thing it should be this rotten, wee bastard sitting next to me who should be lying in the Western, and Ma and me going home on the tram.

*

A few days later I came home from school. Ma was in the house! She looked just like normal. The dinner was on, the fire was lit, she was wearing her wraparound peenie. Then I noticed her right bust was flat; just like a man's chest. I tried not to look, but it kept drawing my eyes.

'They've given me something to put inside ma bra that'll make me look awright. Ah'm a wee bit tender roon there at the minute, so ah huvnae put it in. Ah should be able tae wear it next week.'

I felt myself blush; she had noticed me staring.

'Ah'll be going back an' forrit tae the hospital for the next few weeks. They're gonny be giving me this Radiotherapy Treatment, then after that ah'll be finished wi' the hospital.'

This sounded good. I began to feel better about everything.

Ma was soon back to her normal routine. Going out every day to her wee charring job at some toff's house over in Hillhead. Still smoking, just like she always had. Everybody smoked. My father went back to camp, and his fancy woman. It was just Ma and me again. Within a couple of weeks she began having her weekly night out with Mrs Cameron, 'Aunty Nicky', at the old-time dancing in the F&F Ballroom over in Partick. Things were back to normal.

As the months went past and Ma looked fine I almost forgot her operation and the terrible fear which had gripped me. Everything was going to be all right. Of course, I never asked her if that was her better. I didn't ask in case, maybe, she'd say,

'Well, no' yet.'

As far as I was concerned, if she looked all right, she must be all right.

Ostriches have the right idea.

Thirty Pieces of Silver . . .

'Dr McNicol's arranged for me tae huv a fortnight in the convalescent home at Kilmun.'

Ma stood at the sink peeling tatties as she spoke. She was wearing her 'housewife's uniform' of wraparound peenie, topped off by a Paisley patterned scarf worn as a turban.

'What for?' I began emptying my school bag of that day's books, preparatory to looking at my timetable then loading it up with tomorrow's.

'Jist for a wee break tae build me up a bit. It's sort of like a hotel. Ye get aw' yer meals cooked and spend maist of the time jist reading, listening tae the wireless, and resting. Things like that. It'll be lovely. They're sending yer faither up tae RAF Bishopbriggs for a fortnight so he can look after you while ah'm away.'

'So there'll jist be ma faither and me.'

'He'll be at Bishopbriggs maist o' the time, you'll only see him in the evenings.'

'Huh, even that's too much.'

There was no alternative. A few days later Ma went off for her much-needed holiday. She was really looking forward to it. Surprisingly, the first week passed reasonably well. Each evening, after my father had made the dinner, I'd go out and hang about with my pals until nine. During the week I always had to be in by nine. Once indoors I'd keep out of his way as best I could, a difficult feat in a single-end. I'd settle myself in a corner, reading, or sit by the end of the sideboard and listen to the wireless. Around twenty to ten he'd announce, 'C'mon, you, time ye were in yer bed.'

Five minutes later I would be. He'd wait until I was absorbed in a story, 'Right, put that comic doon, you, and get some shut-eye.'

I'd put the comic on the floor just under the bed-chair, turn on my side, and lie with my eyes shut, listening to the radio until it lulled me to sleep. He always had the radio on.

Although I had to put up with his usual scathing or sarcastic remarks, there had been no 'belts on the lug' forthcoming. Ma not being there to witness them probably spoiled his fun. It was the Saturday night in the middle of Ma's fortnight. Wearing his RAF uniform, bedecked with its five medal ribbons and corporal's stripes, he was all spruced up ready to go out to the pub,

'You can stay oot till half-nine, but make sure you're in for then. Ah might come hame early, and if ah find you're no' in ye know whit you'll fuckin' get when ye dae come in! So, be warned.'

'Ah'll be in.'

'Ye'd better.'

With his advance warning ringing in my ears I watched as, without another word, he set off for his usual 'Setterday night oot'. I listened to the sound of his tackety boots echoing back through the close then, just before he stepped out into the street, he began to whistle. I glanced up at the mantelpiece. Ma's letter was still there, nestling behind the alarm clock. It had arrived after he'd left for the camp. On his return this evening he'd opened it, read it, then stuck it behind the clock. He hadn't bothered to tell me what she'd said, or let me read it. Before reaching for it I carefully took note of its exact position behind the alarm. I wouldn't put it past him to deliberately memorise how he'd placed it so as he'd know if I'd read it. I did the same before removing the two-page letter, noting how it was folded and placed in the envelope. Ma's letter began, 'Dear Bobby and Robert Jnr . . .' She went on to say she was fair enjoying the rest, the meals were lovely and her fellow patients very friendly. Just as I thought she would, she had written a few lines 'just for Robert'. They said she was missing me and, even though she was having a nice time, she was still looking forward to seeing me when she got home. I carefully inserted the two sheets of paper back into the envelope and replaced it behind the clock.

I went up for John Purden. As my curfew wouldn't allow us time to go to the pictures, we went for a donner down one side of Maryhill Road as far as St George's Cross, then returned up the opposite one. The remaining time was spent in Cocozza's. I was safely back indoors with five minutes to spare.

Around ten p.m. I was sitting at the table aimlessly playing with a few foreign coins various uncles had brought me from their wartime travels and listening to a variety programme on the wireless when I heard the sound of him trying to put his key in the lock. As ever, even though I hadn't done anything, I felt that little frisson of fear in my stomach; how drunk would he be? What sort of mood would he be in? As he finally got the outer door opened, I heard voices. Female voices!

'In ye's come,' said my father, 'go on.'

The door into the room opened and in came two women. The elder would probably be in her late forties – older than my father – the younger, perhaps mid-twenties. They would prove to be mother and daughter. The daughter was heavily pregnant. They both smiled at me, the older said, 'Hello.' My father didn't bother to introduce me. Instead, he spoke to me,

'Sit over there.' He pointed to the fireside chair. 'We need the table.' As I rose, the heavy-built older woman said, 'You must be Robert?'

I smiled in return, 'Aye.'

Her daughter also said, 'Hello.'

'It's not "aye",' said my father, 'it's "yes".' He scowled at me. I felt my face go red.

'Och, leave the poor laddie alone,' said the mother. She turned to me, 'It's "yes" in England, and "aye" in Scotland, isn't it, son?'

Glad of the support, I gave a nervous smile, 'Yes.'

She laughed, but I could tell it was not at me.

The two women sat down at the table and my father went to the press and fetched some glasses. On his way back to the table he switched off the wireless.

'We're no needing that bloody thing oan. Never hear oorselves talking.' He pulled out a chair and sat himself down beside the older woman.

I picked up my latest library book, one of Arthur Ransome's 'Swallows and Amazons' sagas, and pretended to read. I wondered who our visitors were. I knew my father had a sister, Jean, who hadn't been seen for years. But surely she would have said. Maybe it was someone who'd grown up in Northpark Street with my father.

Their conversation was all of the remember-this and remember-that variety, until, 'Dae ye think you'll ever get married again, Nell?'

NELL! The rest of what was said for the next few minutes didn't register. I felt my face flush and my scalp tingle. This was Big Nell! I couldn't have been more surprised if he'd brought Hitler back from the pub. This was the woman whose name I'd heard shouted and bawled since infancy. Imagine the wee bastard bringing her into the house. I wondered if she knew my ma had just had a breast off because of cancer, and was awa at a convalescent home. I looked at her. I'd assumed she w

'Big Nell' because she was really tall. She was taller than my father, but who wasn't? she was obviously 'Big' simply because she was hefty-built. How I wished I was older and could say something. For a moment I thought about it, but I was too scared of him. All that would happen was I'd guarantee myself a good hiding once they'd left. Anyway, he'd already brought her into our house. It was done.

I sat for a while looking at my book and listening to them talk.

'Are these your coins, Robert?'

Big Nell was jingling some of the coins I'd left on the table in the palm of her hand.

'Ahh, aye. Yes.'

'Ah've got a tin full of foreign coins in the house. Would ye like to have them?'

The three of them were looking at me. I wanted to say, 'Oh, it's all right, thanks aw the same.' But a wee voice in the back of my mind said, *A tin FULL of foreign coins. There might be some good ones amongst them*. I said, 'Oh, yes, thanks very much.'

They went back to their conversation. I went straight to purgatory. You two-faced bastard! That's Big Nell. How could you say yes to anything she offered you? Just think if Ma ever finds out. I tried to console myself. *If you'd refused he'd have given you a clout for being bad-mannered. Ah, I know, if she does give me them I'll definitely throw them in the midden. Aye, that's what I'll do*. I began to feel a bit better. The wee voice whispered again, *There would be no harm in looking through them first, there might be one or two beauts!* I tried to get back to my book. *I bet you don't throw them in the midden!*

Just before midnight Big Nell and her daughter took their leave. Ten minutes later I climbed into the bed-chair. My father settled 'mself into the recess bed. He put the light out straight away, he was on duty at Bishopbriggs in the morning. I lay in the dark, eyes wide open. Jeez! That was Big Nell. I was terrible at keeping secrets, but I knew it would be best not to tell Ma. It would just cause a terrific row. I determined I wouldn't tell her. And those coins. Probably it was just the drink talking; she'll forget all about them. Anyway, Ma's only away for another week. If she doesn't fetch them in the next few days she won't be able to bring them at all. I wonder how many there are? Eventually I nodded off into a troubled sleep.

In the morning my father was up and away by seven a.m. As it was Sunday he let me lie on, but couldn't resist a parting shot.

'Don't you be lying therr aw morning. Get yerself up by nine.'

'Okay,' I lied. By the time he'd reach the bottom of our street I was sound asleep.

From somewhere far away there was knocking, then I recognised the sound of our letterbox being rattled. I came awake with a start. Jeez! Maybe it's my father. Maybe he's come back for something and hasn't got his key. As I dived out of bed I glanced at the clock – quarter to ten. If it was him, as soon as I opened the door, still in my pyjamas, I'd get a belt. In my bare feet I staggered into the wee lobby and opened the door, whilst getting ready to duck. Standing in the shadowy close was – Big Nell!

She thrust her hand out. 'Here ye are, son.' She pressed a round object into my hand. When she let go, the weight of it caused my hand to drop a few inches. 'That's the coins ah promised ye. Cheerio.' She turned on her heel and walked away.

'Oh! Eh, thanks very much.' She didn't reply.

I was now wide awake, and a little excited at the thought that there must be quite a lot of coins in the tin. I also felt guilty.

I came back into the room, switching on the big light as I did I pulled a chair out from the table and was about to sit on when I realised it was the one Big Nell had used last night. Instead I chose the one her daughter had sat on. The tin of coins I placed in front of me on the bright, floral oilcloth. It was a round, metal Player's Navy Cut tin; the type that held fifty cigarettes. I remembered my Uncle George bringing one for Ma on one of his leaves. Most of the label still remained: the picture of a bearded sailor, framed by a lifebelt. The lid came off easily and I poured a stash of coins onto the table. 'Gee!' There seemed to be coins from all over the world. Amongst them were some silver coins: American quarter dollars and Swiss francs – I knew from my stamp album that 'Helvetia' meant Switzerland. A few days later I took these silver ones into the bank on the corner of Raeberry Street and got eight shillings for them. Somehow, that made me feel better.

At last Saturday came, and Ma was back. She was looking, and feeling, a lot better. She'd even caught some sun. Once Da had left, we quickly settled into our old routine. I felt confident that Ma's operation, and her wee holiday, had finally seen off that cancer thing. If she was *really* ill, she wouldn't look so well. Ma's obviously going to be all right. There's nothing to worry about.

It was a couple of weeks later when Ma noticed how many coins I had now.

'Where did ye get aw these?'

I had been rehearsing; I always found it difficult to lie to Ma.

'Ah swapped some American comics and some soldiers wi' Billy Brittain.'

I willed my face not to flush. I got away with it.

It was no good. During the next couple of weeks every time I played with them I got pangs of guilt. I'd be sitting at the table with the coins, Ma would be bustling about doing something and I'd be conscious all the time that – *Big Nell gave you these!*

At least I managed to keep my mouth shut and she never did find out he'd brought his long-term fancy woman to the house. But the coins had to go. I finished up swapping them for two jigsaws – one of 500 pieces, the other 1,000. When I made them up I found the 500 had two pieces missing. The big one was six short. I didn't bother asking for the coins back.

Uncle George: D-Day + 9 Years

He'd already arrived when I came home from school, another unexpected visit. For him too.

'Uncle George! Ah didnae know you was coming.'

He gave a tired smile. 'Me neither. It's just a flying visit.'

Immediately I sensed I shouldn't get enthusiastic; something wasn't right. There was no spark about him. He was slumped in a fireside chair. He wasn't drunk, but I could smell drink. When I'd come in he and Ma had been sitting at the fireplace, drinking tea. I got the feeling I'd interrupted something, that they still wanted to talk.

'Have you got any homework tae dae?'

'Ma, ye know ah always huv homework tae dae.'

'Well, jist get oan wi' it the noo; yer dinner'll be a wee bit later.'

She and George started talking again, in lowered voices. Jeez! When am I *ever* gonny be considered old enough tae be able tae listen tae big people's conversations? Ah'm fourteen. Ah'm no a wean.

I pretended I was deeply engrossed in my books, doing plenty of page-turning, writing things down, and occasionally leaning toward to study something intently. This lulled them into thinking I was paying no attention. Even so, when they reached crucial bits of their conversation they lowered their voices even more, left a sentence unfinished, or alluded to what they meant. In every case I understood what they were saying. Never missed a word! There were no secrets in a single-end.

The gist of it was that George and Joan had split up, his

drinking being a major factor in the breakdown of their short marriage. But there were others. When he was drunk he'd often knock her about and, the one that I found hard to believe, *he* was jealous of her. With the blindness of hero worship, I couldn't figure out how this man, whom I'd watched attract and discard beautiful women by the dozen, could be jealous. Since childhood I had sat at his side and watched all the women in the room follow his every move, laugh at the least of his jokes, make plain they were available. How could *he* be jealous of just one woman? But he was. I'd heard him say it himself.

As the two people I loved most in the world spoke, I looked at him. It was just over a year since he'd visited to show off his new bride. The gabardine mac was now stained and creased. The honeymoon suit only slightly better. He had a bad pallor. At twenty-eight, the golden boy was sadly tarnished. He would find little comfort with us.

During the two nights he stayed, sleeping in a makeshift bed on the floor, I overheard Ma telling him about her operation, treatment, consultants. He'd always been the 'baby brother' to her 'big sister'. To find out his beloved only sister had cancer, on top of his own troubles, must have left him as low as could be. I listened to them talk for a while about when they were children. Ma, the oldest, was born in 1918. George, the youngest, in 1925. They had been born in Sandyford Street in the Kelvinhaugh district, an old riverside area of the city near Partick. The tenement blocks of Sandyford Street were old even then, having been built in the mid-1800s. Their mother, Maud McIntosh, was well known as a 'spaewife', a fortune teller. She read the teacups – if you crossed her palm with silver. The money came in handy; her husband, James McIntosh, a journeyman brass finisher, was sometimes unemployed in the twenties and thirties. Even when he was in work, money was often short. James was an inveterate gambler.

*

Uncle George, weeks after I got in touch with him, 1997.

Uncle George and I stood outside Cocozza's. Trams wandered up and down the Maryhill Road, slowly finding their way through a murky November evening. He seemed incapable of standing still, preferring to pace to and fro as we spoke. Occasionally he whistled a few bars of 'Paper Doll'. The Mills Brothers' old hit was back in the charts. Sometimes he sang a bit. He stopped pacing, stood in front of me.

'God! Ah'm dying fur a drink. Have ye any money, Robert?'

I could see the pleading in his eyes. I had half-a-crown. I'd been hoping to raise another tanner and that would be enough for two nights at the pictures. At fourteen, half-a-crown was a lot of money to me. But, this was my Uncle George.

'Will ah get it back?' I asked, lamely.

'Next week. Definitely.' He could sense it was almost his. 'Tell ye what, ah'll gie ye an IOU.' He took a penknife from his pocket and, on top of the green-painted junction box that stood on the corner, he scored '*IOU 2/6d – George*.' This made me laugh; the half-crown was his! I handed over the coin and immediately he headed for the nearest pub. I told myself that there was really nothing on at the pictures I'd wanted to see that week.

The following day, while I was at school, he left. As 1953 became 1954 I'd often stand at Cocozza's corner with my pals. I'd lean on the junction box and, when no one was looking, I'd glance down: *IOU 2/6d – George*. If I was on my own I'd sometimes trace it with my finger and wonder where he was. Later in the year the Corporation painted the junction box and my IOU was lost forever. I never saw him again.

Forty-four years later, in 1997, after a major effort I tracked him down to Reefton, a small town in South Island, New Zealand. He had emigrated there in 1956. He had never remarried and his drink problem continued for the rest of his life.

He was very pleased I'd taken the trouble to find him, and we corresponded for just three months until, sadly, a series of

Uncle George's medals

strokes took him to where I couldn't reach him. He died on 12 January 2002, aged seventy-six.

Although it could be said he had feet of clay, when I was a child he was always my favourite uncle. When I think of him, two pictures flash into my mind. The handsome young Marine, smart as paint, brightening up a dismal Glasgow back court as he slips away to meet one girl – while standing up another. Then, late at night, me by his side as he sits at a blanket-covered table playing cards. Uniform tunic open at the neck, cigarette dangling from his lips, one eye shut against the rising smoke as he surveys his cards – and the red-lipsticked, permanent-waved girls watch his every move. And Normandy's Juno beach is just weeks away.

A couple of months after his death I received his medals – four from the Second World War, two from Korea. They now hang framed with a photo of him, aged eighteen, in uniform, forage cap defying gravity on the side of his head.

There was also a money-order for £900! He'd promised me I'd get my half-crown back.

Ring in the . . . What?

'Can ah stay up past the bells the night and go oot first-footing wi' Sammy?'

Ma looked at me. 'How far will ye be goin'?'

'Jist roond oor ain bit. Jist local.'

'Well, make sure ye dae. And don't be drinking anything stronger than ginger. You're only fourteen, remember.'

'Great! Thanks, Ma.'

I dashed round to Sammy's with the good news. It was the last day of December, 1953. Hogmanay. This would be my first venture at being out and about 'after the bells' on my own. Until now I'd always brought in the New Year in the house with my ma and, if he was there, my da. I felt this was another stage in growing up.

'My ma say's it's awright,' I informed Sammy.

'We'll huv tae get oorselves a bottle,' he said, 'ye cannae go intae folks' hooses empty-handed.'

Sammy was a year older and, presumably, a year wiser.

'Ah huvnae enough money fur whisky,' I said. I knew a bottle of whisky was the norm.

'Neether huv ah; we'll jist get something cheap. As long as we huv a bottle of some kind. They know we're jist boys, they'll no expect us tae huv whisky.'

We made our way to the licensed grocers on the Maryhill Road where Sammy purchased a bottle of VP Wine at 3/6d. VP, known by its initials to the cognoscenti as Vomitable Products, was a cheap wine much beloved by its devotees: those wanting to get blotto on a limited budget. Not wishing to be outdone, I topped Sammy by lashing out 3/11d on a bottle of Sanatogen. Only later, to my mortification, did I find out it was a 'tonic' wine, highly recommended for invalids.

'Well, if ah pour it wi' the label turned away from them, naebody will notice.'

As the evening wore on the excitement in the street became palpable as households got ready for the biggest night of the year. All day there had been a queue, of cinema proportions, outside the pawnshop on Garscube Road as folk endeavoured to raise money to ensure they'd have enough food and drink in to entertain visitors. Families, no matter how poor the rest of the year, would be black-affronted if any callers at their house that night found there was a shortage of comestibles.

All day the local butcher's, Craigs and Guthries, had been dishing up 'ashet pies', many ordered weeks ago. All containing the 'Finest Scotch Beef and Kidney'. Bakers were selling 'black bun' and shortbread by the hundredweight. Even so, in half the houses in the street ovens were never cool as grannies came into their own preparing, to their own recipes, dumpling, black bun, shortbread and Dundee cake.

Sniff! 'Nane o' yer shop-bought stuff in this hoose.'

Sammy and I weren't meeting until 'after the bells', so I spent the evening in and out of my pals' houses for short visits, seeing what was happening and soaking up the atmosphere. It was wonderful. For years, at Christmas and New Year, I had often looked up at brightly lit, steamed-up windows in street and back court and wondered what was going on as neighbours prepared for the festivities. Now I could find out.

In every house, as you entered, the dominant smell was of cooking and baking. Grannies, mammies and older daughters bustled about, wiping brows with backs of hands, complaining about men being in the way, and declaring at regular intervals,

'We're never gonny be ready in time for the bells!' They would. But a bit of martyrdom made them feel better.

Some of the fathers and older sons had started their celebrations a trifle early, much to the annoyance of most of the females.

'If you huv any mair you'll never see the bells!'

Face flushed, the older males spent most of their time geeing up the mothers and daughters and regularly trying to steal something from the growing feast being laid out. The nearer it came to midnight, the more food and drink appeared on the table. As I left each house after my tour of inspection, I'd be reminded, 'Don't forget tae come back efter the bells, Robert. This is yer first year oot, so we expect tae see ye.'

'But ah'll be wi' ma pal Sammy fae Maryhill Road.'

'So what? Bring him tae. That door'll be opened at midnight an' everybody's welcome.'

A couple of minutes later I'd be in another pal's house. The man of the house would be at the sink, shaving, or would be in shirt sleeves and braces trying, in vain, to get his back collar stud in.

'Gonny put these studs in fur me, hen?'

'Och, see you, cannae dae a thing fur yersel'.'

'Gie's a wee kiss while yur here, hen.'

'Behave yersel'.'

Daughters in their late teens and early twenties were a delight to watch – I was beginning to take an interest. Girls who just a year or two ago I considered as 'big lassies' were now all of a sudden young women. They'd emerge from the bedroom, hair not combed out, hands behind their back as they tried to zip up their new frock. I'd try not to make it too obvious, but I found it hard to keep my eyes off them. They really were different from us. They'd stand in front of the mirror above the fireplace to do their face and hair. I'd notice how shapely they had become. With a couple of kirby grips held between their lips, forehead already glistening a little because of the heat in the kitchen, I'd wonder why they bothered with make-up to cover their youthful, freshly scrubbed beauty.

I envied the grown-up sons their extra years as I watched them leisurely groom themselves. On coming home from work today, most had headed up to the Steamie for a bath. Now they stood in front of the mirror knotting their tie or Brylcreeming their hair.

'You gonny be in front of that mirror aw night?' a sister would complain.

'Nearly finished, keep the heid,' the Young Pretender would reply, turning to me and winking. 'Got tae get maself jist right for the girls, eh Robert?'

'Aye, that's right, Billy.'

'Huv you got a girlfriend yet, Robert?' the sister would ask. I'd blush and try to think what would be the best reply to that. The father would come to my rescue.

'If he's got any sense he'll keep well away from you lot. You'll never huv any money in yer poaket if ye get mixed up wi' the lassies, Robert.' I'd laugh and blush even more.

'Whit aboot this, then?' All heads turned. The son had put on the jacket of his new suit. 'Gabardine, double-breasted, edge stitching oan the lapels. Twelve guineas, made tae measure at Hector Powe's doon the toon!'

I looked. Gee! Glasgow guys really knew how to dress. When I left school and started working I was going to 'go in my ain can' – just pay my Ma dig money, and have the rest for buying good clothes, going to the dancing and the pictures. That's what most lads in their late teens did nowadays.

'Aw, yer really smart, son.' His mother's eyes moistened as she spoke.

'Better enjoy it while ye can, pal,' his father reminded him. 'When ye finish yer apprenticeship ye'll be off tae the Army for yer two years.'

'Gie us a break, Da. Thanks fur reminding me.'

'Huh! Think yersel' lucky. Ah hud tae dae *five* years withoot the option – and ah hud angry Germans shooting at me at regular intervals!'

Once more I left with invitations to, 'Mind and come back the night, Robert.'

Back home I had something to eat with Ma then the two of us spent what seemed like a long evening listening to the radio. As the sound of Big Ben announced 1954 I, as usual, gave Ma a self-conscious kiss and we wished one another 'A Happy New Year'. She wasn't going to any of the neighbours'.

'When you go oot tae meet Sammy, ah'll jist go tae ma bed for a read.'

Sammy and I rendezvoused at a quarter past midnight. I felt guilty at leaving Ma in the house. If I'd said, 'Will I jist stay in with ye, Ma?' I know she'd have answered, 'Don't talk nonsense. Away oot and enjoy yerself. Ah'm going tae ma bed.' I felt guilty about not offering. Trouble was, I hadn't offered just in case she said, 'That'll be nice, son.' I knew it would be in the back of my mind all night.

'Right, where'll we go first?' Sammy rubbed his hands together in anticipation. The bottle of VP weighed down his jacket pocket, making him look a bit lopsided. We stood in the middle of Doncaster Street and looked up at the host of lit, welcoming windows. Music echoed down, shadows moved across blinds, there were regular busts of laughter and song as folk 'hooched and hawed' to Jimmy Shand. 1954 was being made welcome. Ma was probably in bed. I wondered if she was crying. My father, no doubt, would be at Stranraer bringing in the New Year with his fancy woman.

It was a fine, dry night, not even cold. Sammy and I started with a few quick visits to three or four houses where it was obvious there were good parties in full swing. In each we were made welcome and plied with food and soft drinks. 'Don't you be giving they boys strong drink.' The Mothers Mafia was on the alert in all premises. Offers of a drink from 'oor bottles' were politely refused. 'Eh, ah'm drinking whisky, Robert, so ah'd mibbe better no mix it wi' wine. Jist a wee precaution ye understand. Thanks anywye.'

'C'mon, we'll go up tae the McDonalds',' I suggested, 'they alwiz huv a rerr time at New Year.'

Outside the McDonalds' close stood a low-loader with half a prefab on it. These prefabricated aluminium bungalows, designed to help alleviate the post-war housing shortage, were delivered to the sites in two halves. This was John McDonald's lorry. John, the former owner of the 'biscuit tin on wheels'.

Not having any takers for our wine, we had begun to gulp the occasional wee mouthful ourselves – just to save it being wasted.

'Mibbe we should chap the prefab's door and wish them a happy New Year,' suggested Sammy.

'There's nae light oan. Ah don't think they're in.' We went into paroxysms of laughter. 'Here, huv a try of this Sanatogen, Sammy.' I watched as he took a good swig. He screwed his face up,

'It's murder polis, in't it?' He handed me his. 'Try this, VP also stands fur Virgin's Piss!'

'S'no much better, is it?'

We entered the close and knocked on the McDonalds' half-open door. It was immediately flung wide open.

'Happy New Year!' chorused Sammy and me.

'Happy New Year, boys, and many o' them. Come away in the perr of ye,' said Mr McDonald senior. 'It's wee Robert Douglas and his pal,' he bawled to the assembled company. 'Whit's yer name, son?' Sammy told him. 'May ah announce Robert Douglas and his pal, Sammy – Sammy the Pal,' shouted Mr McDonald. He turned back to us. 'Naebody pays any attention tae me in here. Anywye, boys, ye's are very welcome.' He laid a hand on my shoulder. 'How's yer mother, Robert?'

'Aw, she's no too bad.' That was all I ever said. He squeezed my shoulder.

'She's a grand wee wumman, yer mother. Everybody should look efter their mother.' I could see his eyes were misty. 'Anywye, you enjoy yerself, son. All the best tae ye.'

I felt a bit moist-eyed too what with his sincerity *and* the Sanatogen.

Sammy nudged me. 'C'mon, let's mingle, especially wi' the lassies.'

We began to go round the company, shaking hands and getting kisses from all the women and girls. Most of the teenage lasses kissed us on the lips. One or two lingered. I began to feel a bit light-headed. I hadn't known kisses could do that to you.

'Hey!' said Sammy. 'It's bloody great in here. Ah think we should stay here fur a while.'

John McDonald, prefab deliverer, was in conversation with Alec McKinstrey who lived up my close. Both had served in the Royal Navy during the recent unpleasantness with Germany and now, with a good drink in them, were reminiscing. After exchanging greetings with them I stood listening to their tales.

'Here!' said John, looking around in an exaggerated way to make sure he wasn't being overheard. 'Ah've got a bottle of hame-made stuff, made tae the recipe we used on board ship. Want some?'

'Aye,' said Alec. 'Ah'm gemme.'

John went to the kitchen press and returned bearing an old whisky bottle containing a cloudy grey liquid.

'Wee bit o' sediment in therr, ah think, John.'

'Och aye. Ah think it could huv done wi' a wee bit mair dipstiller, dispiller . . . eh, time,' said John, 'then left tae mature fur a wee while.'

'When did ye lay it doon?' enquired Alec.

'Yesterday moarning!' The two of them went helpless with laughter. 'On board ship it wiz always called "The Coodoo",' said John.

'The Coodoo; why did ye's call it that?' asked Alec.

'Ah'll tell ye later,' said John.

They both swallowed a generous measure, and shuddered in unison. Alec opened his mouth to say something. A sound somewhat akin to the call of a peacock being strangled emerged.

'Noo ye know why we called it the Coodoo,' said John.

Alec managed to get his breath back. 'Ye didnae accidentally bring the turps bottle by mistake, did ye?'

'Are ye for another wan?' invited John.

'Och aye.'

Some forty minutes later their prone bodies were carted through to the front room and laid, side by side, on the bed settee. It would be late in the evening of the first of January before they managed to rise.

By three a.m. Sammy and I had had enough. We had visited nine or ten houses, kissed lots of girls and abandoned our New Year bottles somewhere en route. Tired, but still flushed with pleasure from my maiden voyage into first-footing, I climbed into my bed-chair and lay in the dark, tired but content. My mind still buzzed from all the sights, sounds and laughs.

Ma's voice came from out of the dark: 'Did ye have a nice time, son?'

'Aye. It wiz smashin', Ma. We want tae stacks o' hooses.'

'That's good. Ye can tell me aw aboot it in the morning. Ye'd better get some sleep.'

'Okay. 'Night, Ma. Happy New Year, again.'

'Aye, Happy New Year, son.'

Finding Out

I came in the close, managed to find the keyhole in the dark little corner where our door was, and just as I was about to open the inner door, I heard movement.

I entered the room. 'Hiyah, Ma. Are ye hame al—' It was my father, in uniform. 'Oh, hello Da.' I hadn't known he was due on leave. I could smell beer on him. He must have had a couple of pints before coming home. 'Ma didnae say ye were coming hame.'

'Ah'll be hame a lot more in future. Ah've been posted tae RAF Bishopbriggs.' He looked closely at me. 'Permanently!'

I tried not to let the disappointment show in my face. Jesusjonny. Bishopbriggs was just on the outskirts of the city. Trams ran to it. This meant he would now be home regularly. Just my poxy luck.

'Ah was hoping ye'd be hame before yer mother. Listen . . .' He coughed to clear his throat. He almost sounded nervous. 'You know when your mother had that operation?'

'Aye.' I heard my voice crack. My face felt hot, inside. My whole body went stiff. He's gonny tell me something bad about Ma. Why can't he jist fuck off? All ah ever hear nowadays is bad news about Ma. If ah have tae hear something bad about her ah *don't* want tae hear it from him.

'Dae ye know yer Ma's got cancer?'

'Naw.'

'Well, she has.' He paused. 'And the doctors have given her only six months tae live!'

I burst into tears. Rocky Marciano had just punched me in

the stomach. Six months. I didn't know much about cancer. But I knew what six months were. *Six months!*

'Ah thought she was gonny be awright after yon treatment?'

'It huznae worked. The cancer had already spread too far, even before her operation. There's nuthin' they can dae for her.'

I sat on the fireside chair and cried into my hankie. It was soon soaked. I wished he'd bugger off back to the pub. I didn't want him watching me, he's probably enjoying it. I just wanted to be on my own to get my cry out. I couldn't with him in the room.

'Your ma doesn't know I'm telling ye, but you'll huv tae know sometime. Ah think it'll be best if ye jist carry on as if ye didn't know. Whit dae ye think?'

'Aye, it might be best.' How am I supposed to do that? Every time I look at her, the first thing that will enter my head is, my ma's just got months to live.

'Away and splash yer face wi' cauld watter, then when she comes in it'll no look as if ye've been greetin'.'

I walked over to the sink, its wooden draining board and surround scrubbed white by years of Ma's attention with brush and Fairy washing soap. I turned on the lone, gleaming brass tap. As I splashed my face with cold water I caught sight of my face in its curved spout. I looked like Jiminy Cricket. I wondered how many more times Ma would Brasso the tap.

My father sat down and began to read the *Daily Record*. I started to empty my school bag into the big cupboard. I looked at the timetable pinned on the inside of its door and selected the books I'd need for tomorrow. All the time my head was whirling. Six months. Surely they could still do something for Ma. In six months I would be just fifteen. What's gonny happen to me? He'll still be in the RAF – anyway, he'll want to be away with his fancy woman. I'll not be going to live with her, that's for certain. I'd rather go into a home. Jeez, I wish I was a bit older and working, then I could keep the house on and he could fuck off wherever he wanted. But best would be if I don't lose my ma. GOD, GONNY LET MY MA GET BETTER, PLEASE. SHE'S NO A BIG IMPORTANT WUMMAN BUT SHE'S A REALLY GOOD MA, YOU KNOW THAT. COULD YE NO LET HER GET BETTER? YOU COULD DAE IT IF YE WANTED. IT WIDNAE MAKE ANY DIFFERENCE TAE THE REST OF THE WORLD, BUT IT WOULD MEAN A LOT TAE MY MA AND ME. GONNY DAE IT, GOD. PLEASE.

We heard the familiar footsteps in the close, then the outside door being opened. I pretended to be still footering with my books. Ma came in. I felt like bursting out crying. Maybe it was a good job he was in or I probably would have.

'It's no half raining oot there.'

'Hiyah, Ma!' I had to act like normal.

'Did ye get on all right at the school, the day?'

'Aye, fine.'

She turned to my father. 'Have ye been in long?'

'Naw, half an hour or so. Ah sorted oot ma kit in ma new billet, then they gave me the rest of the day aff. Ah report for duty at eight in the morning.'

'Whit's the arrangement gonny be while you're there?'

'Ah jist come hame every night like ah wiz a civvy. Only if ah'm oan special duty or late duty will ah spend a night in the camp.'

As I listened, it suddenly occurred to me that Ma had shown no surprise when she found him in. She'd been expecting him. She knew he was coming to Bishopbriggs. This must be a special posting, because she's going to get worse. What he'd just told me is really true. Once more a shaft of fear hit me in the stomach. Ma hadn't told me he was coming to Bishopbriggs. If she had, I'd have wanted to know why. My ma's not going to get better. And now he's going to be around the house a lot. No doubt with his face tripping him because he can't get away to Stranraer. The wee bastard will take it out on me. I'll get the brunt of it. Why the fuck am I so unlucky? And my ma? Jeez, ah thought she was gonny get better. What about her? God, why is all this happening tae us?

With the selfishness of youth, and immaturity, I didn't realise fully – or try to imagine – what like it must have been for Ma. At thirty-five, fighting a losing battle with cancer, ill from the radiotherapy treatment, worried to death over what would happen to me, and married to a pig's bastard who would rather be elsewhere. No wonder I'd often come into the house and find her alone, sitting in the gloom, a towel in her lap into which she'd been crying. A hankie wasn't big enough. I'd feel terrible when I'd find her, but never know what to do. I was at that awkward, shy age, where it was embarrassing to kiss or hug my mother. I'd stand beside her, stupid, helpless and upset. Sometimes I'd put my hand on her shoulder. I'd wish she'd stop crying or, to my eternal shame, do her crying before I came home.

It's Off to Work We Go

The compassionate posting didn't last long. The compassion was missing. He soon got fed up with being at Bishopbriggs, having to come home every evening and not seeing his paramour. Within a couple of months he began to engineer rows with Ma two and three times a week, usually by picking on me for the least thing. Eventually, Ma told him to 'bugger off back to Stranraer'. His objective achieved, within days he'd arranged to be posted back to RAF West Freugh in Wigtownshire and off he went. His wife could die without him. But, for Ma and me, life went on.

'Have you made up your mind yet whit you're gonny dae when ye leave the school? Ye'd better get yer thinking cap on; it's only a couple of months tae Easter.' Ma served out the corned-beef fritters as she spoke.

I'd turned fifteen in February '54 and it wouldn't be long until Easter. I'd been so looking forward to escaping the tyranny of Harry Forshaw I hadn't given much thought to what sort of job I should look for. I wouldn't accept the fact that Ma was going to die, yet deep down I must have felt there wasn't a lot of point in getting excited about planning my future. Although he hadn't said anything, I knew that if Ma died, I wouldn't be included in any plans my father had. One way or another, he'd find a way to unload me. Then he'd be free.

'Do ye fancy taking up a trade?' She shovelled some big, fat chips onto my plate.

'Aye, ah might see if ah can start an apprenticeship at the North British Locomotive Company, up in Springburn.' Where had that come from? I hadn't a clue. It had just come into my head.

'What trade are ye thinking of taking up?'

Aw God, Ma. Ah cannae keep making aw this stuff up. She poured me a mug of freshly brewed tea. I thought quickly.

'Ahh, a turner.' The father of one of my pals was a turner. I'd have to keep going through the motions. It would all be a waste of time, but what could I do? She'd never see me through an apprenticeship, but I couldn't say that.

'What diz a turner dae?' I knew she'd ask that. She sat down opposite me and started her dinner.

'Ahmm, they make small metal bits and pieces on their lathe. Bolts and rods and things. It's tae dae wi' engineering an' that.' This seemed to satisfy her. I had no alternative now, I couldn't upset her by not doing anything about it. We would both have to play the game right to the end – as if the future was unlimited. I'd have to start an apprenticeship.

I jumped off the tram just as it turned into the Springburn Road. Like most male Glaswegians from teens onward, I was getting to be an expert at 'The Art of Alighting from a Moving Tram'. This was a rite of passage. Part of being a man. To exit gracefully from a tram in motion – the faster it was going the better – made one appear 'dead gallus'. The technique I had adopted was 'lean backwards off the step, let go the handrail and kick against the step at the same time.' It's not as easy as it sounds. By moving back, at the right speed, you cancel out the forward momentum of the tram. Result? You appear to step off a speeding tram and hit the ground strolling nonchalantly!

Springer once started a rumour that now and again in the city in the vicinity of a tram stop, half a dozen chairs were set up behind a long table. 'Judges' took their places at the table and, as callow youths and young men exited from speeding trams, the judges held up cards giving points.

I stopped the first man who came along.

'Could ye tell me how tae get tae the North British Locomotive Company, mister?'

'Aye, the NB Loco, son.' He pointed across the road. 'Just go doon that street therr, Flemington Street, and turn left intae Ayr Street. Ye cannae miss the big gates tae the works.'

A large red-brick gateway, which would have done justice to Barlinnie Prison, dominated the small street. Its two great, arched doors stood open. Feeling rather intimidated, I passed through them. On the right I could see some people behind a glass partition. I swallowed hard and pressed a button; all the heads swivelled to see who had had the cheek to ring the gatekeeper's bell. I felt my face go red. A plump wee man in a double-breasted blue suit slid one of the two glass windows open.

'What can I do for you, son?'

The aroma of Brylcreem enveloped me. He had the thinnest of pencil moustaches, which looked painted on, horn-rimmed specs and tightly waved hair. I cleared my throat but was still unable to control my voice. This was happening a lot lately.

'I'd like tae see somebody aboot getting a job, please,' I piped.

'You would, would ye,' he said, not unkindly. 'Do ye mean an apprenticeship?'

'Yes, please.' Maybe he was the manager.

'Right, I'll give ye an address tae write tae.' He scribbled on a notepad. 'Write a nice, neat letter tae that address, tell them a bit about yerself and what trade ye fancy learning, and if you're lucky, you'll be called up for an interview.'

'Thanks very much, mister.'

'C'mon, get yerself up, yer startin' work the day. Ye'd better not be late the first morning.'

I came awake in an instant as a whole colony of butterflies took flight in my stomach.

'Whit time is it, Ma?'

'Half past six.'

Ma must have been up for a while; she already had the fire on. I took my pyjama top off and went over to the sink. A kettle of hot water was waiting. I ran some cold into the white enamel basin with its blue rim then poured enough hot in to give myself a good slunge.

'Turn roond, Ma. Ah'm gonny dae ma "below the belt" bits.'

She obligingly turned her back to me, changed the wooden spoon she was holding to her other hand and carried on stirring the porridge. I got to work with the facecloth.

'Right, this porridge is ready.'

'Ah'll huv tae go tae the lavvy first, Ma.'

'Well, hurry up!' I grabbed the lavvy key from its hook by the room door, hurried into the draughty close and let myself into the toilet.

'Jeez!' The place was minging. One of the neighbours must have been in shortly before me. I opened the small, steel-mesh-covered window above the toilet. A breeze straight from the Arctic blew in. As I peed I leaned forward, one hand on the wall, to bring my face near to the window. Better freezing than being gassed. I took a last breath, held it, pushed the window shut, flushed the toilet and made a hurried exit, not breathing again until I was out in the close with the toilet door locked.

'Aw, Ma. Ah widnae go intae that lavvy for at least an 'oor. It's Abraham Lincoln!'

'It's what?'

'Stinking. Ah think auld Mrs Kinsella's been in.'

She shook her head and tried not to laugh. 'Poor auld sowel. Get you hands washed.' She ladled out a big plate of porridge.

'Are ye lookin' forward tae starting work, son?'

'Oh aye. But ah'm a wee bit nervous tae.'

'Och, you'll get ower that. Everybody's nervous their first day. Bound tae be, it's aw new tae ye. Ah wiz the same when ah first started work. It wiz at a french polisher's ower in Partick.'

The tram swayed its tired way up Keppochhill Road. It was seven-thirty. The leather strap I hung from creaked and groaned in protest to the wooden pole which held it. At this time of the morning it was a different world with different passengers. The tram to school was always just before nine and filled with noisy kids. This was nearly all men going to their work. It was a damp, cold morning. Old macs and ex-wartime duffel coats gently steamed in the crowded downstairs saloon, adding to the fetid warmth. There was almost no conversation, most were reading their morning papers. Now and then a sleeve was rubbed down a window so someone could check where we were. I had my ex-army canvas 'small pack' over my shoulder. Last week it had been stuffed with school books; now my piece and a new, shiny tea-and-sugar tin had replaced them.

The glass panel slid open and a waft of Brylcreem welcomed me once more.

'Ah! So they gave ye a start, son. Good for you.' I glowed because he remembered me. 'Now, ah'll jist put yer name in the book, seeing as this is yer first day.' He took his time, writing it in a fine copperplate in the big ledger. The edges of the many pages were multi-coloured, marbled in red, blue and green. 'Right. Now one of the things they'll do today is to give you a 'timecard'. From now on you don't bother coming to this gate lodge. You jist go to whatever department you'll be working in and clock in. Okay?'

'Aye. Thanks, mister.'

That first day of my working life was a kaleidoscope of sights, sounds and smells as, along with two other 'new starts', I was

The assembly shop at NB Loco Works, Springburn. It is my first job when I leave school in April 1954. The works closed in 1962.

shown around the two giant factories that made up NB Loco – Hyde park Works and Atlas Works.

The Milling, Turning and Drilling Shops had a perpetually busy air as dozens of machines hummed and chattered. All had the same smell, the mixture of oil and water used to cool the metal part being turned as the cutting tools bit into it. The foundries were hot, dusty and smelled of scorched sand and wood as molten steel, bronze and brass were poured. I was fascinated by the skill, and artistry, of the Pattern Makers as they made a model, in wood, of the part to be cast. This was pressed into special, damp sand – held in a wooden frame – and a mould made of the part to be cast. As white hot, molten metal was poured into this mould, dangerous-looking sparks, like an out-of-control Catherine wheel, flew everywhere. In the

Fabrication Shop I gaped in awe as large overhead cranes lifted complete locomotives and moved them to other parts of the shop. I held my ears, to protect them from pain, in the Riveting Section. I would find out later that *all* long-serving riveters were deaf to various degrees, many profoundly. As with shipyard riveters, it was accepted as part of the job. By the time you reached retirement you would be deaf. No compensation was paid, or expected!

For my first year at NB Loco I was to be a message boy for the Ratefixers' Department, whatever that was, and I was instructed to report there in the morning. My apprenticeship proper would not start until my second year.

'Right, boys, you can get yerselves away hame a wee bit early, seeing as it's yer first day.' Our guide smiled. 'Don't be late in the morning, mind.'

I headed for the gate with Billy and Vincent, my fellow new starters.

'What did ye's think of that, boys?' asked Vincent.

'It's no half some place, in't it,' said Billy. He stuck a finger in his ear and waggled it about. 'Ma ears are still dingling frae aw the noise in that Riveting Section.'

'Aye, me tae,' I said. 'Anyway, here's ma caur coming. Ah'll see ye's in the morning, boys.'

I sprinted away and just caught a Number 4 as it pulled away from the stop. It was just half past four so I got a seat no bother. As we shoogled back down the Keppochhill Road my head was still full of all the sights and sounds of NB Loco. I was looking forward to getting in and telling Ma all about it *and* getting my dinner. I was starving. Then, as was happening increasingly lately, a little voice somewhere in my head reminded me: How long will it last?

I tried to think of other things. After dinner I'd go round to Sammy's and tell him all about my first day at work. He was already working as an apprentice joiner. Maybe later I'd catch John Purden and tell him. He was working at Malcolm Campbell's the Fruiterer's over on Byres Road.

As I rode on the tram, I was gazing out the window, but not really seeing. My thoughts still on the factory and what tomorrow would hold. I remembered that as I'd left the works I'd noticed a newspaper seller taking up position outside the gates. I know. Ah'll start getting an *Evening Citizen* every night to read oan the tram oan the wye hame. Aye. Just like aw the other Working Men.

Clocking On

I was swept in through the main gate with the stream of men, found the timeclock, and searched for my card. There it was! My heart gave a little leap: *R. Douglas: Ratefixers' Department*. I looked at the confusion of a.m.'s, p.m.'s, days, months, all divided into squares.

A soft Irish brogue trickled into my ear from behind. 'Just put it in the slot, son, and press the handle or you'll have us all late. The machine knows where to stamp it.' It was, as I came to know later, Big Michael.

'Oh, sorry. Right, thanks, mister.' I did as instructed and timidly pressed the lever. I pulled the card out. Nary a mark on it.

'Oi've seen nuns clock in better than that! Give it here. Like this.'

He reinserted my card and with his great ham of a hand gave the handle a firm push. The bell gave a strangulated peal and with a metallic groan the whole apparatus moved forward three inches off the wall.

'Ah, Jaysus!' Michael retrieved my card then pushed the time-clock back into position. 'There you are now, that's how to be doing it.' He handed me my card. 'Now put it back with the rest of them and always use the same niche every day so you'll know where to find it.'

'Thanks a lot, mister.'

The queue which had formed behind me breathed a sigh of relief. They had been having visions of all being docked a quarter of an hour for clocking in after eight. I waited until the Irishman had stamped his card.

'Could ah bother ye for one mair thing: where's the Ratefixers' Department?'

This big, patient man rested a hand on my shoulder – I tilted slightly – and pointed along the broad factory floor. 'Do ye see that wooden building, for all the world like a cowboy saloon? That's it.'

'Oh, thanks again.'

As I walked toward it I took a good look at it. Built of slats of wood, two storeys high with a wooden staircase running up the outside, it was indeed strikingly similar to buildings seen in Westerns. It also seemed strange to have a building *inside* another building. I climbed the stairs, went through the door and found myself in a small lobby with a choice of four doors: *Ratefixers' Office*, *Mr. Ramsay*, *Mrs. Webster – secretary* and finally *Toilet*. I knocked on Mrs Webster's door.

'Come in.' I opened the door. 'Ah! Is it Robert?'

I blushed. 'Yes.'

She was probably in her late forties, slightly plump, with horn-rimmed specs. She wore a flowered overall, reminiscent of the sainted Miss Ivy Ross. We exchanged a few pleasantries then she gave me the basics of what was expected of the department's message boy. Then, 'I'll just see if the Boss is busy.' She pressed a button on one of those wee inter-office communication things they were always talking into in the movies. 'Our new office boy is here, Mr Ramsay.'

'*I'm on the phone at the moment*,' a tinny voice replied. '*I'll buzz you when I'm free.*'

For another couple of minutes we made light conversation until *Buzz!*

'Right, come with me, Robert.'

She knocked then opened the door and I followed her in, already starting to blush in advance. Jeez! That was all I did nowadays. In the last couple of months I'd begun to develop acne and *knew* everybody was looking at it. I could almost hear folk saying, 'Will ye look at the plooks on him, is that no wan o' the worst cases you've ever seen!' I'd recently added another complication, as if blushing and plooks weren't enough. When I blushed, my eyes started to water as well. I was convinced I'd soon be the first person in history to die of embarrassment.

'This is Robert Douglas. This is Mr Ramsay, in charge of the department.'

He reached over the desk and shook my hand. I wasn't used to shaking hands so, of course, went redder than ever and my eyes went all watery. I got out my hankie, pretended to wipe my nose, then gave my eyes a quick dab. The two of them had nothing to do but watch me; no doubt counting the number of spots I had while wondering what on earth they'd got for an office boy. Oh God! I wished I was deid.

As Mr Ramsay went over my duties, I looked at him. Around forty, wearing a blue pin-stripe, double-breasted suit, he could have got a job as James Mason's stand-in.

'That's all for now, Robert. Mrs Webster will take you in to meet the staff.' Oh Jeez, mair embarrassment. Is there nae end tae it?

We entered the main office. Around a dozen men sat at their desks. All wore either brown or grey button-up overalls.

'This is our new lad, Robert Douglas,' announced Mrs Webster. There was a chorus of 'Hiyah, Robert.' I could hardly take so many new eyes all looking at my plooks at the same time. They probably thought I was of Red Indian stock, I was blushing so furiously. I wished the ground would open up.

'Right, I'll leave him in your tender care.'

Mrs Webster closed the door behind her. I was just about to start worrying where to put myself, when, 'Here, son! Bring that chair over and sit beside me and I'll tell you whit goes on in here.'

There was an immediate outbreak of raspberries being blown from all over the office!

'What did Hughie say jist then?'

'Says he'll tell oor new lad whit goes on in here.'

'Bugger me! Who telt Hughie?' There was an outburst of mass sniggering which eventually finished up as laughter. This was great. Nobody was looking at me.

'Could ah come over and listen too, Hughie? I've been here five years and ah still huvnae got a bloody clue!'

I didn't know whether to smile or keep a straight face, but soon found myself laughing out loud. Hughie stuck his hand out toward me. 'I'm Hughie Hudson.'

I liked the look of him right away. In his mid-thirties, he looked like an unmade bed. He was plump, had an unruly mop of black, wavy hair and his top shirt button was undone and his tie loose. He exuded good humour and fun. He winked at me then, in a loud voice, said, 'Let's be thankful, Robert, that on your first day you've fallen into good hands.'

'Aye, and keep an eye on them "good hands", son,' said someone. 'It's no the first time he's got ower friendly wi' the message boy!'

'Here!' responded Hughie in mock seriousness. 'Ah was acquitted of that charge, so it disnae count.' The banter continued for another few minutes, then subsided. I realised I was going to like being the ratefixers' office boy.

Hughie tried to explain what ratefixers did. Basically they worked out the rate of pay that a man on 'piece rate' would be paid per hour, or per item. They timed how long it took a man to make an item on his machine, then how many he should produce in an hour. They then 'fixed a rate' for him while he was making those items. If he exceeded the hourly production he would earn a bonus. The ratefixers' great badge of office, carried in all the top pockets of their overalls, was – the Slide Rule. Over the next few months Hughie, and one or two others, tried to introduce me to the wonders of the slide rule. They failed. Like algebra it remains a mystery to the present day.

They were a good bunch. Mostly in their thirties and forties, the majority had seen war service. Between them they covered all three services and theatres of war: Europe, the Middle East and the Far East. I always looked forward to our dinner break. They would sit at their desks, various flasks and sandwich tins open. Almost without fail, at some time during the period the war, just nine years in the past, would come into the conversation. Often initiated by Hughie.

'Well, I think the Navy was the best service to huv been in during oor fight tae the death wi' Hitler.' Hughie sat back, hoping someone would take the bait.

'Who are you kidding?' said Frank. 'You were in the Army, so how come ye think the Navy was best?'

Hughie, with feet up on his desk, took a sip of tea. 'Aw that rum, bum and baccy.' There was a mixture of laughs and titters.

'He's right, mind,' said George. 'They sometimes ran short of rum and baccy, but there wiz never any shortage of bum, wiz there, Ralph? Famous for it, the Navy.'

'Notorious, ye mean,' added another voice.

'Could we have a bit of respect, if you don't mind,' interjected Ralph. 'That's the senior service you're casting aspidistras at.'

'Senior Service! They're a fag. Look!' said Hughie, pulling a twenty packet out of his overall pocket. Ralph shook his head in despair.

'Talking about fags', said George, 'was it just the Army that got them bloody Victory-Vs foisted on them?'

'Naw, we got a couple of issues of them in the RAF as well,' vouched Frank.

'We never got them in the Navy,' said Ralph, 'we only got the best fags. They were good enough for you pongos and Brylcreem boys.'

'Whit's pongos and Brylcreem boys?' I asked. Ralph sighed.

'A "pongo" is the Royal Navy's nickname for a soldier, "Brylcreem boys" were the RAF.'

Hughie interrupted him. 'And Victory-Vs were these terrible fags the government gave us as a free issue during the war. You could tell somebody wiz smoking wan a mile away. Smelled as if they were burning an Egyptian tramdriver's jockstrap.'

'Man, they were bloody awful, weren't they,' remembered Frank. 'Do ye no think it was mibbe the Germans that sent us them? You'd be lying in your tent at night, dying for a smoke. Then you'd hear somebody nearby say, "Ah'm gonny have tae have one." Ye'd hear a match strike, immediately followed by a paroxysm of coughing then, "Fuck it!"'

'Aye, that's right,' said John. 'Every time ah took a draw ah used tae cough.'

Hughie looked up. 'Every time ah coughed ah used tae shite maself!' There was the usual burst of laughter.

'Ye didn't.'

'Ah did,' said Hughie. 'Ah hud dysentery at the time.'

'Yes, but the big debate was, why did they taste so bad? What was in them?' said George.

'Camel shite!' said Hughie.

Frank put on his serious face. 'I read that, originally, it had been good tobacco which had been stored in one of Wills's warehouses. It had been bombed, set on fire and the water from the firemen had soaked the tobacco. When it was dried out it wasn't good enough for top-class fags, so they made a deal with the government to make it into these free-issue fags – to be called Victory-Vs.'

There was a moment's silence.

'It wiz definitely camel shite!' said Hughie.

After working a 'week's lying time' I went home on the Friday of my second week with my first pay packet. All thirty shillings and sixpence of it! On the way home that evening, every few minutes I'd put my hand into my inside pocket to check it was still there.

As I came into the house Ma was making the dinner. A fire crackled in the grate, the brasses shone, I could smell Cardinal floor polish. In between regularly checking I hadn't lost my wages, I had also been rehearsing for this moment. I held the unopened brown envelope up between finger and thumb.

'There ye are, Ma, my first pay packet.'

As she took it I shyly kissed her on the cheek. Her eyes moistened.

'Isn't that nice, son. Ah hope ye have many more of them.' She opened it and extracted the red ten-shilling note. 'Here ye are, that's yer pocket money.' She put the pound note and the sixpenny piece into her worn, brown leather purse.

As she busied herself with the dinner I sat at the table, elbows resting on the flower-patterned oilcloth covering it. I stretched the ten-bob note between my fingers. Great! I could go to the pictures at least three times this week *and* buy sweeties every time. Maybe even a five Woodbine. Ah think ah'm gonny like being a working man.

Lord of the Dance

'Are you no away tae the dancing, yet?' Uncle Jack looked at me as though considering reporting me to the polis. Every time we had visitors during the summer of 1954 somebody would ask that question. You leave school, get a job and start going to the dancing. It was written down somewhere. Tribal. Another rite of passage. It has always been debatable whether Glasgow should have been known as Tramcar City or Dancing City.

I shifted uncomfortably. 'Ah huv been thinking aboot it. Ah don't think it'll be long till ah'm away.' Truth told, I'd rather have had a night at the pictures. Nobody could see your acne at the pictures. But the pressure was on. Uncle Jack persisted.

'Everybody starts going tae the jigging when they leave the school. Best puckin' night oot in the world.' He drew on his Capstan Full Strength. 'Aye, a night doon the Locarno or the Barrowland. Ye cannae beat it. Time ye wur away.'

'Aye, so ah will,' I answered lamely.

I finally gave in. Ma loved dancing and hoped I would too, so she kept pressuring me.

'Well, you'll huv tae gie me some lessons, Ma.'

'Nae bother. If ye take efter me you'll pick it up in nae time.'

For the next three weeks, I'd come home from work, have my dinner, then the table would be pushed back to reveal our 'bijou' dance floor. Ma would then attempt to initiate me into the pleasures of the quickstep, foxtrot and modern waltz, all executed using a basic 'one, two, chassé'. There was always at least one, often two, dance-music programmes on the wireless every evening; Geraldo, Victor Sylvester, Edmundo Ros et al.

'These orchestras are aw great tae dance tae,' said Ma, 'they're aw strict tempo.' Whatever that meant.

At the end of my third week of intensive training, Ma considered I was ready to be loosed upon the unsuspecting female population of Glasgow. I had my doubts. Another reason for my graduation came in Ma's declaration that, 'Ma feet'll no stand up tae another night of you stepping oan them!'

The Dennistoun Palais was chosen for my debut. When Saturday came I immersed myself in that other great Glasgow ritual – 'Getting Ready for the Dancing'.

A bath was taken up at the Steamie in Cameron Street, even though I'd already had one the previous week. A shave was deemed necessary. I was now shaving twice a week. A generous dollop of Brylcreem was applied to the locks and an attempt made to mould the front into a 'Tony Curtis', the back combed into a DA (duck's arse). Finally, and fatally, in an attempt to improve my adolescent looks I burst a couple of reluctant plooks from the current crop. Over the previous few months my acne had developed into a severe case, Acne Vulgaris. Not just spots, but large eruptions akin to small boils. I was extremely self-conscious of them and they just about dominated my young life. I was also discovering that the day before you were going somewhere there would always be a severe outbreak. How did they know?

'Have you been squeezing them plooks again?'

I stood at the mirror, on the brink of tears as I applied flesh-coloured ointment to the now-inflamed, still-weeping spots.

'Och, ah'm no going oot. Look at the state of me, who'd want tae dance wi' me?' I eyed myself in the mirror. My face looked like a relief map of the Grampians. Ma came over.

'Ah've told ye, ye should'nae squeeze them. Anyway, naebody will notice at the dancin', the lights are low so they'll no see them. You'll huv tae go. Ah've jist about crippled maself teaching ye, so get yerself away.'

Finally, I stood ready for inspection. Hair combed, teeth cleaned, shoes polished, trousers pressed and tie knotted into a 'Windsor'. I was wearing my best, only, clothes. Navy blue blazer and grey flannels, brushed and pressed to within an inch of their lives. At fifteen, I looked like any other middle-aged man.

After what seemed like a long tram journey, I alighted at, then approached, the imposing brightly lit frontage of the Dennistoun Palais. People were homing in from all directions. I easily passed the scrutiny of the doormen, who, after one look at my polka-dot face under the bright lights of the canopy, took a step back in case I was infectious. I entered the large ballroom, found a quiet shadowy corner and settled down for the evening. I'd said I would start going *to* the dancing. I hadn't said anything about *dancing*.

I spent the next two hours watching the dancers glide by, occasionally dabbing the two spots with my hankie in case they were still leaking. At the interval I bought myself a glass of Vimto – neat! Venturing onto the dance floor wasn't even considered. I didn't have the courage to approach some unsuspecting lassie and ask her if she'd like to dance with El Spotto. During the evening I'd watched quite a few blokes ask a girl to dance and she'd refused. No way was I going to put myself in that position. I'd drop dead of humiliation.

Well into the second half of the evening, a woman appeared in front of me, blocking my view of the floor. I leaned to the side to see past her.

'Would you like to dance? This is the 'Ladies' Choice'.'

I looked to the left and right; there was nobody near. Jeez!

It's me she's asking! I swallowed hard. Ma had never mentioned this. I felt myself blush; at least my face would be all the same colour for a few seconds.

'Oh, thanks very much.'

Reluctant as I was to dance, I knew it would be extreme bad manners to refuse. All my years of sitting in the Blythsie watching Cary Grant, George Sanders and the rest of them had shown me how to conduct myself in society! She led me onto the floor, took hold of my left hand and placed my right on her waist. The band struck up – and all Ma's lessons and instructions left the building. I couldn't even remember what foot to step off with. Oh God! This is gonny be a disaster. She'll probably limp off the floor in about two minutes and everybody will wonder what I did to her.

'This your first time at the dancing?'

I blushed. 'Aye.'

'Thought so. Me and my pal huv been watching ye. You were jist gonny sit therr aw night, weren't ye?'

'Aye.' Bigger blush.

'How old urr ye?'

'Fifteen.' Mega blush.

'Och well, you've plenty of time.' I looked at her. She was probably in her late twenties, dark-headed, quite attractive. We were attempting to do a quickstep. I had set off by immediately standing on her toes, from then on it deteriorated. I couldn't remember one thing Ma had taught me.

'I'm awfy sorry aboot that.'

She winced. 'It's awright.'

As we approached the bandstand I realised, with horror, I couldn't remember how to turn. I could barely recall how to go straight. Just feet from disaster my partner assumed command and wrestled me onto another direction.

'Ah'm no very good at turns.' Double-mega blush.

'Och, you'll learn.'

'If you're gettin' fed up lugging me around, it'll be awright if ye don't want tae finish the three rounds,' I offered.

'Naw, not at all. We'll huv oor three dances,' she said, gamely.

Finally, mercifully, it was over. I thanked my partner profusely and accompanied her as she hobbled back to her friend.

In years to come I'd sometimes think back to my first night 'at the Dancing' and the kind-hearted girl who knew I'd sit all evening if she didn't ask me to dance. I wish her well.

It was around eleven p.m. when I got home.

'Did ye have a good time, son?' I knew Ma wanted me to love dancing as much as she did.

'Aye, it wiz good, Ma.' I tried to sound enthusiastic.

'Were ye up dancing?'

'Aye,' I answered, truthfully.

'Many times were ye up?'

'Ah never bothered tae keep count, Ma.'

'Did ye no get a wee click?'

'Well, there wiz wan very nice lassie I danced wi'.' I was pleased with that answer.

'How many times did ye dance her?'

'Aw, Ma, gie us a break, will ye.' She finally let it go.

Later, I lie in my bed-chair, supposedly reading the *Wizard*. I run the evening's events, well, non-events, over in my mind.

'Ma?'

'What, son?'

'Will ye gie me a few mair lessons? There's wan or two things I'm no quite sure o' yet.'

'Aye. We'll find a dance music programme the morra night and shove the table back.' I try to get back to Mosquito pilot Sergeant Braddock and his faithful navigator Bourne as they carry out a daylight raid deep into Germany. My thoughts are straying. *That's me working. I've just about started going to the dancing.* As I lie there musing on such weighty matters my eyes begin to close, the *Wizard* slips from my fingers. I can't be bothered to get it. Braddock will have to circle Dortmund until tomorrow.

Ma takes her cue and switches off the bedlight. The click momentarily brings me back from the edge of sleep, but not for long. As usual, my favourite lullaby comes reverberating through the night: a late tram, at speed, making its way down the Maryhill Road to St. Georges Cross. Since infancy this has been my night song. Why is it so soothing, so appealing? In my mind's eye I always see it from above. A moving pool of light speeding along the dark, empty street, its wheels singing as it accelerates down the gentle slope. The sound echoes and re-echoes off the silent tenements, fainter and fainter into the still night. I am asleep before the last note fades.

Miracles Only Happen in the Movies

Saturday afternoon. My favourite time of the week. I was on a five-day week at NB Loco but Ma had to work Saturday mornings at her wee charring job. I'd struggle out of bed about ten a.m. because I was hungry, have a big bowl of Puffed Wheat, then go back to bed. By the time she was due in, about ten past one, I'd be washed, dressed and anticipating her arrival. I'd hear the familiar footsteps in the close then her key in the door.

'Ah'm starving, Ma.'

'Huh, yer always starvin', you. Pit the kettle oan.'

'Ah've already filled it.' I struck a match, turned the gas on, then tentatively kept moving the lit match in and out toward the loudly hissing ring. I was feart of the gas and, no matter how many times I lit it, it still made me jump when it ignited.

'Jeesusjonny! Will ye get that ring lit before ye gas us – or blaw the hoose up.'

I braced myself and moved the match nearer. *Phoppp!* A hot blue flame caressed my hand. *Ohyah!* Ma shook her head and tried not to laugh.

'Whit ye got for eating, Ma?'

'Ah got three well-done rolls oot the City Bakeries and four slices of nice roast beef oot the cooked meat shop. So, we'll huv one and a half rolls each wi' plenty meat oan them.'

'Did ye get a wee snaster for efter?'

'Of course. It's Saturday, in't it?'

'Whit did ye get?'

'You'll find oot efter ye've had yer sanny.'

Ten minutes later found us sitting at the table with mugs of tea, eating crusty rolls spread thick with butter and stuffed with roast beef. Sometimes, for an extra treat, she would bring in a tin of Nescafe instant coffee. I loved opening the small, round can with its brown label. I'd lever off the tightly sealed lid, cut open the gold foil and . . . Heaven! The most beautiful coffee smell rose up from the fine, rich brown powder. Two mugs of coffee, made in a pan with mostly milk, would accompany our lunch.

As we ate, Ma would tell me of the happenings at the big house she cleaned over in Hillhead. Toffs, they had a son and daughter ages with me. Their life and schooling seemed to be much like the weekly adventures of Smith of the Lower Third, whose exploits I followed avidly in the *Wizard*. Ma would tell me of them coming in and out in their school uniforms and caps, carrying hockey sticks, cricket bats and rackets. I soaked it all up and wished I could see them.

'Right!' Ma reached into her red and black Rexine message bag and delicately lifted out a paper bag with the City Bakeries logo on it. She laid it on the table, opened it and gently inserted a hand – Ma would have done well in Bomb Disposal. I watched every move. She withdrew her hand.

'For you, a custard tart.'

'Oooh, ah like them.' She put her hand back in.

'And another custard tart!'

'Aw, thanks Ma.'

'And for me . . .' Again she reached inside.

'A fern cake,' I forecast.

'Right,' she said, putting the little round cake on her plate.

'Why dae ye always get a fern cake, Ma? They're identical tae the other cakes oan the same tray. They jist draw a wee fern in chocolate oan the icing.'

'Aye, ah know. But ah jist like them.'

This was our regular Saturday routine. We both looked forward to it.

*

We were now into the second half of 1954. Nine months or more had passed since my father had told me Ma had just six months to live. I began telling myself she was now over her cancer. In reality she was starting to decline, but I didn't see it. I didn't want to. As she hadn't died after the six months was up, she must have got better! I never asked her, in case I heard something I didn't want to. And she never spoke about it.

'Dae ye want tae come doon tae the Empress wi' me the night?' The Empress was a theatre just off St George's Cross.

'Who's on?'

'Frank and Doris Droy and wan or two good supporting acts.'

'Yeuugh! Ye want me tae go doon and see them two. Ah've spent a better night wi' the toothache!'

Ma laughed. 'Och c'mon, you're always going tae the pictures wi' yer pals. Come and keep yer auld mammy company for a change.'

'Well, awright then. Are we going tae the second house? It's alwiz mair fun when the pubs have come oot. Some of the hecklers are funnier than the acts. Ah suppose we'll be going up tae the gods as usual?'

'Aye, it's only a tanner tae get in.'

'Mind me tae take a cushion. Sitting on yon big widden steps gies me a sore bum long before the interval.'

As the summer wore on I had adjusted well to life as a 'working man'. All my pals had now left school and were working, some of the older ones even trying a bit of courting. At fifteen, my sole interest was going to the pictures. As I now had a few shillings in my pocket I usually went at least three times a week. My two main pals were John Purden, whom I'd grown up with, and Sammy Johnson, whom I'd palled up with on my first day at NKS. We were all film fans.

I climbed up to the top landing and knocked John's door. It was opened by Robert, one of his older brothers.

'Is John in, Robert?'

He turned his head to the side. 'John! Robert Douglas for ye.'

Robert went back into the house. I stood by the open door looking into the dark lobby. The smell of cooking and sounds of conversation drifted out. They were a big family, the Purdens. The oldest sister, Jessie, had been a GI bride and had lived in Kansas for quite a few years now. She often sent parcels over with foodstuffs, sweets – and American comics for the younger ones. John appeared.

'Hiyah, Robert.'

'Fancy gawn tae the pictures the night?'

'Is there anything good oan?'

'There's a Robert Mitchum picture oan up at the Roxy, gangsters, supposed tae be good.'

'Right. Gie me ten minutes tae finish ma dinner. See ye at Cocozza's.'

As the Number 23 tram took us up the Maryhill Road we sat working out what extras we could afford to buy to add to the evening's entertainment.

'How much have ye got?' asked John. I had a quick tally.

'Three and tenpence.'

'Ah've got four and eleven. We're stoating! That's plenty. Whit will we get for going in?'

'Jist five Woodbine will be enough, win't it?' I said.

'Aye. Whit else? Two Crunchies?'

'And mibbe a bar of McCowan's Highland Cream Toffee,' I suggested.

'Good idea. Toffee lasts fur a long time.'

I handed him my contribution so as he could go into the sweetie shop. 'Don't forget, John, hang on to enough fur oor tram fare when we come oot. Ah don't fancy walking; it might be raining.'

'Right. If there's tuppence or thruppence left ah'll jist get two or three Penny Dainties. That'll definitely be enough sweeties fur the whole show.'

Five minutes later we settled into the seats the usherette had led us to with her torch. As our eyes slowly adjusted to the dark the projector did its best to pierce the haze of blue smoke drifting up from the audience. John and I gave ourselves up to the drama on the screen. Soon, we were no longer in a suburban cinema in Glasgow: we were standing in the shadows of a warehouse on Frisco's waterfront. Ten minutes later we'd be questioning a gorgeous dame in a hacienda-style bungalow in LA. Well, somebody has to do it.

As Mitchum lit up another Lucky we would take a few cool draws on oor Woodbines, trying hard no tae cough, then 'nip' them for later as we only had two and a half each.

For the best part of three hours I'd be lost, taken out of myself, worries pushed as far back in my mind as possible. Then the film would finish and real life would intrude.

John and I came out of the Roxy and joined a small queue at the tram stop opposite. The cool night air began to blow away the spell, and comfort, of the movie. Ten minutes later we were swaying our way back down the Maryhill Road. As usual, we talked about the movie we'd just seen then discussed what we should go and see a couple of nights from now. As we chatted away, he couldn't know how much I envied him. When we got off at our stop and then split up outside his close, he'd be going upstairs to a house where his parents and brothers and sisters were. I'd be going round to our one room where my poor, sick ma was waiting, trying her best to be cheerful for my sake. 'Was the picture good, son? Dae ye want something tae eat?' She'd have a welcome fire waiting for me and soon we'd be sitting with tea and toast and I'd tell her all about the film and re-enact bits for her and she'd say, 'Eh, that wiz almost as good as seeing it maself, son.' And I'd be thinking, why can't we go on like this for years and years, jist Ma and me? Then I'd look at her. Really look at her. And I'd know we couldn't.

Later, I'd be lying in the bed-chair reading the *Hotspur*, and she'd be above me in the recess bed and she'd say, 'Better put the light oot, son. You've got your work in the morning.'

I'd put the *Hotspur* down and she'd click the light out.

'G'night, Ma.'

'Night night, son.' Then she'd add, 'Don't let the bugs bite!' Just a bit of the rhyme she'd always say when I was little. So I'd laugh and say, 'Aye, if they bite squeeze them tight, Ma.' But really, her voice coming out of the dark saying that childhood thing made me unbearably sad. She was saying it to comfort herself, to take her back in time. In the dark she could be twenty-five again and me a wee boy, and him in Italy. I think she was happiest during the war. 1945 hadn't brought her peace.

Now and again when she thought I was sleeping, I'd hear her having a wee cry to herself because she was so miserable. Sometimes I'd ask, 'What's the matter, Ma?' But she'd always say, 'Oh, nothing. It's jist yer faither.'

Most of the time I wouldn't say anything. Just put my hankie on my pillow near my eyes and have a quiet wee cry along with her until I fell asleep.

As 1954 wore on into autumn and then the start of the winter months, that's how life was. On 7 November Ma turned thirty-six. I got her a card and a box of Fry's chocolate mints, her favourites. There was nothing from my father.

It was now a year since he'd told me the doctors had given Ma six months. Only will power and the worry of what would happen to me if she wasn't there kept her going. She weighed about seven stones now, yet still kept trekking over to Hillhead to her wee job because we needed the money. No longer could I fool myself that she must be getting better. All I had to do was look at her. She was very ill. There was no betterness for her. This was a terrible admission to make to myself. Ma was thirty-six. She was my whole life and she was going to die.

Soon after I accepted the fact of how ill Ma was, I decided to start keeping some of the notes she was always leaving me. Whenever she was away visiting somebody and thought I'd be home before her, she would always leave me a note. She didn't like me coming into an empty house so, at the very least, I'd come home and find a note waiting for me. Over the years there would be an average of one or two a week. After I'd read them they'd just be scrunched up and thrown on the fire. I now realised I perhaps didn't have too much time left if I wanted to have some to remember her by. Ma's notes. They were so much part of my life.

I had almost left it too late. I only managed to collect three before she became too ill to go visiting anymore and the notes stopped. Even so, they are typical of her notes – and her punctuation – she was very fond of using inverted commas. The three I have are from November 1954. To start keeping them was an acceptance that she would die soon. She wouldn't get better without a miracle.

Miracles only happen in the movies.

Robert
I'm away to Mrs Cameron's
if you need anything else for a meal
get it marked in Miss Spence's.
Ma..
PS You can use 1 pt milk but
leave the rest till I come in..

Robert Wash out your
Hankies with "hot" water
before you go to bed also
your "Dusters" for your
work Ma

Dear, "Robert,"
I've taken a "notion," to visit
"Rutherglen", to-day but if Alice is out I'll
be right back "Home," again but if
not I've left you two eggs "they are
boiled," also take "Krispees" if you want
and you can have 1 pint milk leave
the rest.. If you go out remember
your key and if the fire is too
far down let it go out if not put
some more coal on and leave it
safe.. See you tonight.. "Ma."
P.S., Hope you have some money?..
Mind to turn off the gas..

Three notes from Ma.

Ae Fond Kiss

It was still November. I came home from work to find Ma sitting alone, her eyes red from weeping and still making an occasional dry sob.

'What's the matter, Ma?' I went over and stood by her, putting my hand on her shoulder. I had never seen her so upset. Between sobs she told me that my father had arrived home an hour or so ago. She had written to him a few days previously. As usual he had been for a few pints first. She had told him he should be here all the time now as she was finding it difficult to manage. He, of course, had no wish to be separated from his lady love. One word had bothered another and he'd announced he was going straight back to Stranraer. As he opened the door to leave he'd turned round.

'Anyway, I'm jist waiting for you tae die so's ah can get married again – so fuckin' hurry up, will ye!'

Those were the last words he spoke to her. He would never see her again.

Ma buried her face in the towel she held in her lap. 'How could he say that tae me? How could he?' She hadn't the strength to sob anymore.

'Ma, you know he's a bad wee get. When he's had a drink he jist says the worst word in his belly.'

The enormity of what he'd said began to dawn on me. I remember looking at her and the terrible state he'd left her in. I vowed to remember this moment. Never to forget. Or forgive. It was almost the end of the month. It may be coincidence, but after that day Ma seemed to lose heart and go downhill quickly.

*

It was 8 December. As I opened the house door all was in darkness. No fire, no smell of cooking. No Ma. A few days earlier she had stopped going over to her wee job in Hillhead. She was too unwell. Nevertheless, she had still struggled out of bed each evening to have the fire lit and the dinner on for me coming in from work. Neighbours had done her shopping and Dr McNicol called in every day. I tried to reassure myself; maybe she'd felt a wee bit better and was round at somebody's house. But if that was the case, she'd have been back in time to put the dinner on. I began to get worried. If she was away somewhere she'd have left a note. She always left a note.

I decided to light the fire so the room would look a bit cheerier when she came in. As I laid the paper and sticks in the grate, somebody knocked on the door. I opened it and found old Mr Lawrie from two-up standing there.

'Ah, your mother said you'd be home about this time, Robert. Can I come in, son?'

'Oh aye, sorry. C'mon in, Mr Lawrie. Ah was jist gonny light the fire before me ma comes hame.'

I had a funny feeling as I looked at him. I noticed he held a piece of paper in his hand.

'It's about yer mother I've come to see ye, son. She wasn't very well today, so one of the neighbours sent for the doctor. Well, he thought she needed a wee bit more attention than she could get in the house, so he arranged for an ambulance to take her to a St Margaret's Hospice in Clydebank.' He handed me the piece of paper. 'That's the address. Dr McNicol says the visiting time is from seven till eight in the evening.'

I had never heard the word 'hospice' before. I thought Mr Lawrie had been trying to say 'hospital'.

'Jeez! Clydebank? That's pretty far away. It's ootside the city boundary, isn't it? Ah wonder why they've taken her aw the way oot there. Ye'd think they'd jist huv taken her tae one o' the city hospitals for treatment.'

He looked at me. 'Aye, well, maybe they couldnae find a bed for her nearby,' he said.

'Aye, that must be whit it is.'

He gave me directions on how to get there. It entailed taking the subway to Partick, then a bus from Dumbarton Road out to Clydebank. A bus. Jeez, I wasn't used to taking the bus. It was a fairly long journey, and included a fair amount of walking too.

I had a quick wash at the sink, then headed round to Bundoni's for a fish supper, which I ate as I walked to Kelvinbridge subway station to start my journey.

It was around ten to seven when I got off the single-decker bus in Clydebank, and it was settling in to be a raw, blustery December night. I got directions for the road where the 'hospital' lay and set off at a good pace; the visiting would be starting soon. Within minutes it began to rain.

Eventually I found it. Dimly lit, it consisted of large, detached houses set back from the road. They were all surrounded by walls, drives leading up from their gates. Many of the houses were hard to see from the road because of trees and bushes in their gardens. By now the rain was blowing in squalls. My navy blue trench coat was sodden, drips from its hem wetting my trouser legs. I wore no cap; water ran down my neck from my wet hair and soaked my shirt collar. As I walked the length of the road, trees behind the walls swayed in the wind and showered even more water onto me. There was no sign of a hospital, just big houses. I was almost in tears with frustration; it was twenty to eight. Ma would think I'd let her down. Because it was such a rotten night there was no one around to ask. I set off back down the road again. There was a man walking his dog!

'Mister, can ye tell me where St Margaret's Hospital is? I've been up the length of the road and ah cannae see it; it's aw just hooses.'

'It's no a hospital, son. It's just one o' the houses. It's whit they call a "hospice".'

'Oh! Ah've been looking for somewhere big, like the Western Infirmary, so ah huvnae really been looking at the hooses.' I felt stupid for not knowing what a hospice was. It must be what you call a small hospital.

'It's the third gate on the left. There's a sign just inside the gate; it's a wee bit hidden by the bushes.'

'Thanks, mister. Ah wish ah'd seen you earlier. Ah'm soaking.'

'Aye, it's a terrible night. Cheerio, son.'

Within minutes I was ringing the bell of the hospice. I looked at my watch: five to eight. Ma will be saying, 'He didnae come.' The front door was opened – by a nun!

'Oh, my name's Robert Douglas. Ah've come tae see my mother, Janet Douglas. Ah'm awful sorry ah'm late but ah've had terrible trouble finding the place.'

I must have looked like a drowned rat. My hair plastered to my face, trench coat shining and dripping with water, my collar a wet misery round my neck.

'Mmm, visits are just finishing, but we'll give you a little time.'

I stepped into the tiled hall. It was dimly lit and drably decorated. I got the impression once the visits were finished the place would settle down for the night.

'She's just in here.' The sister opened the door of the first room on the left. There was Ma, sitting up in the bed just inside the door.

'Aw, Ma, whit a job I've had finding the place. Ah've been up and doon the road twice. Did ye think ah wiznae coming?'

'Ah knew ye'd come, son. It's a long way by yerself. Ah'd an idea ye might have trouble finding it. And look at ye, yer wringing wet. Here, take ma towel and dry yer hair and take yer mac off and put it ower the radiator tae dry a wee bit.'

As she spoke, I looked at her. She looked really ill, sitting up sort of hunched against a couple of pillows. Her voice was low, tired, as if she'd no energy. The only light on in the room was Ma's bedside lamp. There were two other beds. I could just make out a grey head on a pillow in one. An old lady was propped up on one elbow in the other, watching us. Smiling and continually nodding as she did.

'Ah don't know why they put me in here. That old soul ower there is dying, and that other poor cratur is senile, so ah've naebody tae talk tae unless one o' the nuns comes in.' She looked at me. 'Have ye had something tae eat?'

'Aye, ah got a fish supper oot o' Bundoni's.'

'Good, that'll stick tae yer ribs. Are ye awright for money?'

'Ah think so. How long are ye gonny be in here, Ma?'

'Maybe a couple of days. Ah'm needing a rest and feeding up a bit.' She took her purse off the bedside table. 'Ah'll give ye a pound in case ye need it, and here's another ten bob. When ye come the morra night bring me forty Craven "A", will ye.'

The door opened and the nun came in.

'I'm sorry, but I'm afraid you'll have to go.'

It seemed to be barely ten minutes since I'd arrived. I stood up and put my mac back on. It was still wet.

'Right, Ma, ah'll not forget yer cigarettes, and ah know where tae come now. Ah'll be right oan time the morra night so's we'll huv a long visit.'

I looked down at her; she looked so frail. The nun was standing watching and, as usual, I felt embarrassed about kissing Ma. I looked at her again. I leaned forward and she turned her face up. I kissed her softly on the lips.

'Goodnight, Ma. Ah'll see ye the morra.'

'Aye, cheerio, son. See ye the morra night.'

The front door closed behind me and I stepped from the porch into the unrelenting rain. When I got to the bottom of the drive

I stopped and looked back. I could see the glow of Ma's bed light through the window blinds. I pictured her sitting up in bed and remembered how ill she'd looked. I was glad I'd kissed her.

I set off along the road and then, in spite of the rain, I stopped once more. I took a final look back. I could just glimpse the faint light from her bedroom window through the swaying branches.

It was after ten when I got in to our cold, empty house. I was wet, miserable and dispirited. I lit a couple of gas rings to warm the place up, had some toast, then got into my pyjamas and climbed into the big bed. I set the alarm. Too tired to read, I switched out the bed light. I had kept my socks on and now tucked my pyjama legs into them. I pulled Ma's pillow over and half-turned my face into it; there was the faint scent of California Poppy or Evening in Paris. Whatever it was – it was Ma. I lay in the dark, curled up to try and get warm, and thought of all the nights we'd cuddled up together in here when I was a wee boy. Lying there, that was just how I felt, a wee boy who was missing his mammy. I murmured softly into her pillow, 'Night night, Ma. Don't let the bugs bite. If they bite, squeeze them tight. Night night.'

As I said it I could see her in her room in the hospice. Just a lamp for company.

Raining From a Clear Sky

'Robert! The Boss wants ye in his office.'

Hughie and I walked back together to the Ratefixers' block. That's funny, I thought. When they're looking for me they usually just send another message boy, not one of the ratefixers.

'He probably wants me tae go oot tae the City Bakeries and get him a couple of custard tarts for his teabreak.'

'Aye, maybe.'

I looked at Hughie. He wasn't full of his usual bounce. Jeez, I hope I'm not in trouble. I racked my brains to try and recall something I'd done – or hadn't done. Hughie was always full of fun and tormented the life out of me when he got the chance. He must know I'm in trouble.

We made our way through the noisy Fabrication Shop, past the giant locomotives being built for South African Railways, then climbed the stairs up to our wooden office. I closed the door against the clamour of the shop floor.

Mrs Webster pointed. 'Just go in, Robert, he's waiting for you.' No smile or anything.

As always, I gave a wee rap on the door and went straight in. Mr Ramsay sat behind his desk. As I entered, a policeman and old Mr Lawrie from our close stood up. *Mr Lawrie?* I felt my skin tingle. A giant hand seemed to press down on top of my head. I wished I had the courage to say, 'Look, I don't want to hear what you're about to tell me, jist let me go back to my job and everything will be awright.' But I didn't. I knew it wouldn't do any good. A terrible, frightening thought came into my head – MY MAMMY! I didn't want to take that thought

THIS FORM TO BE FILED FOR FUTURE REFERENCE

TELEPHONE MESSAGE

From St Margaret's Hospice, Clydebank. Telephone No.

Date 9/12/54 Hour 1.50 pm Recd. by

Inform ~~[illegible]~~ Robert Douglas (16) 14 Doncaster Street
that his mother Janet Douglas died to-day, and
to get in touch with the Hospice (Clydebank 1141)

NOTE This boy is residing with a neighbour at
that address – make enquires.

Message attended to by Date Hour

Remarks

we

The message the policeman handed me as he told me Ma has died.

to its conclusion. They were about to talk to me. I couldn't stop them.

'Is this the boy?' asked the policeman.

'Aye, this is Robert,' said Mr Lawrie. He gave a sad smile. I didn't want him to smile like that.

'You're Robert Douglas, son?' The policeman held a folded piece of paper in his hand.

'Aye.'

I willed him not to say any more, then I could still go out to Clydebank tonight. Even if it was pouring with rain I'd get there early and my ma and me would have a nice long visit and I'd not be shy about kissing her when it was time to leave. But that could only happen if he didn't say . . .

'I'm afraid your mother, Janet Douglas, died this morning out at Clydebank.'

Why did he have to say that? I couldn't go and visit her now. He handed me the torn-off sheet of 'Police Message Pad'.

I didn't know what to say with them all looking at me, so I blurted out, 'Aye, we were expecting it. She had cancer.'

I immediately wondered why I'd said that. I hadn't expected it. I knew she had cancer, I knew she wouldn't get better. After last night's visit I knew she was very ill. But she was my mammy and she was not going to die. But she had. And I'd said, 'We were expecting it.'

'Just get yourself away home, son,' said the Boss. 'Don't come back till after the funeral. You'll be paid while you're off. I'm very sorry to hear about your mother.'

'Thanks, Mr Ramsay.'

'We'll travel back home together, Robert.' Mr Lawrie put his hand on my shoulder as we left the office. Mrs Webster smiled.

'See you next week, Robert.'

Going down Keppochhill Road on the tram, Mr Lawrie and I spoke about anything and everything, except Ma. After what seemed an interminable journey, we entered our close.

'Would you like to come up and Mrs Lawrie will make you a wee spot of dinner or a sandwich?'

'Thanks very much, Mr Lawrie, but ah'm no hungry.' I just wanted to get through that brown door and be in the house on my own where nobody could see me.

'Aye, I don't suppose you will be, son.' He stopped at the foot of the stairs. 'Come up later if you feel like it. I'm very sorry about your mother, Robert. It's a sad loss for you.'

I could feel the tears starting. In the shadows of the back close I hoped he couldn't see them.

'Thanks, Mr Lawrie.'

I turned to the door and had difficulty getting the key in the lock as the tears brimmed in my eyes. I could hear Mr Lawrie starting up the stairs.

I shut the front door, glad at last to be alone. Ma's brown coat, with its 'coney collar', hung from a nail on the back of the door. I looked at it, then buried my face into its folds, pushing it up with my hands onto either side of my face so that I had to breathe through it. I could smell nothing but Ma. For a while I cried silently into it, standing in the dark in our small lobby. But crying silently wasn't enough. My chest was bursting and sore with all that wanted to get out. I went into the room, shutting the inner door behind me. Just as I'd seen Ma do many times; it was now my turn. I went to the press door and unhooked the towel from behind it, sat in the fireside chair, pressed my face into the towel and cried and howled and broke my heart for my lost ma. I cried until there were no more tears, then I sobbed great, dry sobs until, exhausted, I fell asleep.

When I awoke, the room was dark and cold. For a precious second I didn't know where I was – or what had happened. Then I remembered. And broke my heart all over again.

I wondered if my father would find out. I had no intention of telling him.

Later that evening I took a tram up Maryhill, then walked down the gentle slope of Oran Street. Mrs Cameron, 'Aunty Nicky', and the girls would have to be told. As I entered their close, I remembered the times, during and after the war, when I'd come up here with Ma for the Saturday-evening card games – Nap, Chase the Ace, Card Dominoes and Newmarket. Ina and Nancy, Aunty Nicky's two girls, and I would be allowed to stay in the kitchen to watch the adults play if we behaved ourselves. We seldom did, so would be banished to the front room.

I knocked on the familiar door. Ina, the oldest girl, opened it,

'Oh, c'mon in, Robert.' I followed her into the kitchen. 'It's Robert Douglas,' she announced.

Aunty Nicky sat on one side of the range, Nancy, who was my age, sat opposite. Mrs Cameron had been my mother's 'best maid' when she'd married my father. Although she was twelve years older than Ma, they had been great friends since they'd met at work in 1936.

'How's your mother, Robert?' Aunty Nicky looked at me.

'Aaah, Aunty Nicky, ah've come up tae tell ye . . . ma ma died this morning.'

Immediately, in unison, the three of them began to wail. Mrs Cameron rocked back and forth. Sometimes I could hear her say, 'Oh my God! My pal, my lovely pal, whit'll ah dae withoot her.'

I took the tram back down the Maryhill Road and went up to Sammy's to tell Lottie and Frank. Although Sammy and I were great pals, our parents didn't know each other. They were, of course, sad for me. They offered me something to eat and I spent the rest of the evening with them, sitting round the fire, talking. It seemed such a long time since the policeman had spoken to me. Their bell rang.

'Dearie me,' said Frank, a worried look coming over his face and almost going into 'Stan Laurel' mode. 'Ah wonder who that is at this time of night?'

Lottie sighed and drew on her Woodbine. 'Well, we'll no know unless ye open the buggerin' door!'

As usual, when Lottie started on Frank, I got the giggles; then felt guilty for laughing on the day my ma died. As Frank made for the door he looked at me.

'Don't you encourage her when ah'm oot the room, mind.' I could tell he was just trying to make me smile.

We listened as he opened the door. Voices drifted in from the long lobby, then footsteps. Frank came in first.

'It's your father, Robert!'

My heart gave a leap. The police must have told him, too. He entered, wearing his uniform and, as usual, smelling of beer. Frank and Lottie made some polite condolences; they knew the situation. I realised this was the first time they'd met him. Sammy just stared at him.

'Are you coming round the house, Robert? It's gone ten.' It always sounded strange when he called me 'Robert'. You could tell he wasn't used to it.

'Aye.' I stood up. 'Ah'll probably come roon again the morra.'

'Aye, of course, son. Any time you like.'

'See ye the morra, pal,' said Sammy.

We said our goodnights and stepped out onto the cold landing. The door shut behind us and I started down the curving stairs, my father behind me. I hadn't taken three steps when he laid his hand on my shoulder and started to speak, 'I'm sorry about y—' I immediately shrugged his hand off and braced myself for the statutory 'belt on the lug'. It wasn't forthcoming!

As we descended I thought, Who does he think he's kidding? It's only a month since he was telling Ma, 'Just fuckin' hurry up and die so's ah can get married again.' Now he's trying to show me sympathy. I wished I was a few years older and could grab him by the throat, slam him up against the wall and tell him a few home truths.

Maybe it's best I'm not older. In just one day I could finish up an orphan.

We were back home barely five minutes.

'Ah'm no havin' your mother lying in the house for the usual three days. Ah don't think it would be good for you.'

'That's awright wi' me. Ah don't want tae see ma ma in a coffin.' My last memory of her in the hospice had been bad enough.

It was some time later when it dawned on me why he didn't want Ma lying in the house. It wouldn't be because Ma didn't look nice, or to spare my feelings. If Ma had been brought home for folk to come and pay their respects, as the 'grieving husband' he would have to be present most of the time. All of Ma's friends and neighbours knew the sort of life he'd given her. Standing looking at Ma in her coffin, with him in the room, would have proved too much for some of them. Annie Dunn and Esther Sinclair most certainly wouldn't have been able to hide their contempt for him. The volatile Irene Barrie would probably have taken a swing at him. He knew that.

Next morning when I rose I had a nagging worry. I wanted to ask him for something and knew I'd have to choose the right moment. Ma's wedding ring had been pawned a couple of days before she'd been taken into the hospice; the ticket was in the Sharp's Toffee tin on the mantelpiece. I badly wanted it to remember her by. There was little else. The timing would be crucial. Ask him when he was in the wrong mood, he could quite easily refuse to let me have it. He was rotten enough.

About half an hour after breakfast he was sitting reading the paper, still drinking his tea. It was now or never. I tried to keep any tremor out of my voice; I didn't want him to know how important this was to me.

'Oh, Ma's wedding ring is up the pawn. If ah get it oot can ah keep it?'

'Huh! Shows how much it meant tae her.' I bit my tongue. I watched his face as he pondered it. He never looked up. 'Aye, ye can huv it. It's nae use tae me.' He resumed reading.

'Thanks.' This was such a relief. I wanted it so much. He never offered to give me the money to get it out, but I didn't care. I preferred to redeem it myself. I reached up for the tin and retrieved the ticket.

Minutes later I was climbing the familiar wooden stairs to the pawn. All the ingredients were there: stiff cubicle door, smell of mothballs, and the pin-dropping silence. Yet, it wasn't the same anymore; I wasn't with Ma. John duly appeared.

'I'll redeem this, John.'

I wondered if he knew about Ma. I gave him the buff-coloured ticket and the required eleven shillings and sixpence. He dis-

Ma, late summer 1954.

appeared for a minute, then returned and placed Ma's slim, nine-carat ring in my palm. It was mine now. I looked at it, closed my hand round it and determined it wouldn't see a pawnshop again.

Going downstairs to the Garscube Road I slipped it onto my finger. It fitted fine.

The funeral, at Lambhill Cemetery, was held in appropriate weather: cold, blustery rain. Ma's brothers, James and Bill, had come through from West Lothian. I gave Uncle Bill the Craven 'A' cigarettes I'd got for Ma. Granny Douglas and Aunties Nicky and Alice were there, as were some neighbours Ma had been friends with. I felt sorry for Granny Douglas, she'd miss all the cuppas and wee 'bites to eat' Ma used to give her unknown to my father.

Hardly anyone spoke to my father. My father, Ma's two brothers Jim and Bill and I took hold of the four blue braided cords attached to her coffin. I looked at Ma's name on the brass plate on the coffin lid – *Janet McIntosh Douglas*. As we lowered her into the grave, the thought came into my mind of how glad I was that I'd overcome my shyness and kissed her goodnight. That last kiss was my only comfort.

After the funeral everyone just dispersed. My father hadn't laid on any refreshments, no doubt for the same reason he hadn't had Ma lying in the house. He couldn't face the mourners. As he and I were driven off in the only car, alone, I wondered where my Uncle George was. He'd stayed with us that couple of nights the previous year, then vanished. Would I ever see him again?

With the funeral over, I began to wonder what was going to happen to me. I was a couple of months off sixteen, too young to keep the house on. I didn't earn enough, anyway. My father still had around eleven months to do in the RAF. One thing was for certain, I wouldn't be going to live with his fancy woman. That would be letting Ma down.

My father already had it all worked out.

Last Post

'You'll have tae make up yer mind what you're gonny dae.' It was the day after Ma's funeral. He wasn't going to waste any time. My father sat across the table from me as we ate our dinner. 'Ah'll eventually be getting married again, so you'll have tae either go and live at her house . . . or ye can join the RAF Boys' Service. You'll learn a trade there.' He paused. 'So, whit dae ye think?'

Whit dae *ah* think? I looked at him. With all the thoughts that were flashing through my mind it would have taken half an hour to tell him 'whit ah think'. Ma was just buried yesterday and it was quite obvious he wanted rid of me. He knew there was no way I'd go and live with his fancy woman. I looked at him.

'Ah might as well go intae the Boys' Service.'

He had a job to keep a smile off his face. He knew he was only giving me *one* choice. He'd got rid of his wife. Now, twenty-four hours later, he'd got rid of his son.

'We'd better get doon tae the recruiting office sharp. The next entry is in February; we'll huv tae get ye signed up before the closing date.'

He had obviously been making enquiries. I would love to have said, 'Huv ah time tae finish ma dinner?'

The next morning found me sitting in front of a recruiting sergeant in Union Street while my father waited outside. He had coached me before I went in. I told the sergeant I'd long fancied being a Boy Entrant and was really looking forward to it. If I'd said, 'Two days ago I'd never heard of the Boys' Service, my father's pushing me into it,' I'd have been shown the door. A couple of weeks later a letter arrived, informing me I'd been accepted for the next entry at RAF Cosford, near Wolverhampton on 16 February 1955. Further details to follow.

The nine weeks from Ma's death to going into the RAF was a strange time. I still went to work and came home at night, but there was no Ma. Nothing was the same. My father was posted back to Bishopbriggs so as he could look after me. When I came in from work he had the dinner made and the fire on, but the house was different now. He'd try to make conversation, actually attempting to be on good terms with me as though the past hadn't happened. His approach seemed to be – it's just you and me, now that your mother has gone, so we'll have to make the best of it. I couldn't believe the change in his attitude, nor was I having any of it. He was about to get rid of me so, to salve his conscience, he intended to do 'father impersonations' for the few weeks before I left.

In the evenings, after dinner, I'd go out with Sammy or John. If they weren't around I'd go out alone even if it meant just sitting in Cocozza's. I didn't want to spend any time with him in the house. It was too unnatural to have him talk civilly to me, to try and make jokes. I wasn't used to it. I found it unsettling because it was all put on.

During this period he never bothered me. I came in and out as I pleased. With Ma not there to 'bait' it probably wasn't fun anymore to pick on me. After a fortnight or so he was obviously dying to go down to Stranraer. I told him he could go down every weekend if he wanted, I would look after myself. So he did. I spent a lot of time up at Sammy's, especially over the festive season. My father spent his Christmas and New Year at Stranraer. He didn't bother getting me a present or a card.

*

I was always welcome at Frank and Lottie's, and it was nice to be with a family. As ever, they were good for a laugh. When I was up there the sadness would be kept at bay for a few hours, especially when Lottie would have a 'wee refreshment' and the Frank and Lottie Show would hit the road. They had just acquired their first television set, a sixteen-inch Baird, in time for the festive season. Lottie wasn't keen on it.

'We'll put the telly oan, Lottie, and bring in the New Year wi' the singer Robert Wilson and his "Hello to 1955" show.' Frank smiled as he reached for the 'on' switch.

'Touch that fuckin' knob and ah'll brekk yer fingers!' Lottie's command issued from the cloud of Woodbine smoke that surrounded her. Frank withdrew his hand smartly and immediately assumed his Stan Laurel persona. I tried not to laugh out loud.

'Goodness me,' he said, 'are ye not wantin' tae bring the New Year in wi' Robert Wilson?'

'Ah'd rether bring it in wi' Crippen!' responded Lotisha.

I snorted the mouthful of ginger beer I'd just taken out through my nose and back into the glass.

Lottie looked at me. 'Is it no' a bit early fur party tricks?'

Frank scratched his head; I began to take a stitch.

'Ah don't know why we bothered buying a telly if we're jist gonny listen tae the wireless.' He then decided, like Chamberlain, to make 'another appeal to reason' – with the same result. 'Mibbe the boys would like tae see a wee bit of telly.'

'Fuck the boys!' snapped Lottie, winking at me.

I held my side and let out a low moan as the stitch really kicked in. Frank tutted.

'Is that no terrible?' He looked at me. 'Ye shouldnae laugh at her, you'll jist make her worse.'

'Piss up ma kilt,' said Lottie. She'd obviously been reading *The Short Guide to Repartee*. She lit up another Woodbine. This was better than anything the telly had to offer.

*

Late at night, reluctantly, I would leave their warm home and come round to my cold, empty one. My father was away at his fancy woman's. That's when it would hit me most, switching on the light and illuminating our sad wee room. The glow I'd carried round with me just melted away. I'd light the three gas rings to heat the place up before I got undressed for bed. The house was always cold now. Every single item in the house reminded me of Ma, yet at the same time said, she's dead.

One weekend, when he was away, I spread a newspaper on the table, took Ma's hairbrush and combed all her brown hairs out of it. Using a needle, I took ages to line them all up side by side until I had a small lock of her hair. I tied it with a piece of thread then placed it in a small, stainless-steel tube.

A few days before I was due to leave I asked my father if I could have the few photos we had of Ma. He said I could. The photos, the notes she'd left me and her wedding ring, were the only tangible memories I had of Ma. Once the house was given up this was all I'd have.

On the evening of 15 February 1955, Sammy came down to the Central Station to see me off. I had turned sixteen just six days earlier. It was bitter cold as we stood on the draughty, deserted platform, our hands deep in our pockets, occasionally stamping our feet. As we spoke, our breath froze instantly into clouds of condensation. The locomotive which would pull the train, and me, out of Glasgow stood in the shadows giving off a smell of steam and cinders so strong you could taste it. Now and again it gave a great sigh. I nodded in the direction of the concourse.

'When ma faither got called up during the war, ma ma came doon here and caught him wi' his fancy woman seeing him off. Gave the two of them a right sherrackin in front of the crowd.'

'Did she! The same fancy wumman?'

'Naw, this wiz another wan.'

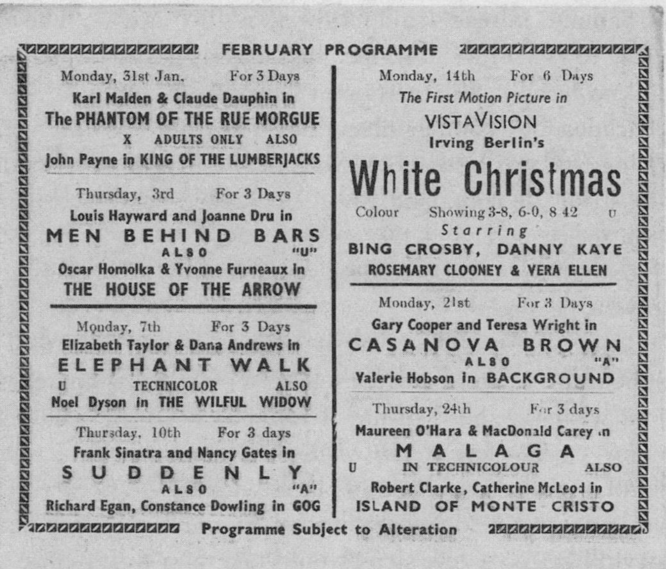

FEBRUARY PROGRAMME

Monday, 31st Jan. For 3 Days
Karl Malden & Claude Dauphin in
The PHANTOM OF THE RUE MORGUE
X ADULTS ONLY ALSO
John Payne in KING OF THE LUMBERJACKS

Thursday, 3rd For 3 Days
Louis Hayward and Joanne Dru in
MEN BEHIND BARS
ALSO "U"
Oscar Homolka & Yvonne Furneaux in
THE HOUSE OF THE ARROW

Monday, 7th For 3 Days
Elizabeth Taylor & Dana Andrews in
ELEPHANT WALK
U TECHNICOLOR ALSO
Noel Dyson in THE WILFUL WIDOW

Thursday, 10th For 3 days
Frank Sinatra and Nancy Gates in
SUDDENLY
ALSO "A"
Richard Egan, Constance Dowling in GOG

Monday, 14th For 6 Days
The First Motion Picture in
VISTAVISION
Irving Berlin's
White Christmas
Colour Showing 3-8, 6-0, 8 42 U
Starring
BING CROSBY, DANNY KAYE
ROSEMARY CLOONEY & VERA ELLEN

Monday, 21st For 3 Days
Gary Cooper and Teresa Wright in
CASANOVA BROWN
ALSO "A"
Valerie Hobson in BACKGROUND

Thursday, 24th For 3 days
Maureen O'Hara & MacDonald Carey in
MALAGA
U IN TECHNICOLOUR ALSO
Robert Clarke, Catherine McLeod in
ISLAND OF MONTE CRISTO

Programme Subject to Alteration

Blythswood programme for February 1955. I took it as a souvenir when I left to join the RAF Boys' Service.

Sammy gave it a bit of thought. 'He's been a right wee shitbag, your faither, huzn't he?'

'Aye, ye could say that.'

There was some activity from further up the platform as a guard walked quickly along the length of the train toward us, slamming any open doors shut with a solid *clu-thunk* as he came.

'Ah think ah'd better get oan, otherwise, if ah'm lucky, ah'll miss it.' I looked at Sammy. 'Ah really don't want tae go. Ah don't want tae leave Glesga – but there's fuck all ah can dae aboot it.'

Sammy stuck his hand out. 'All the best, Robert. Write me when ye get the chance, let me know whit it's like.'

I was near to tears. I wanted to say, 'Thanks for being a good pal, Sammy.' Instead I said, 'Anyway, it's no' as if we'll be losing touch. Your ma says ah can come tae your hoose for ma leaves. Ah'll no be going tae ma faither's, that's for certain.'

I headed for a compartment door. The train was nearly empty. My luggage was a shoe box, wrapped in brown paper and tied with string. It contained my mementoes – and two pairs of nylon socks.

'See yah, Robert. Look after yourself.'

'Aye. Cheerio.'

As the train began to move, I felt butterflies. I was apprehensive about what lay ahead of me. There was no turning back now. Sammy took a few steps, waving all the time, then was left behind. I wished I could swap places with him. A twenty-minute tram ride and he'd be getting off at our usual stop on the Maryhill Road. A few steps would take him to his close then, two flights up, and he'd be walking into their warm house. I could see Frank and Lottie sitting at the fire and turning round as he came into the living room.

'Is that Robert away? Are ye hungry, son? Will ah make ye a sandwich?'

I wondered if I was going to be an unlucky bastard *all* my life?

As I sat in the empty compartment and the train gathered speed, in my mind's eye I could see our single-end, looking as it always had, receding further and further into the distance. I knew I wouldn't see it again, as he'd arranged to give it up within the next couple of days. I had the same feeling as when I'd turned the couple of times to look back at Ma's light in the hospice window.

I tried to drum up a little enthusiasm. C'mon, this is your first time in England. It'll be exciting. All those towns you've only heard of, you'll be amongst them soon. I was heading for

RAF Cosford, just a few miles from Wolverhampton. You'll be in the Midlands! It'll be smashing! A few days from now you'll probably be walking round the streets of Wolverhampton looking in the shops, going to the pictures, listening to the way they talk. It'll be wonderful! Will it?

I'd bought myself a paperback at the kiosk in the Central: *Rommel: Desert Fox*. I tried to get into it, but my mind kept straying. You don't live in Glasgow anymore. You don't live anywhere. And nobody gives a fuck. I felt like crying, but instead dozed off.

I awoke feeling lousy: hot, sticky and far from home. I looked out of the window to try and catch my first glimpse of England, but it was still dark. I wasn't sure if we were out of Scotland.

Occasionally we'd race past a factory yard and I'd get a glance of someone walking between buildings or sitting, solitary, in an office. I'd wonder who he was. After his night shift, would he be going home to wife and kids and a big fried breakfast? I bet he was happier than me.

Then, I'd look at the reflection of the compartment and me in the dark window. It was like looking through a one-way mirror into an adjoining one. This dimly lit, isolated figure looked back at me. Neither of us knew where he was going. What lay ahead for us? I stretched out full length on the bench seat and slept fitfully. Every time I came to, for just a second I'd think I was in bed at home. Then I'd realise I wasn't.

At last, as it was becoming light, the train edged into Wolverhampton. I gazed out at street after street of red-brick terraces. They looked as though they'd be better to live in than tenements. In the grey light people hurried along, wrapped up, going to work. Many rode bikes, more than you'd see on a Glasgow morning. It was all so different.

As we slowed to pull into the grimy station, I took my first good look at English folk. The platform was crowded. Many of the men more gabardine macs, lots of women in tweedy costumes and small hats. It seemed all very *Brief Encounter*. Trevor Howard and Celia Johnson were out there, somewhere.

Within minutes of stepping onto the platform, waiting RAF personnel had shepherded all the new recruits onto a local train which would take us the few miles to Albrighton Halt, the station for RAF Cosford. Most of the passengers were civvy workers going to the camp. They paid no attention to us recruits, reading their papers and chatting as we trundled along. They'd seen it all before. At Albrighton we climbed into waiting 'three-tonners' and, minutes later, jumped back off again inside the camp. We lined up for our first roll-call then marched off, after a fashion, for our introduction to Air Force cuisine midst the unforgettable smell of a mess hall: the staleness of past meals and greasy washing-up water hung permanently in the air, easily overwhelming the smell of the meal being served.

I managed the cornflakes; they hadn't yet found a way to bugger them up. The tea was insipid, the fried egg cold and greasy, the bacon fatty. I was a confirmed 'Jack Sprat'. The sausages were thin and hard. The whole meal was, at best, lukewarm. I recalled Sammy's definition, 'LUKEWARM: It looks warm – but it isnae.' We had fallen about the classroom laughing at that. Further along the table I heard an English voice refer to the sausages as 'dog's dicks'. For the only time that day, I smiled.

After breakfast, the day became a bewildering blur of drawing kit, being interviewed and attending lectures until, by early evening, I found myself in a new uniform whose thick, woollen trousers were jaggy and made me itch. I sat on a bed in a billet surrounded by twenty or more other boys. This wooden hut, one of dozens, was our new home. We then had to try to fold and fit our mountain of new kit into our wooden lockers.

RAF Cosford, 1955. The unhappiest time of my life. I'm on the right, aged 16. Tommy Green, also from Glasgow, is on the left.

The hut had the stale smell of a thousand previous applications of wax polish which had been driven into every crack and crevice in the floorboards by the heavy 'bumpers' used for polishing. As the evening wore on, the smells of toothpaste, soap, Brylcreem and sweat were added, bringing the billet back to life.

I sat on my bed and listened to accents from all over the British Isles, some of which I couldn't understand. For all these boys this was a dream come true. They had waited impatiently for the day when they would leave school and be able to join up. Now it was here. They ran around chattering to one another, making friends. Pillow fights were breaking out, guys were acquiring nicknames. It was all very 'first day of the new term'.

Two months before I had never heard of the RAF Boys' Service. Now I was 1930545 Boy Entrant Douglas. R. I had just signed on for ten years: the minimum. This was certainly not the happiest day of my life.

As the evening wore on I became more and more miserable and depressed. Sitting in that billet my situation seemed to bear down on me. In the last couple of months I had lost my Ma, home, pals and city. Now I was faced with ten years of being where I didn't want to be – in the RAF. It loomed in front of me like a life sentence. I was so 'down' all I wanted to do was cry. I began to long for 'lights out' so as I could go to bed and cry and no one would see me. The evening seemed to drag on and on. Everybody else was having a great time. I lay on my bed and pretended to read my biography of Rommel. The fact I'd bought it in Glasgow was somehow a comfort. Now and again lads would speak to me and I would force a smile as I replied. I hoped they would think I was just a quiet type.

December 2004 was the fiftieth anniversary of Ma's death. Half a century since I came downstairs from the pawnshop and slipped Ma's wedding ring onto my finger. It's still there.

Like anybody my age, I feel I just don't know where the time has gone. I managed to escape from my ten-year sentence in the RAF by 'working my ticket'. It was daunting as a sixteen year old making my way in the world, but I was my Ma's son, and whenever there were decisions to be made, I would think: what would Ma want me to do? As the years passed and I became a man, it became a case of: what should I do? The result was usually the same.

I've laboured on the docks in Glasgow and down a pit in West Lothian. I've been a soldier, a prisoner officer in Birmingham and Durham jails, and latterly, until I retired, I roamed the Northumberland countryside working for the electricity company. At the age of fifty, I started to write. I've more to tell you, but it must be another time. For now, my thoughts return to that cold billet in Wolverhampton.

At long last an NCO came in and switched the lights out. Everyone carried on talking and laughing, but that was fine, they would leave me in peace.

I lay in the dark, hundreds of miles from where I wanted to be. I had never felt so alone. I wondered what I had done to deserve all this. From somewhere in the depths of the camp a bugler began to blow 'Last Post'. Its beautiful melancholy only added to my misery. It seemed to carry echoes of the last tram, making its way in the night down the Maryhill Road, reminding me of all I'd lost. I placed my left hand on my pillow so Ma's wedding ring just touched my lips. Then, amid all the happy banter, I cried myself to sleep.